AF770756

Entitlement

Entitlement

The Paradoxes of Property

Joseph William Singer

Yale University Press

New Haven & London

Published with assistance from the foundation established in memory of Calvin Chapin of the Class of 1788, Yale College.

Copyright © 2000 by Yale University.
All rights reserved.
This book may not be reproduced, in whole or in part, including illustrations, in any form (beyond that copying permitted by Sections 107 and 108 of the U.S. Copyright Law and except by reviewers for the public press), without written permission from the publishers.

Printed in the United States of America.

Library of Congress Cataloging-in-Publication Data
Singer, Joseph William, 1954–
Entitlement: the paradoxes of property / Joseph William Singer.
p. cm.
Includes bibliographical references and index.
ISBN 0-300-08019-0
1. Property—Social aspects. 2. Property—Philosophy. I. Title.
K720 .S56 2000
346.04—dc21 00-043271

A catalogue record for this book is available from the British Library.

The paper in this book meets the guidelines for permanence and durability of the Committee on Production Guidelines for Book Longevity of the Council on Library Resources.

10 9 8 7 6 5 4 3 2 1

For Max and Lila Singer
my first teachers

Property rights serve human values. They are recognized to that end, and are limited by it.

—*Chief Justice Joseph Weintraub*
Supreme Court of New Jersey, 1971

What we do cannot be understood except in relation to those we touch.

—*Justice Jack Pope*
Supreme Court of Texas, 1978

Contents

Preface

> The notion of responding to a responsibility confronts us with a paradox. It clearly involves an element of choice and a complete absence of choice. Responding to a responsibility to which one is called upon to respond is not the act of a subject. But neither is it simply a matter of being "subject to" a responsibility. To be responsible is a mode of existence that cannot be reduced to either the passive or the active voice.
> —*Johan W. G. van der Walt*

In the musical *Fiddler on the Roof,* a beggar complains when Tevye gives him less than his usual amount. Tevye responds, "*Nu,* I had a bad week." "So you had a bad week," responds the beggar. "Why should I suffer?"

A quip, perhaps, but based on Jewish law. The word for charity in Hebrew—*tzedakah*—means righteousness. *Tzedek* is justice and a *tzaddik* is a righteous person. There is no other word in Hebrew for charity. The right to a share of the world's wealth—a realistic opportunity to obtain the means necessary for a human life—is a matter of justice. It is a fundamental principle about the structure of human society. It does not depend on the "kindness of strangers" but on something deeper and more secure—obligation. Obligations may give rise to entitlements. But it is the obligation that comes first.[1] It is a *mitzvah* to give charity. We Jews often use the word *mitzvah* colloquially to mean "good deed," but *mitzvah* means "commandment." We are commanded, we are obligated to act with *tzedek,* justice. Part of what justice demands is that we make it possible for every individual to obtain a living. The ability to earn and to use property is a necessity for human life. Access to property is therefore a fundamental component of social justice.

In a remarkable exposition of the story of Noah, Aviva Gottlieb Zornberg explains that the great sin of the generation that faced the flood was their "pursuit of ecstacy" in a manner that "excluded attention to other people."[2] They lacked love, which "is to be identified with curiosity, with that attentiveness to the self-made worlds of others."[3] In contrast, "the righteous man . . . is defined by his capacity to nurture the needy"[4] as Noah nurtured the animals. Charity is not a right that a "special interest group" demands. Rather, justice and righteousness impose obligations on both individuals and the community to ensure that each person, created in the image of God, has access to the means of life.

These views are not in fashion today. Republicans and Democrats alike competed for the honor of being the party responsible for ending "welfare as we know it." We have abolished the "entitlement" to welfare and substituted a time-limited right to assistance that will be cut off whether or not the family still needs help and whether or not that need is the result of a failure to take personal responsibility for oneself and one's family. The idea of compassion—of concern for those who face rough times—seems to have been completely obliterated from our political rhetoric.

There were—and are—substantial problems with the welfare system, and I do not mean to defend it in its current or its pre–welfare reform version. I do mean to defend the notion that one "personal responsibility" we have is to be responsive to the needs of others, especially the most vulnerable among us. Those most vulnerable include children who cannot be held responsible for the "irresponsibility" of their parents. How to respond is a complex question; not to respond is a sin.

I did not write this book alone. I want to thank Martha Minow, Greg Alexander, Keith Aoki, Milner Ball, David Barron, Larry Blum, Kent Greenfield, Jon Hanson, Todd Hinnen, Elinor Horne, Larry Kramer, Jenny Nedelsky, Avery Rimer, Fred Rowley, Lila Singer, Max Singer, Judy Smith, Avi Soifer, Vicky Spelman, Carol Steiker, Laura Underkuffler-Freund, André van der Walt, Johan van der Walt, and Eric Yamamoto.

I especially want to thank Patricia Fazzone for her expert administrative assistance and for her insights on the connections between spirituality and the work of the world.

This book is dedicated to my parents, Max and Lila Singer. They were the first to teach me that attending to the needs of others in times of distress is not a matter of charity but of justice. They continue to teach me about *tzedakah* through their daily lives and their numerous "charitable" activities. My mother, the teacher, continues to teach through her leadership work with the League of Women Voters. My father, the engineer, has engaged in preventive maintenance with Interfaith Neighbors, an organization funded by synagogues and churches which works to make sure people don't become homeless. Both of them have taken turns in leadership positions at Monmouth Reform Temple. Their work reflects Maimonides' insight that the highest form of charity is to enable others to become "self-sufficient" so that they are no longer in need of "charity." "You shall strengthen [your brother] . . . and he is to live beside [literally, 'with'] you" (Leviticus 25:35).

My parents passed on to my brother, my sister, and myself the teaching of their parents. My mother's parents, Harry and Flora Braunstein (ז״ל), worked for many charitable organizations and received dozens of plaques thanking them for their work in raising money for good causes. They did not do what they did in order to get plaques or recognition; they did it because they were good people and because the righteous person "is defined by his capacity to nurture the needy."[5] I have two of their plaques, one with my grandfather's name and one with my grandmother's name, in my study to remind me of what they thought was important and what they tried to teach me.

My father-in-law and mother-in-law have similarly taught me about the importance of serving others. Newton Minow has devoted his life to the "public interest" and has recently turned his attention to protecting children from the wasteland of current television programming. Josephine Minow also has been highly active in numerous charitable activities; her service on the board of the Chicago Historical Society brings home to me the importance of remembering the past in order to learn from it.

Martha Minow helped me to organize and clarify the ideas I hoped to present in this work. Martha is a model for me of someone who is both for herself and not for herself alone. I owe her more than I can say. Mira Judith Minow Singer, as her name implies, brings forth light. In the usual way of chlidren, but with particular tenacity, Mira has demonstrated again and again that there is no end to the "why?" questions we can ask. And why, she might ask, is that? The

Talmud notes that we cannot "stand on" (understand) the words of Torah unless we have "stumbled over them."[6] Explaining this teaching, Avivah Gottlieb Zornberg notes that "to discover firm standing ground it is necessary to explore, to stumble, even to fall."[7] But why, Mira would ask? Because "only a vision in which the plot is unclear, in which anomalies bewilder serene faith and integrities are torn apart, can open the possibility of human action."[8] As human beings, we confront an "eternal oscillation between extremes of fear and love, certainty and courage, in the face of perplexity," and "in this world, what is most needed is not fear, which deprives man of initiative beneath the sleepless eyes of God, but love—the capacity to act in a world where absolute clarity is not obtainable."[9] But why? Why do we need love, Daddy? And so on . . .

Joseph William Singer
Cambridge, Massachusetts
5760/2000

Introduction

Any owner of that lot next door has the right to do with it as he pleases.
—*Jonathan Larson*

Property rights are, by nature, social rights; they embody how we, as a society, have chosen to reward the claims of some people to finite and critical goods, and to deny the claims to the same goods by others. Try as we might to separate this right from choice, conflict, and vexing social questions, it cannot be done.
—*Laura S. Underkuffler-Freund*

At the start of the twenty-first century, faith in private property as a mode of social and economic organization is as strong as it has ever been. Since the collapse of the Soviet Union and the fall of the Communist regimes in Eastern Europe in 1989, it appears that no alternative exists to the market economy. The nations of the former Soviet bloc have converted institutions previously controlled by the government to private ownership. Market solutions to social problems are being implemented in Asia, Africa, and Latin America. In the 1990s a Democratic president supported the movement to end "big government" and championed the demise of "welfare as we know it." We appear to have grown disenchanted with both the New Deal and the welfare state.[1] We are skeptical about the virtues of regulation and government-sponsored entitlements. The idea of taxation for public purposes seems almost quaint.

What is left when we deregulate? When people speak about deregulation, they do not advocate the abolition of the state or the rule of law. They are not anarchists. What they propose to do is to allocate power over material resources to private owners and to liberate those owners from governmentally imposed restrictions on their freedom to manage their property as they please, as long as their actions do not interfere with the legally protected rights of others. What is left, in other words, is the institution of private property.

Property is on the political agenda. The United States has witnessed a burgeoning property rights movement.[2] Some businesses and landowners are angry about environmental regulations and local zoning laws that limit their ability to develop their land. The Republican party's 1994 "Contract with America" proposed legislation in the House of Representatives to protect all private property owners from any new federal regulations that would limit their freedom to use their property as they wish if those limitations would reduce the market value of the property by 10 percent or more.[3] This radical legislation would have required compensation for any changes in law that affect property values and, as Joseph Sax notes, could have required the public "to pay pornographers, slum landlords, and owners of leaking toxic dumps to cease their activities, so long as no previous law prohibited that same conduct."[4] A similar bill, introduced in the Senate, proposed a figure of 33 percent as the trigger for a right to compensation.[5] In 1995 the House passed a more limited statute, entitled the Private Property Protection Act,[6] which was geared to protect some owners from property devaluations resulting from certain federal regulations without regard to the public interests served by those regulations. Several states have already passed such legislation.[7] In addition to these legislative developments, the Supreme Court has been receptive to arguments to expand constitutional protection for property rights. It has altered the law in some significant respects and has suggested that further protections for property owners from government regulation might be forthcoming.[8]

What is property? One might think this was a simple question. Property is about rights over things and the people who have those rights are called owners. What powers do owners have over the things they own? Owners are free to use the property as they wish. They have the right to exclude others from it or grant them access to it. They have the power to transfer title—to pass the powers of ownership to someone else. They also are immune from having the property taken away from them without their consent, or they must be adequately compensated if the property is taken by the state for public purposes. We typically presume that the owner has, not just one or two powers, but all these powers—a full bundle—over the property.[9]

Of course, we know that some limits on property rights do exist and may be justified. Owners are generally not free to use their property to harm others. Property rights are sometimes limited for other reasons as well, such as to prevent racial discrimination. When ownership rights are limited, we imagine those limits to be exceptions to the general rule that owners can do whatever they want with their property. The burden is always on others (meaning nonowners or the state) to explain why the owner's rights should be limited, and in today's political climate that burden is quite heavy.[10]

In the words of Sir William Blackstone, property is "that sole and despotic dominion which one man claims and exercises over the external things of the world, in total exclusion of the right of any other individual in the universe."[11] Since regulations are conceptualized as limits on the preexisting rights of the owner, property and regulation are understood to be opposites. Protecting the rights of owners enhances liberty; it gets the government off our backs. Protecting property means that the government lets us do what we want with what we own. It also means that those who do not own something are obligated to refrain from interfering with the rights of the owner. These duties are not regarded as meddlesome government regulations; rather, they are viewed as the necessary correlative to government protection of property rights. The more protection we have for property rights, the less government regulation we have, and vice versa.

This way of thinking about property is pervasive. We can call it the *ownership model.* We see it in political life, where debates between Republicans and Democrats about public policy revolve around the question of when regulation is justified. The burden is always on the party seeking to "regulate" to justify limitations on property rights. The baseline is freedom from government restrictions on private actions. Philosophers call this *negative liberty.*[12] Protection of property rights does require individuals to respect the legal rights of others. Sometimes this means that owners may have to limit what they do with their property. A murderer cannot claim innocence on the grounds that he owned his gun and that, as an owner, he was entitled to do what he wanted with his property. Even land owners may be required to limit their property uses when they harm neighboring property, as in the case of industrial pollution. At the same time, the harm limitation is understood narrowly. We presume that most uses of property are *self-regarding,* in that only the owner is legitimately interested and others have no legitimate claims to control what the owner does with her own property. Substantial freedom to control one's property without interference by government regulation is believed to promote both individual autonomy and economic efficiency.

We see the ownership model in academic discourse, as well. Philosophers and political theorists ask whether private property is justified and what limits, if any, can legitimately be placed on the rights of owners.[13] In analyzing these questions, philosophers usually take the ownership model for granted. Full control by an owner is the core concept that defines a private property system. Jeremy Waldron, for example, argues that the "organizing idea" of property is ownership, "the idea that it is for a certain specified person (rather than for anyone else or for society as a whole) to determine how a specified resource is to be used."[14] Although philosophers are aware that many conceptions of property are possible, and that limits on full ownership rights are pervasive in modern legal systems, their normative analysis takes the absolutist conception as the starting point. "When philosophers argue about the justifiability of private property, they are not interested (at least in the first instance) in the detail of the property rules of any society in particular."[15] If ownership means presumptive control by an owner, and if the existence of ownership rights is a good thing, then limitations on the rights of the owner must be justified by sufficiently strong reasons to overcome the presumption of legitimacy. Of course, philosophers disagree vehemently about how much regulation is appropriate. But whether they are libertarians or liberals or communitarians, they all tend to frame the issue in the same way: How much community control should be imposed on individuals?

Economists also often take the ownership model as gospel. They start from the assumption that resources should be privately owned, that owners should be free to use their property as they like, and that they should be free to exchange it at will. They presume that the legal system determines how property is allocated initially and that the interesting question is what limits to place on use or exchange when markets work imperfectly and therefore do not allocate resources efficiently.

Of course, the ideas of ownership and free exchange do not solve all problems for economists. Harold Demsetz remarks that "the world does not deal in absolutes."[16] Property rights cannot be absolute, any more than other legal rights can. "On the margin, economic man is prepared to trade off some freedom for some security, some privacy for some wealth, some freedom for some paternalism, and vice versa."[17] At the same time, like most economists, Demsetz assumes that the concept of private property provides presumptively applicable answers to such problems. He notes that "the prima facie case for private property solutions is strong," even though "some mixture of systems is required."[18] Property as ownership forms the baseline for much economic analysis. Demsetz observes that sometimes "attenuation of private rights is in order. But in these issues, as lawyers well know, it is important where the burden of proof lies."[19] He argues that economic considerations strongly favor looking to private property rights for a solution, "even if principled doubts may arise about it."[20] This language suggests that we can identify who the owner is and that owners are entitled to control their property unless some market imperfection can be identified and a public policy response can improve on the market's performance.

Lawyers who adopt the economic model similarly presume that the most efficient system of property law identifies an owner for every valuable, scarce resource and allows free transfer of those property interests through market exchanges.[21] Richard Posner argues that "if every valuable (meaning scarce as well as desired) resource were owned by someone (universality), ownership connoted the unqualified power to exclude everybody else from using the resource (exclusivity) as well as to use it oneself, and ownership rights were freely transferable or as lawyers say alienable (transferable), value would be maximized."[22] Regulations that limit the rights of owners are presumptively inefficient since they prevent them from acting to satisfy their preferences by using property or selling it to someone who values it more. Imposing regulations decreases business investment, lowers the number of jobs, and winds up hurting the very persons it was intended to protect.

Under this view, regulation of markets is justified only when markets work imperfectly. For example, regulation may be justified to prevent owners from using their property to harm others; such a rule might require owners to pay damages to those harmed by their property uses. This forces owners to internalize the external costs of their property uses and is justified when government action can respond to those externalities more efficiently than the market itself can.[23] Economists recognize that strong protection for property rights may result in unacceptable inequality, but they suggest that such problems be addressed through redistributive programs rather than through manipulation of the law of property or contracts.[24] This model is so well entrenched that U.S. economists are traveling the world over to preach it both to countries emerging from Communist rule and to the so-called developing countries.[25]

OWNERSHIP VERSUS PROPERTY

The ownership model is pervasive, but it is also misleading and morally deficient. By conceiving of property as ownership, we invite owners to use their property without regard to the needs of others. We encourage them to consider their self-interest alone—to act as if no one existed but themselves. Ownership, as we use the term, abhors obligation; for obligations, if they exist at all, are understood to limit ownership. In this conceptual framework, ownership and obligation are opposites, as are property and regulation. If property means ownership, and if ownership means power without obligation, then we have created a framework for thinking about property that privileges a certain form of life—the life of the owner. In the conceptual space framed by the life of the owner, we are invited to live as if we were the only ones that mattered. We are invited to live as if we were alone.

Yet we know that we do not live alone—and neither do owners. The fact that owners do not live alone has surprising implications. "Property," Joseph Sax writes, "does not exist in isolation."[26] The recognition and exercise of property rights affects the interests of others, including other owners and nonowners. When we recognize that this is so, it becomes much harder to define what ownership means.

Since the legal realists wrote in the first half of the twentieth century, lawyers have understood two crucial points about property. First, the institution of property comprises a bundle of rights which can be disaggregated into distinct entitlements owned by different persons.[27] Property rights are not always bundled together and owned by the same person. More often that not, several people may have powers to control various aspects of the same piece of property. Second, property rights describe relations among people and not just relations between people and things.[28] Legal rights impose duties on others to respect those rights, and the exercise of one's legal liberties may affect others in ways they would wish to avoid.

But for all the sophistication of the legal-realist conception of property, we in fact remain mired in an absolutist paradigm. Scholars, lawyers, and judges all revert to the ownership model with surprising frequency. This is a problem, because ownership is flawed as a description of both the social practice and the legal structure of property systems. As a concept, it has its uses, but more often than not it misdescribes the ideals that underlie the institution of private property, as well as the legal rules that define the basic structure of property rights. The ownership model also sometimes allocates burdens of persuasion in a manner that is morally unacceptable as a framework for criticizing and judging alternative property regimes.

When we consider the actual practices of our legal system, and the norms that justify property rights, we see that we face tensions within the concept of property itself. Such tensions are far more common than is generally realized. Because property law must adjudicate these tensions among competing property claims, property requires regulation. Indeed, because property rights conflict, it is often impossible to tell which government actions are regulatory and which are deregulatory. When one property right clashes with another, government cannot remain neutral; it must choose which property claim will prevail. Viewed in this light, the distinction between regulation and deregulation breaks down. Whatever government does, it will be regulating the structure of property rights. Deregulation is simply not an option.

The ownership model also fails to acknowledge the fact that property rights often conflict with personal (nonproperty) rights. Property rights are not the only rights we care about. Nor it is obvious that property rights should prevail in a clash with personal rights. Personal interests often take precedence over property claims, and for good reason. Because of conflicts among legally protected interests, regulation is inevitable, and limitations on property rights are far more pervasive than one would think.

The ownership model is premised on the view that the meaning of property is clear and is not a matter of controversial political or moral judgment. This view assumes that property rights have a built-in structure and content and that it is easy to tell when a government action constitutes a regulatory limit on the preexisting rights of the owner.[29] Controversy comes in only when someone attempts to regulate or limit the rights of owners. This view, prevalent though it may be, is mistaken. Property does not come in a preset package. There is no simple definition of property that can be posited without making controversial value judgments about how to choose between conflicting interests. When we examine social conflicts, as lawyers do, we see over and over again that property rights conflict, both with each other and with other important legally protected interests. Dealing with these conflicts brings questions of political and moral judgment *inside* the property system itself. The question is not whether to regulate owners; the question is what kind of property system to create in the first place. To address this more fundamental question, we need a new model of property that goes beyond ownership as an organizing category.

Although we live in an age that champions deregulation, we do not, in fact, live in an age of laissez-faire—far from it. We do not grant owners absolute rights over their property; our actual law of property in the United States is not even close to that model.[30] Despite the recent surge of support for deregulation, many laws limit the prerogatives of owners. Zoning laws, consumer protection laws, workplace safety rules, banking rules, building codes—all these types of measures for regulating owners' rights are quite popular. Although we face enormous battles about affirmative action, almost no one is arguing to get rid of the antidiscrimination laws in their entirety. Although we see great anger at particular applications of zoning and environmental laws, hardly anyone is calling for wholesale abolition of them. We tend to forget that, despite recent affirmations of the end of big government, we retain a host of regulations that enjoy widespread support. We may live in an age of deregulation, but we also live in a regulatory state.

Private property and regulation are not mortal enemies. In fact, private property cannot exist without regulation. A private property regime is not, after all, a Hobbesian state of nature; it requires a working legal system that can define, allocate, and enforce property rights. Because property regimes adjudicate conflicts between separate property rights, and between property rights and personal rights, private property itself is a form of regulation. Moreover, many regulations protect property rights and even enhance them. Zoning laws, for example, which keep factories from locating in residential districts, are instrumental in preserving the market value of homes by ensuring the continued suitability of the neighborhood for family living.

The truth that property requires regulation is often lost in the overheated rhetoric that portrays owners as victims of power-hungry government bureaucrats. Despite public support for many limitations on property uses, our current political language is bereft of means to justify these popular regulations in terms that seem politically acceptable. People say they want deregulation, and yet they support substantial regulation of property. Nor are they naively mistaken when they extend such support. Although some regulations may be unjustified and counterproductive, many are essential to the fair and efficient operation of the market and to the basic structure of social relations that allow human beings to flourish in a free and democratic society. The result is a huge gap between rhetoric and reality, between what people say they want in general and what they say they want in particular. Those who profess to favor deregulation often find themselves supporting particular regulatory regimes that protect significant individual interests—including interests in property.

Our ideology and our practice diverge in sharp and irreconcilable ways. Laura Underkuffler-Freund usefully explains that the *idea* of property revolves around absolutist conceptions, but that the *institution* of property in the real world involves—and has always involved—substantial limitations on the rights of owners.[31] The prevailing ideology makes it hard for people to justify regulations that they in fact favor. It also leads them to be skeptical of regulations that support rather than undermine property rights. Worst of all, our romance with the absolutist conception of property often blinds us to our better selves. We do not place property rights ahead of all other rights; we do not believe, when rights conflict, that property rights should automatically triumph over personal rights and liberties and over the interests of the whole society.

The absolutist conception does not do a good job of expressing our values. This is true no matter what one's political ideology may be. Even libertarians, who support minimal government interference with both property and liberty, will better express their own values and better understand the choices implicit in creating a private property system if they can appreciate the limitations of the absolutist conception of property. The absence of a politically acceptable discourse for property impedes debate between liberals and conservatives. Both sides support certain forms of property regulation. We will better understand both our current legal practices and our moral commitments if we can regenerate a notion of property that recognizes the legitimate role of regulation in the public interest. The absence of such a moral discourse has impeded efforts to engage in reasonable policy making.

Owners do not live alone. Hannah Arendt noted that it was a fundamental truth about the human condition that "men, not Man, live on the earth and inhabit the world."[32] The "human condition of plurality [is] *the* condition . . . of political life."[33] Because this is so, the institution of private property inevitably raises questions about the character of social relations and the nature of governance. Property is a form of power, and the distribution of power is a political problem of the highest order. Thus the property problem goes beyond deciding whether to recognize particular property rights, or when to limit them; rather, it forces on us more urgent questions: What shall property be? What shall it mean? What kind of property regime should we construct?

BUNDLES OF RIGHTS

An alternative to the ownership model was invented by the legal realists in the early twentieth century. Working from the premise that property comprises a discrete group of rights, they suggested that property be viewed metaphorically as a bundle of sticks loosely tied together, and that particular sticks (rights) could be taken out of the bundle and given to various people. This meant that we could not just make one big policy decision to adopt a private property system. Rather, we had to make specific policy judgments about the rules that should govern particular sticks in the bundle.[34]

The legal realists emphasized that property rights concern, not power by owners over things, but relations among people. Property rights place duties on others to respect those rights. The right to exclude nonowners, for example, regulates nonowners by requiring them to stay off the owner's property. Similarly, when an owner is free to use her property as she likes, she is at liberty to use it in ways that may be disagreeable to others. In either case we understand property rights to comprise relations among persons with respect to the control and use of valued resources. Many economists have embraced this model and suggested that we consider the efficiency of particular entitlements rather than supposing that property rights only come in pre-set bundles. Once we understand that ownership comprises a collection of more specific entitlements, it makes sense to examine each entitlement separately to determine which legal rules result in its efficient allocation or fair distribution.

This new model has much to recommend it. Yet it also has problems. Lawyers and economists sometimes act as if the bundle-of-rights model has shoved the ownership model completely out of the picture. This assumption is false. In analyzing property rights, we often adopt unconscious presumptions about who owns the particular entitlement we are discussing. Such presumptions place the burden on the other party to justify redistributing the entitlement. Where do these presumptions come from? They tend to come from conventional understandings of ownership. Those understandings have their origins in culture, history, and law. The importance of the cultural underpinnings of property cannot be overstated.

When I go to lunch with my students, I sometimes order a cup of coffee. When the waiter serves the coffee, I pick up the cup and ask them, "Who owns this cup?" It is obvious to everyone that the restaurant owns it and is only loaning it to me so that I may drink the coffee I have purchased. I am not to understand that the price of the coffee includes the cup; I cannot take it home and put it in my cupboard. This is so even if the menu listed a "cup of coffee." How do I know this? I know this because I grew up in the United States and learned at some early age that when I get up to leave a restaurant, the forks and spoons and plates *and* cups stay on the table. My knowledge is based on custom rather than law. The presence of such customary norms is essential to the operation of a market. What is perhaps more surprising is that such cultural norms are also essential for any system of property law. The existence of such norms raises the possibility that they can be changed, either by social action or by law reforms. They also raise the question of legitimacy.

Imagine if you were the manager of a bank in Russia and were just granted ownership rights in a factory. You might imagine that owners can do what they want with their property, and you might have no conception of how to run a business. You might plunder the business, take what you can and fail to make a serious attempt to turn it into a profit-making enterprise that could sustain both you and the workers over the long term. You might do this, especially if you thought that owners have rights without obligations. You might do this because everyone else is doing it or because you do not know what it means to run a business.[35] You might be good-hearted but have no idea how to manage a profitable business.[36] A Western economist who advises the political leaders of the country that private ownership will unleash the benefits of private enterprise might be surprised if this policy did not work in the way he envisioned. He might not realize how much the economic success of the West is premised on cultural norms about proper conduct and regulations that limit the ability of owners to act in ways that destroy the legitimate interests of others with whom they engage in consensual capitalist relationships.

Another problem with the bundle-of-rights model is that it does not adequately direct our attention to a central problem in constructing property law—choosing rules that respond to and promote human relationships that comprise a defensible form of social life. The legal realists understood property rights as relationships only in the formal sense. They acknowledged that rights impose duties on others and that liberties impose vulnerabilities on those affected by the exercise of those liberties. In deciding whether those duties and those vulnerabilities were fair, they suggested that lawmakers balance the interests of those harmed by entitlements against those who benefit from them. This balancing solution did not take seriously the idea that legal rules both respond to and shape the contours of social relations. They did not, in other words, take the character and structure of social relations as an important independent factor in choosing the rules that govern market life. Economists may similarly fail to give sufficient attention to the moral and customary underpinnings of market societies. The idea of balancing interests is a useful one, but it does not quite get at what is at stake in constructing property law. What is at stake is a vision of social life.

The ownership model envisioned a society of equal individuals, widespread ownership of property, decentralization of power, and a particular mixture of freedom of action and limits on freedom of action to promote security of persons and property. It was associated with a laissez-faire economic philosophy and was the backbone of the so-called classical legal thought that was prevalent around the end of the nineteenth century and in the first decades of the twentieth century.

In the 1910s and 1920s the legal realists argued that the ownership model did not adequately achieve this social vision. They noted that the laissez-faire policy left a great deal of inequality in the distribution of both property and power. To rectify these inequalities, they sought to justify regulations of property in the public interest. They had a vision of property that included attention to such problems as monopoly power, unequal bargaining power, minimum labor standards, and consumer protection. The realist vision was motivated by a desire to vindicate the legitimacy of Progressive legislation, such as the antitrust laws and minimum wage and maximum hours legislation, which had been viewed with suspicion or even struck down as unconstitutional by the courts.

What the legal realists lacked, however, was a way to explain why their vision of social life was better than the laissez-faire vision. The adherents of the ownership model, for example, viewed labor contracts as freely negotiated agreements; they understood any legal restrictions on such agreements, such as minimum wage legislation, as infringements on the liberty interests of both parties. They also saw them as takings of the property rights of the employer without just compensation because they rewrote existing contracts and forced employers to admit people to their property on terms that they had not chosen. The realists, in contrast, believed that employers had market power that could be used to coerce employees to agree to unfair terms. Where the classical legal theorists saw freedom, the realists saw coercion. Where the classical theorists saw a deprivation of property rights, the realists saw an abuse of property rights that prevented others from acquiring similar rights. What the realists needed—and what was missing from the bundle-of-rights model—was a way to argue persuasively that their vision of social life was better than the laissez-faire vision. Balancing interests does not get us very far. What we need is a way to address value choices directly and honestly. This requires elaboration of the ways in which property norms affect social relations, and normative argument about which forms of social relations meet our substantive goals of promoting justice, liberty, equality, and democracy.

Paradoxically, scholars who focus on developing the implications of substantive norms such as liberty, autonomy, equality, and social justice tend to use the ownership model. They do so because the absolutist conception of property expresses strong and widely shared claims about the power of individuals to shape their own lives. I have argued, however, that the ownership model hinders our ability to address these normative goals adequately. It does so because ownership is a woefully inadequate conception of what property is. It hides from our view consideration of the systemic consequences of alternative property regimes, and it takes our attention away from considering which relationships can be characterized as just and which ones should be seen as oppressive.

Legal scholars who focus on substantive norms of economic efficiency tend to use the bundle-of-rights model. Their approach to the concept of property and property law appropriately directs our attention to a more nuanced understanding of the complexity involved in defining, allocating, and enforcing property rights. They are especially interested in exploring the social consequences of alternative property law rules. On the other hand, they tend to defer consideration of what they call distributive considerations, by which they mean not only problems of the distribution of wealth but also problems of fairness and justice. In so doing, they wrongly suppose that distributive concerns can be usefully segregated from efficiency concerns. Although the bundle-of-rights model acknowledges complexity, some of its modern adherents wrongfully eschew consideration of the norms of liberty and social justice that must inform our construction of the meaning and content of property and property law. We need an alternative to both the ownership and bundle-of-rights models. My goal is to unite what is best in both these approaches by directing our attention to the ways that property law responds to and is shaped by social relations.

ENTITLEMENTS AND SOCIAL RELATIONS

Property law defines entitlements and obligations that shape the contours of social relations. Property is something we must collectively define and construct. It is not given to us whole; it does not emerge fully formed like Athena from Zeus's head. It is closer to a piece of music that unfolds over time. Like music, property gets its sense of stability from the ongoing creation and resolution of various forms of tension. The tensions that inform property are the tensions inherent in social relations.The solutions to the problems of property conflicts lie in understanding the connection between property and human relationships. Relationships sometimes form stable patterns, but they are also ongoing and constantly renegotiated. They may even end. Their beginnings and endings, their shape and character over time, are topics of intense human interest. And perhaps surprisingly, it turns out that the law of property is intimately connected with them. Judging whether a property right is justified requires us to consider the ways in which the recognition of legal rights in property structures social relations.

What are those ways? First, property law establishes minimum terms for social interaction among individuals. In so doing, it identifies individual interests that will be granted legal protection and defines the contours of those interests by reference to an implicit conception of a defensible form of social life. In structuring property law, we must be attentive to the consequences of alternative property rules and regimes for the structure of social relations and of social life in general. Shaping property law with these goals in mind precludes the adoption of a grand theory that would allow rule choices to proceed in a fashion that reduces all questions to a single model. Some theorists suggest that the tensions within property should be addressed by adopting a single normative goal, such as economic efficiency, the promotion of social welfare, or the protection of individual rights. They sometimes attempt to convince judges that they should seek only a single, well-defined goal, such as efficiency, while leaving other, more political goals, such as distributive fairness, to the legislatures. Other theorists propose that property rights be defined by reference only to a single normative formula, such as choosing those rights that would be chosen in a suitably defined constitutional bargaining situation where the contracting parties were ignorant of which side they would occupy in any future dispute.

Even if we adopt one of these approaches, we will not avoid the need to make difficult judgments. Tensions within the concept of property will reemerge when one tries to apply welfare or rights theory. Those theories do not resolve difficult questions cleanly. Rather, they structure argument in ways that highlight relevant concerns. Because I believe that a variety of values are relevant to choices about property law, I will argue that it is wrong to exclude from consideration factors that most people would consider relevant. There is a lot we can say about how to choose between alternative property regimes, especially when we realize that those choices are about the shape of social life. We cannot reduce the relevant considerations to a simple formula that protects us from the need to make difficult, controversial judgments.

Second, property law both responds to and shapes social relations by norms and rules that take into account the systemic effects of alternative entitlement structures. Paradoxically, property is both an individual entitlement and a social system. Property rights are generally understood to be the most quintessentially absolute and the most quintessentially individualistic of legal rights. But the idea of private property also assumes that there will be many owners. Many of the legal rules governing property rights are designed to make the system of property ownership run smoothly. They focus on creating a social environment in which individuals can effectively exercise their entitlements.

Some rules, such as antitrust laws, limit the accumulation of market power to ensure that individuals can enter the system freely and on fair terms. Owners are not entitled to monopolize markets in ways that prevent others from entering the market and becoming owners themselves. Similarly, the rules that prohibit racial discrimination in public accommodations and in the housing and employment markets ensure equal access to property without regard to race. These rules not only protect individual rights; they also structure a market system that does not allow opportunities to be formally conditioned on race. Other rules, such as environmental laws, protect against the cumulative effects of individual actions. Development by a single owner may have no harmful effects, but similar development by many owners may devastate the environment. Limits on each owner may be necessary to preserve property for all.

Many rules of property law are not only geared to protecting particular individual interests but are also designed to sustain the system of personal and market relations that allows those interests to flourish. They are like rules of the road that limit how people drive to ensure that everyone may drive safely and expeditiously. They are akin to constitutional provisions that establish the institutional structures for self-government or define certain social arrangements, such as slavery or racial caste, as out of bounds. Systemic rules define property regimes.

Property law sometimes responds to social relations. Customary conduct or a pattern of interaction may establish legitimate expectations that diverge from the results that would be suggested by assigning entitlements to the formal title holder. Sometimes the law respects those informal expectations by adopting property rules that privilege informal sources of property rights over formal ones. At other times, the law steps in to channel social conduct by declaring certain types of relations as out of bounds. This occurs, for example, when the law requires landlords to use court proceedings to evict tenants and gives the tenants some time to find a new place to live, rather than allowing landlords at will to change the locks on the door of the apartment and throw the defaulting tenant's belongings out on the street. More than we realize, the shape and content of property law define a form of social life.

OWNERSHIP AND OBLIGATION

Our political rhetoric, court opinions, and scholarly discourse all revert to the ownership model with surprising frequency. Both the ownership and the bundle-of-rights models obscure or deny something important: *owners have obligations as well as rights.* We know this to be true, but our language for talking about property denies it. It is a knowledge that we suppress by the way we frame discussions about property.

There is a tension hiding inside our property system, a tension between liberty and obligation. We tend to reconcile this tension by privatizing obligation. After all, one might believe that owners should be encouraged to act in a caring manner toward others but that it is wrong for government to mandate such behavior. This conception attempts to separate the private and the public world. The private world is where owners are free to satisfy solely their own interests or to look outside themselves and tend to the interests of others if they like. The public world is where limits are placed, through regulation, on the liberty of owners to act as they please. Because our political and legal tradition places the burden of persuasion squarely on the shoulders of government to justify regulation, owners are often not called upon to justify themselves even when they act in a manner that adversely affects others. Morality and obligation become private matters that cannot be mandated by government regulation without infringing on liberty. There is little space in this normative world for legally mandated obligations. The public realm of law protects liberty, while the private realm of individual choice allows a space for moral action if one is so inclined.

This reconciliation is attractive, but it cannot work. The idea that owners have no legal obligations to others wrongly supposes that property rights hardly ever conflict with other legally protected interests. If owners can exercise their legally protected rights in property in ways that adversely affect the legitimate interests of others, then those property rights must be limited, *by law,* to protect those interests. A legal system that allowed right holders to exercise their rights without regard for the legal entitlements of others would be a legal system in name only.

It is well understood that owners cannot use their property to harm others, but it is not well understood how difficult it is to define what that means. Moreover, in some cases owners may be both morally and legally obligated to use their property in ways that benefit others. Although owners are entitled to use their property for their own purposes, they are not entirely free to ignore the ways in which their property use affects others. A property system that allowed owners to act without regard for the interests of others would be self-defeating. Property regimes require individuals to respect the property and nonproperty rights of others. Although they operate to a large extent on the principle of self-interest, they also demand extraordinary cooperation to succeed. Indeed, as Carol Rose has shown, the entire institution of property would fall if most people did not believe that it is right to respect the property of others. Property cannot exist without trust.[37]

> Property itself is fragile—much more so than one would think from its sheer persistence. A central feature of this fragility is this: property entails the cooperation of others. You cannot have property all alone. Even the rule of First Possession, seemingly so quintessentially individualistic, depends on the recognition and acquiescence of others; they must know what you are claiming, and tacitly agree to let you hold it—even against their own interests.
>
> A property regime thus depends on a great deal of cooperation, trustworthiness, and self-restraint among the people who enjoy it.[38]

As Frank Michelman has trenchantly observed, "No trust, no property."[39]

Ownership entails not only the granting of rights but also the adoption of obligations. In making this point, I am moved by two underlying concerns. The first is an intellectual one. Liberals and conservatives alike will better understand their own values and achieve their own goals if they comprehend the internal tensions within the property concept and within property law. Exploring the tensions and paradoxes intrinsic to property rights and property systems will force thoughtful people to recognize unavoidable conflicts within the value systems that motivate alternative property regimes and help them better articulate the reasons for resolving those conflicts one way or another. These tensions sometimes require owners to act in the interest of nonowners and other owners rather than out of their own self-interest, narrowly considered.

The second goal is a political and moral one. I hope to counter, in a small way, the individualist turn evident in current political life. Everywhere we face the invitation to act out of self-interest and to limit the role of government—of any collective power—in enforcing mutual obligations among citizens. I want to demonstrate that mutual obligations among property owners and between owners and nonowners are dictated partly by the enlightened self-interest of owners themselves and partly by considerations of justice. Some obligations on owners of property toward nonowners are morally justified even when this entails some measure of sacrifice of self-interest. Some obligations legitimately rest on owners to share their wealth to enable nonowners to have an opportunity to become owners. Some obligations legitimately rest on the poor, such as limitations on the kinds of contracts poor persons can enter, when those limitations are needed to create a form of social life responsive to human dignity.

Defining the legal structure of property requires hard choices to be made about alternative forms of social life. Property owners have moral obligations to nonowners as well as obligations to other owners. Some of those obligations can and should be made legally compulsory. Owners have obligations both to share their wealth with the dispossessed and to use their property in a way that is compatible with the interests of nonowners in being able to enter the system to become owners themselves. This commitment to an egalitarian conception of property rights can be justified, not merely by external moral arguments, but by the very arguments that support recognition of private property in the first place. Provocative and destabilizing as it may seem, the very norms that justify protecting the rights of owners justify limiting those rights to ensure that the property system protects the ability of nonowners to become owners on relatively equal terms with those who already can claim legitimate property rights.

All this means that there is no core of property we can define that leaves owners free to ignore entirely the interests of others. Owners have obligations; they have always had obligations. We can argue about what those obligations should be, but no one can seriously argue that they should not exist.

Chapter 1 Paradoxes of Property

It was easier to make a revolution than to write 600 to 800 laws to create a market economy.
—*Jiri Dienstbier*

It would be as absurd to argue that the distribution of property must never be modified by law as it would be to argue that the distribution of political power must never be changed.
—*Morris Cohen*

Water is a valuable resource in Texas. Between 1964 and 1971 the Friendswood Development Company dug wells on its property in Harris County and began to withdraw "vast quantities of underground water" from those wells for sale to industrial users.[1] Neighboring property owners began to complain that Friendswood was drawing water from underneath their land, as well as its own. The neighbors depended on the water contained in the underlying aquifers to help support the surface of their land. In 1973 those neighbors sued Friendswood and its corporate parent, Exxon, for undermining the subjacent support for their land.[2] They argued that if Friendswood did not stop withdrawing so much water, their homes and businesses would sink into the earth. Their property would become either completely unusable or extremely expensive to fix and redevelop. According to the plaintiffs, even if it was generally lawful to withdraw water from wells on one's own land, an owner like Friendswood had no right to do so in a manner that would destroy the property rights of everyone else in the county.

Friendswood regretted the harm to its neighbors but pointed out that it was merely using its own property in a lawful manner. It had the right to withdraw water from beneath its own land, and no existing regulation limited its freedom to do so. On the contrary, prior court decisions in Texas clearly provided that owners had the power to withdraw as much water as they liked from their own land, even if this had the effect of pulling water away from neighboring land. Friendswood claimed that it had reasonably relied on this prior case law in investing in its property and that it would be unfairly surprised if the court retroactively limited its privilege to withdraw water freely from its land. The neighbors responded that they had property rights too. Whatever property right Friendswood had to withdraw water from beneath its land did not go so far as to include the power to destroy everyone else's property with impunity. The case eventually reached the Texas Supreme Court for resolution. What was to be done?

Let us assume that one of the judges deciding the case strongly supports property rights and believes in limiting government regulation of property as much as possible. In her view, infringements on property rights are as oppressive as infringements on liberty interests such as free speech or privacy. In fact, this judge views unwarranted limitations on property rights as a substantial interference with liberty because they prevent owners from using their property as they like. Liberty includes the ability to live your life on your own terms. If the only place you can live is in someone else's house, then you are subject to the control of the owner, who may evict you from the property. Only if you own property yourself can you be sure that you can do what you like. Property is thus necessary to liberty, and restraints on property can directly inhibit liberty. Such limitations also constitute a form of theft because they result in expropriation of property rights without compensation. Limiting an owner's land use for the benefit of others, if done without adequate justification, uses some people for the benefit of others; it therefore treats individuals as means rather than as ends in themselves. It also counts the interests of some to be more worthy of protection than the interests of those whose liberty is restricted. Protection of property rights is thus directly related to individual interests in autonomy, equality, and dignity. How will this judge analyze the case?

She will have a problem. The case presents a conflict of property rights—Friendswood's and the neighbors'. Here the interests in free use conflict with interests in security. One way the judge might resolve the conflict is to rely on her libertarian instincts and take the side of free use and "deregulation." She might rule in favor of Friendswood because she believes land owners should have the freedom to use their land as they wish unless a legitimate preexisting regulation clearly prohibits them from doing so. No statute or regulation limits Friendswood's ability to withdraw the water. Nor is its action clearly prohibited by any preexisting common law doctrine. In fact, as Friendswood pointed out in its brief, prior cases in Texas regarding water use supported its claim.

The judge might further conclude that this result is not unfair to the neighbors because they, like Friendswood, are equally free to use their property as they wish. She might even conclude that the neighbors acted negligently in building homes in an area that was prone to flooding or to sinkholes. If they want to prevent Friendswood from using its land as it wishes, they are free to bargain with Friendswood to induce it to stop its lawful activities. If they are unable or unwilling to come to offer Friendswood enough money to induce it to give up its property rights, then Friendswood has the same right to use its property as they have to use theirs.

Another possibility is that a strong supporter of property rights like our judge just might side with the neighbors. After all, by withdrawing water from underneath neighboring land, Friendswood has caused direct physical harm to its neighbors' land. It does not matter that all of Friendswood's activities took place on its own land. An owner who sends noxious fumes to neighboring land both physically invades that land and substantially interferes with the use and enjoyment of the neighbors' property. Such actions are prohibited by the common law doctrine of "nuisance." Moreover, under trespass doctrine, Friendswood has no right physically to enter its neighbors' land against their will, and it certainly has no right to destroy it. Friendswood, by its actions on its own land, has caused physical harm to its neighbors' property even if it has not physically entered their land. Recognition of property rights necessarily requires the government to act affirmatively to prevent such harms to property.

Does it make a difference that the destructive action is itself a use of someone else's property? The owner of a gun does not thereby acquire the legal right to kill other people. A real estate developer has no legal right to use explosives to demolish a building on her own land in a way that will harm neighboring structures. Although it is true that restricting Friendswood's withdrawal of water would infringe on its liberty interests (and, arguably, its property rights), the failure to protect the neighbors would constitute an abdication of the government's responsibility to protect the property rights of the neighbors. Regulation of Friendswood's land use does not unfairly restrict its property rights; rather, it prevents Friendswood from invading and destroying the property of others.

What about those prior Texas cases in which the courts held that owners have the right to withdraw as much water as they like even if their actions dry up their neighbors' wells? Friendswood claims that it relied on this case law when it invested in the equipment and infrastructure necessary to withdraw the water and market it. In response the judge might argue that the right to dry up a neighbor's well does not necessarily mean that one has the right to destroy the land in which the well sits.

This is because Friendswood's withdrawal of water benefits society by making water available for use on the market. Nor has Friendswood interfered with any property rights that the neighbors may have in the water itself, because before the water is pulled to the surface, they have no claim to ownership of it. Only by withdrawing the water from below can a land owner actually possess it and claim full ownership rights in it. Friendswood's withdrawal of water from beneath the neighbors' land therefore does not deprive them of legitimate, preexisting property rights.

Destruction of the land, in contrast, harms both society and the neighbors by destroying scarce and valuable real estate that is impossible or expensive to replace. It also infringes on the neighbors' preexisting property rights in the land. Thus, it was unreasonable for Friendswood to interpret prior Texas cases affirming the right to withdraw water and reduce it to possession as encompassing a right to do so in a way that would destroy others' property rights in their land. The *Friendswood* case involves the wholesale destruction of a county; no prior case that authorized the free withdrawal of groundwater comes close to allowing injury on such a scale.

In the *Friendswood* case, then, the judge faces a fundamental conflict between two distinct property rights—the right to use one's property as one sees fit and the right not to have one's property physically invaded or destroyed by others (including by other owners). In this situation, protection of property rights may provide an argument in favor of "government regulation" to prevent one owner from using her property to destroy the property of others.

Our judge, as a libertarian who believes that government should both provide strong protection for property and minimize interference with individual liberty, faces an acute dilemma. The liberty interest of one owner, Friendswood, conflicts with the security interest of other owners, the neighbors. The libertarian impulse favors deregulation to free owners from restrictions on their liberty, but the propertarian impulse suggests that this is an appropriate case to use government power to limit the freedom of individuals to seize or destroy property rightfully owned by others. This judge's political and moral commitments arguably create a conflict between liberty and property.

Would our judge be in any better shape if she adopted liberal views favoring government regulation of property? Yes and no. Adoption of a pro-regulation position would allow the judge to acknowledge that regulation of property is essential to prevent owners from using their property so as to inflict harm on others—including other property owners. But the advocate of regulation cannot get off so easily. After all, regulating Friendswood's use of its property not only prevents harm to the neighbors but also inflicts harm on Friendswood. Regulation has the effect of protecting the neighbors' property rights at the expense of Friendswood's freedom to use its land. Such a restraint on Friendswood's liberty arguably infringes on a preexisting property use—the production of water—a use that was thought to be socially beneficial before it started undermining the support for neighboring land.

Although liberals are more accepting of the need for regulation of private property than conservatives are, it is not obvious how to determine when regulation is legitimate and when it is oppressive. After all, liberals are as interested in individual liberty as are conservatives. Although they do not often associate liberty with the ownership of property, it is not clear why they do not do so. It is true, from the liberal perspective, that use of one's property may be oppressive to others by constituting an exercise of undue power over them; at the same time, it is not the case that *all* uses of property are oppressive. Some property uses are necessary to provide a setting within which individuals can exercise liberties that liberals care about, such as free speech, religious activity, and private family life, without undue government interference. For this reason, regulatory limits on property should concern liberals as much as conservatives.

Regulation of an owner's use of her property to prevent harm to neighbors inflicts harm on the one who is regulated by depriving her of the freedom to use her own property as she desires. If we are as concerned with liberty as we are with property, we must figure out what to do when these principles conflict. When these principles are attached to property claims, as they are in this case, the regulator must determine which property right should prevail.

There is no easy resolution to this conflict. One possibility is Richard Epstein's suggestion that "each person can do with his own land what he pleases as long as he does not physically invade the land of another."[3] Would this principle apply in the *Friendswood* case? In one sense, Friendswood has not physically invaded the neighbors' land; all its actions take place on its own land. It has not entered or sent any physical objects onto the neighbors' land, as it would if it spewed noxious fumes onto their property, for example. On the other hand, it has physically affected the neighbors' land by drawing water away from underneath the neighbors' property. This physical effect might well be viewed as akin to a physical invasion.

A second possible solution to the conflict is to adopt a principle that owners have no right to harm their neighbors' property, whether or not they have physically invaded it. As John Stuart Mill wrote, "The only purpose for which power can be rightfully exercised over any member of a civilized community, against his will, is to prevent harm to others."[4] But this principle also is hard to apply here. After all, it cannot be the case that *all* harms are prohibited. If property rights were protected absolutely from interference by neighbors, then an owner who first established a business in a community could claim a monopolistic right to be protected against competition. Home owners who built first in an area near the shore would be able to prevent their neighbors from building on adjacent lots if their homes would block the first home owners' view of the ocean. Thus a legal rule that protected owners against all conceivable harms would be unacceptable because it would interfere too much with the liberty interests of other owners. It is necessary, then, to determine which harms should be prohibited and which should be allowed.

Both advocates and opponents of government regulation face a problem here. They agree that we should protect property and liberty. But when various property rights conflict, and when liberty interests conflict with security interests, one must choose between the conflicting claims. One cannot solve this dilemma by voicing a strong allegiance to property rights; nor does a commitment to liberty from unwarranted regulation solve the problem. Conversely, support for regulation does not provide a solution. It acknowledges that we must choose between the principle of protecting individuals from undue interference with their free use of their land and the principle of protecting property owners from having their property damaged by the actions of others, but it cannot tell us how to make that choice.

The judges on the Texas Supreme Court split in deciding the *Friendswood* case. The six in the majority agreed with Friendswood's assertion that prior cases had established a rule of law authorizing the company to withdraw as much water as it liked without liability for any harm to neighboring owners. By so doing, those prior cases had created an exception in property law, which generally prohibits owners from using their property to cause substantial, unreasonable harm to neighbors. However, the majority changed the law in *Friendswood* by establishing a negligence test, under which Friendswood would be liable if its future actions in withdrawing water were deemed to be unreasonable. The two dissenting judges not only found that existing law already protected the rights of neighbors from unreasonable harm by Friendswood's actions but would have adopted a nuisance test rather than a negligence test to measure reasonableness. Under nuisance law an owner's actions may be deemed unreasonable if they cause more harm than good, even if the one causing the harm had not acted negligently. Thus an owner who could not have foreseen the harm her actions would cause to neighbors might still be found to have committed a nuisance if the gravity of the harm outweighed the utility of the conduct.

All the judges agreed that Friendswood could no longer enjoy absolute freedom to withdraw water but had to act in a manner that took into account the effects of its conduct on its neighbors. At the same time, the majority and minority approaches interpreted previous Texas property law in diametrically opposed ways. The difficulty they had in choosing how to define what constitutes reasonable land use was both a disagreement on principle (which rule best served the competing legitimate interests of property owners in the community) and a disagreement on precedent (how to interpret existing law).

THE PROBLEM WITH OWNERSHIP

In 1995 Texas passed a statute called the Private Real Property Rights Preservation Act.[5] The legislation grants owners the right to enjoin any new land use regulation that "restricts or limits the owner's right to property that would otherwise exist in the absence of governmental action" and causes the market value of the owner's property to drop by at least 25 percent. The owner is not entitled to an injunction if the government regulation restricts a use that "constitutes a public or private nuisance" or if it prevents a "grave and immediate threat" to life or property. The legislation also allows a restriction on property use when necessary to counter a "real and substantial threat to public health and safety" as long as the restriction will "significantly advance the health and safety purpose" and "does not impose a greater burden than is necessary to achieve the health and safety purpose."

Suppose an owner of a single-family home contends that a city zoning ordinance limiting residential construction to two stories reduces the market value of her property by more than 25 percent. Can the owner obtain an injunction prohibiting application of the ordinance to her property? What is extraordinary about this statute is that the answer to this question is not clear. Ordinary zoning laws protect the public by separating incompatible land uses, but it is not at all clear that such laws prohibit "nuisances" or "real and substantial threats to public health or safety."

This statute represents a recent trend in both politics and law. We live in an age of deregulation. What is left after we deregulate? Private property. And what is property? In thinking about property, our organizing concept is *ownership.* We want to identify a person or entity as the owner of every resource, and our assumption is that the owner has a full bundle of powers over the property and that those powers are close to absolute.

The *Friendswood* case dramatizes a crucial problem with this conventional understanding of property. Property appears simple, but in practice it generates conflict, exhibits ambiguity, and defies definition. The Texas statute presumes that it is possible to compare the value of property with and without government regulation. But as *Friendswood* demonstrated, the existing rules of property are less than clear. The majority in *Friendswood* believed that existing rules of law allowed the company to withdraw as much water as it liked and that any limitations on this privilege would constitute changes in the law. The dissenting judges felt just as firmly that existing law prohibited Friendswood from using its property so as to substantially and unreasonably harm its neighbors' property.

Suppose that the *Friendswood* case had never been heard by the courts. Instead, the Texas legislature passed a law prohibiting the withdrawal of water if it would undermine subjacent support for neighboring land. Let's call it the Subjacent Support Act of 2000. Suppose further this law substantially reduced the market value of Friendswood's land—for example, by more than 25 percent. Does the Private Real Property Rights Preservation Act grant Friendswood the right to enjoin operation of the Subjacent Support Act?

Again, the answer is not clear. Depending on the viewpoint of the judges in the majority, the hypothetical Subjacent Support Act may or may not constitute a new government rule restricting preexisting property rights. Does the act fit in the health and safety exception? Perhaps, but perhaps not. After all, undermining subjacent support does not affect health as clearly as chemical pollution does. Nor does it directly undermine safety—as long as neighbors have sufficient warning to abandon their sinking homes. The Texas legislature assumed that the background rules of property law, such as the law of nuisance, were sufficiently clear and uncontroversial that a court could determine when a regulation limited preexisting property rights and when it merely clarified or codified them. But, as we have seen, this is more problematic than it appears.

Moreover, the Texas legislature assumed that regulations legitimately limit property rights only to prevent traditional common law nuisances or to avert substantial harm to health or safety. Two important facts are missing from this set of assumptions. First, the legislature seems to have assumed that property was never traditionally subject to limitations by legislative action in situations that did not constitute traditional, common law nuisances. But of course this is not the case. Already in the nineteenth century it was commonplace for legislatures to pass legislation that defined which types of land use constitute unreasonable interferences with neighboring property rights.[6]

Second, the legislature could not imagine that regulations (such as zoning laws) might be enacted, not to prevent harm, but to protect private property itself. Zoning laws do not merely prevent harm. They are enacted to enable owners to enjoy the fullest benefits of their property by separating incompatible uses (residential, commercial, industrial) and at the same time avoid overcrowding and congestion. The legislature that passed the Private Real Property Rights Preservation Act seems to have assumed that any land use regulation that goes beyond prohibiting common law nuisances must invade property rights rather than protect them. The underlying premise is that owners have absolute freedom to use their property as they wish. This conception ignores traditional doctrines of property law designed to protect owners from the actions of others that would have the effect of unduly hampering the owners' ability to enjoy their property. These doctrines are in no way exhausted by the law of nuisance.[7]

The law of servitudes, for example, allows owners to use the institution of contract to impose land use restrictions on an entire neighborhood. Public enforcement of private covenants restricting land to residential use is designed to protect property rights as constructed by private owners. A recent law reform proposal by the American Law Institute, the Third Restatement of Property on Servitudes,[8] would modernize this hopelessly archaic area of the law, and many property law scholars hope that many of its recommendations will be adopted by court rulings or legislation. The Texas legislature appears to have assumed that new regulations which alter existing rules of property law necessarily take away property rights; it could not conceive that they might actually *protect* such rights. Modernization of traditional rules of the common law of property has been a consistent practice in U.S. courts since the beginning of the republic. The assumption that ownership means free use led the legislature to ignore traditional rules of property law that protect the security of property owners and allow changes in property rules to readjust the balance among property rights.

The Texas legislature, in other words, thought that the core meaning of property was sufficiently clear and noncontroversial that it could pass a law protecting individual owners from retroactive application of any new legislative restrictions on property rights without thereby infringing on property rights themselves. Conflict within the concept of property or among property rights and the need to manage tensions within the property system are, this legislation suggests, quite unnecessary. Yet the disagreement between the majority and minority opinions in *Friendswood* shows that this confidence is misplaced. Property is more complicated than it appears.

The traditional concept of property is ownership. Every thing has an owner, and the owner gets to control the thing.[9] The owner can use it, keep others from using it, and decide when to transfer ownership to someone else. No one can take the thing away without the owner's consent. These rights are presumed to be absolute, at least until some law intervenes to limit them—typically in order to prevent an owner from harming other people. But the harm limitation is considered minimal; most uses of property are self-regarding—that is, they are of no legitimate concern to anyone except the owner. So, when you own a thing, you have the right to do with it pretty much whatever you want. Regulations of property rights are presumed to be invalid. A heavy burden rests on the advocate of a regulation to prove that it is justified by the public interest in preventing harm to others.

Although property seems to be about power over things, it has long been understood that property rights (especially legal rights) describe not only relations between owners and things but *relations among people*—between owners and nonowners and among owners. Each property right involves not merely the owner and the land but also a decision, in the words of Laura Underkuffler-Freund, to "reward the claims of some people to finite and critical goods, and to deny the claims to the same goods by others."[10] Property represents a decision to use the power of the state to allocate the thing to the owner and to prevent others from using the thing without the owner's consent. The owner's lawful privilege to use the thing makes others vulnerable to the effects of the owner's actions; in such cases the law authorizes the actor to harm the interests of others. Moreover, rights are protected by giving owners the power to control the behavior of others—the nonowners of the thing. The owner's right to exclude others entitles her to call on the state to keep others from interfering with her ability to control the property.

In imagining the meaning of property, people call on a particular set of core conceptions, images, examples, and pictures of the social world. Property is about ownership, and the core image of ownership is ownership of a home. The core conception is the notion of absolute control; ownership is the ability to do what you like with your own, without having to account to anyone else for your actions. The image of the social world is one of many owners, each with absolute powers within the boundaries of their property. Together, these conceptions and images describe the following social relationships:

Single owner with consolidated rights. For most people, the core image of property and prime aspiration of ownership is the home. In this image, ownership is vested in a single person or entity. It is easy to tell who the owner is, and the various rights in the ownership package are all held by the same person. Unitary ownership and consolidated rights mean that we need not worry about the conflicts that might emerge if there were more than one owner of the same thing.

Title. The single owner holds title to the property. That means the law recognizes that she alone is allowed (entitled) to enjoy all rights in it. Formal procedures identify the title holder by defining the events that create property rights (such as state grant, first possession, or labor) and the transactions that transfer those rights (such as contracts, conveyances, gifts, or inheritances). Whether we are talking about initial acquisition or subsequent transfer, the concept of title is based on the assumption that it is always possible by means of clear, formal criteria to identify the owner and to determine the identity and extent of the property.

Historical entitlement. Ownership rights are created at a particular moment in time and fixed for all eternity. They can only be changed with the consent of the owner. Changes in the world or in the environment in which the property is located have no effect on the owner's rights. Nor does it matter if a particular use of property generates changing effects over time as the social context changes. Neither the identity of the owner nor the package of rights in the ownership bundle can change without the owner's consent. Only two moments matter: the moment of initial creation or acquisition and the moment of transfer. Events that happen in between or after them have no effect on the rights of the owner.

Boundaries. We know the extent and the limits of the property by a physical description of the space that is to be controlled by the owner. The boundary separates the owner from nonowners. The owner's property rights are absolute within the boundaries of the property and nonexistent outside those boundaries.

Absolute powers. Within this bounded space the owner has a host of powers and can use the property in almost any way she likes. If the property is her home, she can use it to eat, sleep, entertain guests, watch television, and raise children. She can invite other people in or exclude them. She can let them stay or ask them to leave. She can transfer the property on terms chosen by her at a time chosen by her, and no one, including (perhaps especially) the government, can take the property from her without her consent.

Control of things. The ownership concept directs our attention, first and foremost, to the relation between persons and things. It focuses attention on the owner's control of the thing that is owned. In so doing, it takes our attention away from the fact that an owner's legal rights over a thing make other people vulnerable to effects of the owner's use of it. Making the owner-thing relation central suppresses our consideration of the relationships structured by property rights.

Many owners and self-regarding uses. Although we are aware that there are many owners, we often assume that each person's use of her property concerns herself alone. It is assumed in the simple ownership model that property use has few or no effects on others for which the owner need account. Economists would say that there are no *externalities;* no one but the owner is affected by either the recognition of property rights in the owner or the ways in which the owner uses the property. From a moral standpoint the owner's activity and rights are *self-regarding;* they legitimately concern no one but the owner. Conflicts among owners appear minimal in this picture and, given the self-regarding nature of ownership, the rights of owners appear obviously to trump the rights of nonowners.

Harm. Ownership rights can be limited only to prevent harm to other people. It is accepted that not all harms are preventable and that not all harms are illegitimate. Differentiating between harms one should bear as a member of the community and harms one should not have to bear requires a determination of the interests of owners and nonowners that merit protection by the legal system. In defining those rights of security of person or property, however, the burden of persuasion traditionally rests on the party seeking to restrict the "free" actions of the owner whose conduct is supposed to have caused the harm. The ownership model is captured in Jonathan Larson's play *Rent* (1996) when the landlord, Benny, says that "the owner of that lot next door has the right to do with it as he pleases." This idea is commonplace in American culture and has a strong intuitive appeal.

Things are not as simple as they appear. The picture of the social world embodied in the ownership model is problematic, because it obscures tensions within the concept of property and among the rules needed to implement a property system in practice. Problems emerge when abstract property concepts meet the disputes over property that arise between people in the real world. The ownership model fails to acknowledge the substantial limitations on property rights that are necessary to protect the interests of both owners and nonowners harmed by the exercise of those rights. Conflicts among owners are quite prevalent. In some cases one owner's exercise of her lawful property rights interferes with other owners' rights in their own property. We also need to restrict property rights in situations where they impinge on nonproperty rights we hold as dearly.

I want to explore the ownership model by examining situations of conflict over property rights. We can do this best by exploring some basic rules of property law that are generally taught to first-year students in most law schools. Lawyers, unlike philosophers, tend to begin their study of a subject by examining concrete disputes that arise in the real world; they develop principles, not by making abstract deductions from concepts or theories, but by attending to the competing interests that characterize social interactions. This focus on cases directs our attention to the social world, where owners interact and come into conflict with one another. When we do this, several things become apparent.

First, both the concept of property and our social and legal practices exhibit internal tensions. Property describes a bundle of rights, and often some of those rights come into conflict with others in the bundle. This conflict occurs, not because property is an incoherent concept, but because property is not just an individual entitlement but a social institution involving many owners. In practice, the interests of some owners impinge upon and may interfere with the interests of other owners. When this happens, the legal rights of one owner must be limited to protect the legitimate interests of the other. Property rights cannot be fixed entitlements but are contingent, to some extent, on the social context in which they are exercised. These internal tensions within both the property concept and the institution of property are far more pervasive than is generally recognized.

Second, by focusing on disputes about property, we will discover that property rights are related to a variety of values, such as autonomy, security, distributive fairness, economic efficiency, promotion of the general welfare, and social justice.[11] These values are of different kinds; they are incommensurable, in the sense that they cannot be measured or valued according to a single metric. Property therefore exhibits inevitable tensions among the values that justify and shape it.

Third, it will become clear that the relation between property and regulation is ambiguous and problematic. In contrast to the view that regulations limit property rights, we will see, some regulations actually protect property rights. When we understand why this is so, we will see that property is itself a form of regulation. The relation between property and regulation is a contested one; regulations seem to threaten property, yet property cannot exist without regulation.

Starting with disputes will clarify what is involved in implementing a property system in the world. It will reveal facts about property as an entitlement and as a system that are important when examining property from a moral point of view. The tensions that arise when we implement property in practice are relevant in understanding the concept of property itself. If our institutional practices require us to understand property rights as inherently limited, we may do well to revise the way we talk about property so that this realization is at the forefront of our attention. Continuing to adhere to an absolutist conception of property may blind us to morally relevant facts. For this reason, we will make better judgments about how to understand and construct property if we start in the messy real world rather than in the fantasy world of theory.

Law students learn that the bundle of entitlements that attend ownership of property consists of privileges, rights, immunities, and powers. *Privileges* (or *liberties*) are rights to do something on or with your property; they confer freedom to act. *Rights* (or *claims*) describe entitlements to control the behavior of others by preventing them from interfering with specific legally protected interests of the owner. While liberties describe what you are allowed to do with your own property, without interference by the state, rights describe your powers to prevent others from interfering with your use or possession of your property. *Immunities* are rights to be secure from having others take property without the owner's consent. *Powers* involve the freedom to transfer ownership rights or alter entitlements in oneself or others. Each of these basic entitlements creates characteristic tensions that will emerge when we look at particular cases.

THE LIBERTY TO USE PROPERTY VERSUS SECURITY FROM HARM

Sometimes property owners use their property in ways that cause significant harm to owners of other properties. In *Friendswood* one owner used its property in a way that interfered with other owners' use and enjoyment of neighboring land. Every day in the papers we read about similar disputes. A factory spews pollutants onto neighboring property. A pig farm emits foul odors that make neighboring homes uninhabitable. A homeowner decorates her house and lawn with a lavish Christmas display that attracts hundreds of cars to a quiet residential neighborhood. An owner allows his property to be occupied by drug dealers, making neighboring owners feel unsafe and drastically reducing the market value of their homes. Similar disputes arise among tenants in apartment buildings or unit owners in a condominium complex. For example, noisy tenants in a second-floor apartment may disturb the sleep of the tenants downstairs.

Such cases present conflicts between freedom of action and security. One owner claims that she should be free to use her own land as she wishes; the neighbor adversely affected by that use claims an entitlement to have his property be secure from harm. Neither a strict adherence to the defense of property rights nor a general philosophy of protecting owners and promoting liberty by decreasing government regulation tells us what to do. When property rights exist on both sides of a dispute, we need a way to choose between conflicting claims.

Four approaches might be adopted to adjudicate such disputes. First, one might grant owners complete freedom of action to do what they like on their land as long as they do not physically invade their neighbors' property. As we already discovered, this principle does not give a clear answer in the *Friendswood* case; no physical invasion occurred there, but the defendant's conduct directly caused a physical effect. More important, this approach authorizes owners to engage in actions that substantially harm their neighbors' property interests. Property rights will lose much of their value if owners are free to harm or destroy their neighbors' property at will. And as *Friendswood* illustrates, there are many ways to harm your neighbors' property without leaving your own. When the harm is substantial, it is simply implausible to claim that one's status as an owner entitles one to destroy the ownership rights of everyone else.

Second, one might adopt the opposite principle—that owners have no lawful right to harm their neighbors' property interests. Owners would be guaranteed absolute security, or at least compensation and restoration when one's rights are violated. This principle is no better than the first, and for the same reason: it goes too far. Preventing any harm at all to the property interests of neighbors would inhibit liberty interests too greatly. It would also effectively confer monopoly rights on first developers, who could claim that competitors' plans to develop neighboring properties might cause them harm. A strict principle of security from any harm would protect the rights of some at the expense of the many, sacrificing equality. Neither absolute free use nor absolute security will work. We need some kind of balance between them.

One could adjudicate the dispute between freedom and security by adopting a historical approach that grants the right to the party whose use was established first. This third principle also is hard to implement in practice. What events or actions are necessary to establish the right? If Friendswood purchased its property with the intention of using it to withdraw water, is that sufficient to allow it to harm the property of owners who built later? Conversely, does the fact that others owned property in the neighborhood with the intention of building homes on their land limit Friendswood's power to use its land in the way it planned? If purchase of the land with the intention of developing it in a certain manner is an inadequate rule (because it is too hard to tell what other people's intentions are and this will make property rights too uncertain), does the construction of a building bind everyone else in the world? Suppose the area is one in which any construction is likely to affect the water table under the ground. Does the first builder in the area acquire a right to prevent development on the fifty parcels surrounding her own? Does the first builder have no obligation whatsoever to anticipate construction next door and build her own home or warehouse or factory in a way that would enable it to be supported even if others develop as she did? An absolute historical rule is problematic because, like the rule of absolute security, it effectively confers a monopoly on the first actor and prevents others from using their property as she did. The only way around this dilemma is to allow some harms to be committed and to make judgments about which types of use should and should not be privileged on the ground that they were established first.

The fourth option is to split the difference and allow land uses that commit harm as long as they are reasonable. This is the approach generally taken by the law of nuisance, the basic common law doctrine that addresses land use conflicts. The law provides remedies for harms only if they are both substantial and unreasonable. As the Iowa Supreme Court ruled in 1984, "One's use of property should not unreasonably interfere with or disturb a neighbor's comfortable and reasonable use and enjoyment of his or her estate."[12] In determining whether a land use constitutes a nuisance, courts compare the gravity of the harm with the utility of the conduct. To remedy a nuisance, a court may order the offending owner to pay damages and may issue an injunction requiring the owner to terminate the activity or alter it so as to avoid the harm.

In deciding whether a use constitutes a nuisance, courts are interested in two kinds of factors: a utilitarian calculus of the relative social value of the conflicting activities and a justice-oriented consideration of what constitutes a fair distribution of the benefits and burdens of land ownership. The utilitarian concerns compare the extent of the harm and the "social value that the law attaches to the type of use or enjoyment invaded" with the social value it attaches to "the primary purpose of the conduct" causing the harm, as well as the cost and difficulty of avoiding the harm.[13] The social value test requires an explicit balancing of the interests of the parties with the goal of maximizing social welfare by outlawing only those activities that cause more harm than good.

As to the fairness factor, the central question is whether the owner should have to bear a particular harm for the good of society. A nuisance is more likely to be found if the harm is substantial and "causes observable effects that most of us would find disagreeable,"[14] if the conduct is not suited to the locality, or if the harm is of such a nature that a property owner should not be forced to suffer it. A nuisance is less likely to be found, however, if the harmed party "came to the nuisance." In other words, if before you closed on your new home you already knew that the next-door neighbor raised pigs, you will have trouble convincing the courts to offer you relief from offensive smells. In such cases the unfairness of allowing an owner to commit substantial harm to neighboring owners must be compared with the unfairness of limiting the property rights of an owner whose use was established first in an area where it was not initially committing any harm to its neighbors.

The law of nuisance therefore adjudicates land use conflicts by requiring the decision maker to consider the ultimate normative bases for property (justice and social welfare) and to apply these norms carefully to the facts of each case. The indeterminacy of this rule of law is obvious; it cannot be applied mechanically. Rather, it requires judgment.

Conflicts over land use, such as the conflict between Friendswood and its neighbors, teach us several things. First, property rights cannot always be defined by reference to ownership alone. Because property interests owned by different people often come into conflict, it is crucial to understand the effects that claiming or exercising a property right may have on others. Sometimes, one owner's exercise of her legal rights harms other owners in a way that is or should be prohibited by the legal system. Typically in a land use conflict one owner's free use interests are at odds with the security interests of another owner or owners. In such cases it is not possible to reason from a fixed right or entitlement to determine who wins the dispute. Exercising one entitlement may harm similar or different entitlements held by others. Friendswood cannot plausibly say that it should win the lawsuit because it owns its property and has a legal right to do what it pleases with its land; the neighbors are also owners, and the effects of Friendswood's claim would be to deny completely *their* property rights.

Second, property requires regulation. Giving Friendswood an absolute right to use its property as it likes would authorize it to destroy the property of all its neighbors; but if the neighbors have absolute rights too, the law cannot leave them vulnerable to such a violation of their property. We have here, not just a clash of rights, but a clash of the *same* right—the right to private property. Resolving this clash between free use and security—two of the particular entitlements in the bundle of rights that make up ownership—means that one right or the other must be limited; the state has no choice but to privilege one right over the other. Deregulation is not an option. The only question is how to draw the line between the conflicting rights. This is a regulatory decision. It is true that the neighbors in *Friendswood* do not necessarily see themselves as asking for regulation. What they want is protection of their interests in controlling their property. But, of course, this requires that Friendswood's property rights be regulated to protect the property of others.

Regulation has two different meanings: the limitation of free use and the alteration of established property rights. According to the first meaning, any government action preventing Friendswood from sinking its neighbors' homes into the bay would constitute a regulation. The second meaning associates regulation with any law that alters existing property rights. In this view, because zoning laws limit free land use in order to protect the interests of other owners, any law that removed a restriction on the use of land (and would therefore be deregulatory under the first definition) would take away a previously recognized property right and thus would count as a regulation of property. Under this second definition, a law authorizing Friendswood to destroy its neighbors' property might infringe on the neighbors' preexisting rights to be protected from nuisances and thus constitute a regulation taking the neighbors' property rights.

Depending on how one looks at it, the same law might be viewed by some as regulatory and by others as deregulatory. This is of crucial importance because of the stigma that has attached to the term *regulation* in American politics since the 1980s. Calling a proposed legal rule a regulation can make it hard for supporters to win its passage. On the other hand, if supporters can characterize a piece of legislation as deregulatory, it may automatically be viewed as justified and may therefore escape careful scrutiny and thoughtful criticism. The outcome of legislative initiatives often hinges on who wins this battle of rhetoric and succeeds in placing the burden of persuasion on the other side.

Third, land use conflicts cannot be resolved by resorting to definitions or fixed claims. They require the exercise of judgment and the application of social norms. I do not mean to argue that land use conflicts must always be decided case by case. General rules may indeed be formulated to adjudicate particular classes of cases. For example, the law in almost all states allows owners to build on their property even if they thereby interfere with their neighbors' access to light and air. But whether we engage in case-by-case adjudication or regulate through rigid rules, we must consider the goals and values to be served by property rights and the property system to determine which rules to promulgate or which property interests should prevail in particular cases. As Joseph Weintraub, the great Chief Justice of the Supreme Court of New Jersey, explained, "Property rights serve human values. They are recognized to that end, and are limited by it."[15] Property is defined not by reference to a fixed conception but by reference to human values.

The nuisance doctrine, for example, resolves land use conflicts by requiring courts and juries to assess the reasonableness of one owner's land use in light of the harm it causes to others. This solution, of course, is a nonsolution. It requires a judgment of some kind. Either we balance the interests of the parties, or we consider the overriding interests of the community, or we make a moral judgment about which uses to favor. In any case, this solution to land use conflicts requires the exercise of judgment. It answers the dilemma by restating the problem. In so doing, it forces us to attempt to articulate the considerations of justice or utility that prompt us to want to rule in favor of freedom or security in particular cases or classes of cases. It calls for us to make a judgment and forces us to explain the factors that lead us one way or the other. It forces us to face the tension within the concept of property and within the legal institution of property head on, without flinching or turning away.

Disputes over property use can be solved only by reference to human values, to a normative framework that helps us choose between freedom and security. In this sense, the nuisance doctrine redefines property as *containing* within it the normative values and tensions that characterize such disputes. As Laura Underkuffler-Freund explains, the traditional view of property—the "absolute approach"—assumes that "property is objectively definable or identifiable, apart from social context; and that it represents and protects the sphere of legitimate, absolute individual autonomy."[16] In contrast, in the "comprehensive approach" to property prevalent in the era of the Founders, property "did not represent the autonomous sphere of the individual to be asserted against the collective; rather, it embodied and reflected the inherent tension between the individual and the collective."[17] This is partly a tension between the individual and society, but it is also a tension between individuals. Property owners worry not only about their relation with state power or society as a whole; they also worry about the conflicts that arise when the exercise of property rights by one owner impinges on those of another.

Fourth, the values implicit in choices among property rules are not only in conflict; they are various and incommensurable. How do we compare the value of freedom and the value of security, and choose one over the other? Because land use conflicts often involve legitimate freedom and security interests on both sides, arriving at a resolution by choosing among alternative rules is often difficult. In the *Friendswood* case, the company claims a liberty interest in free use of its own land as well as a security interest in its established investment. Because the prior rule of law seemed to authorize it to withdraw water without liability, it invested in reliance on that rule and reasonably expected that the state would not retroactively declare its actions unlawful. On the other hand, the neighbors claim a strong security interest in the continued existence of their land and structures; their autonomy as individuals and as owners is threatened if Friendswood has the power to destroy their homes and businesses. Similarly, we face conflicting claims about which rule will best promote the general welfare or economic efficiency. Friendswood can claim that the production of water is crucial to the economic livelihood of the community and that this benefit from the company's actions outweighs the harm to the surrounding owners. The neighbors can counter that the general welfare will be better promoted by inducing owners to show concern for their neighbors, most of whom also own land, by using their property in a manner that minimizes external harm to others.

Cases like *Friendswood* confront us with difficult judgments. Fairness claims can be made on both sides, and each of the parties can plausibly argue that their approach to property rights promotes economic efficiency or social welfare. Worse still, we may face an intractable conflict between incommensurable values. Suppose we conclude that the social need for production of water is so great that it must go on despite the harm to the neighbors. We may at the same time conclude that it is unfair to place the cost of this socially beneficial activity on the neighbors because it strips them of legitimate preexisting property rights and because this harm is both of a kind and a magnitude that they should not have to bear for the good of society.

One solution is to split the difference and allow Friendswood to continue withdrawing water while requiring it to pay damages to the home owners who are injured. This decision might maximize social utility (allowing production of the water) while achieving distributive justice (by providing compensation to the victims of the socially beneficial conduct). But the compensation is unlikely to be adequate here, no matter how high it is set. After all, the result of Friendswood's actions is not just to impose a monetary loss on the neighbors; it is to disrupt their lives and destroy their homes and perhaps the entire community. Personal, emotional connections with their homes and community cannot be replaced with money. In such a case, we face a difficult choice between incommensurable values—values that cannot be adequately described or measured on the same scale and are not reducible to cash. In such cases, the protection of property rights forces us to make a hard decision, to make a choice that will occasion regret, whichever way we go.

THE RIGHT OF EXCLUSION VERSUS THE RIGHT OF ACCESS

Similar conflicts over land use also arise between owners and nonowners. After all, property rights are not the only rights protected by the legal system, and nonproperty-based rights sometimes trump property rights.

Consider the right to exclude nonowners from one's property. The Supreme Court has noted that the "power to exclude has traditionally been considered one of the most treasured strands in an owner's bundle of property rights."[18] In many ways, the power that owners have over their property derives from their legally delegated power to call on the aid of the state to exclude nonowners. Any legal rule that limits the owner's right to exclude therefore bears a heavy burden of justification. Or does it?

Think about a shopping center. Can it exclude customers on the basis of race? Of course not. The law prohibits businesses open to the public from discriminating on the basis of race. In addition, federal and state laws now prohibit such businesses from discriminating on the basis of religion, national origin, or disability. Many states prohibit discrimination in such facilities on the basis of sex—although no federal law does so. It is now firmly established that owners who serve the public—such as malls, restaurants, motels, and theaters—have an obligation to allow access to their property and to do business with customers without invidious discrimination. Public accommodation laws are supplemented by other antidiscrimination statutes, such as those requiring businesses to allow tenants and employees to enter their property even if the owner of the business wishes to exclude them or refuse to deal with them.

Public accommodation laws fit awkwardly with the conventional conception of ownership. The usual statement of the common law is that most owners have the right to exclude nonowners unless that right is limited by a civil rights statute. In this view, the right to exclude is presumptively absolute, and the statutorily created right of equal access to public accommodations is a limited and narrow exception to the basic principle. The traditional formulation of the problem places all property rights on one side, with owners, and suggests that nonowners have a right of access to others' property only in exceptional circumstances. On one side of the dispute is a property claim and on the other side is an equality claim. In this formulation, civil rights laws appear to limit property rights.

This way of conceptualizing the problem ignores the fact that public accommodations laws not only limit the property rights of the owner but *transfer* one of those rights to nonowners. Public accommodations laws grant members of the public a limited right of access to businesses open to the public. The owner's right to exclude is limited by a competing public right of access to the property. A right of access to property possessed by another is a property right. In fact, we have a name for such a right: it is called an *easement*. The most common easement is a right of way for passage, as in a road over another's land. Although we do not ordinarily see public accommodations laws as granting property rights to the public, there is no logical or historical reason to view them as doing anything less.

In *Nollan v. California Coastal Commission*[19] the Supreme Court considered a California statute that authorized a public zoning agency to deny beachfront owners a permit to expand their homes unless they agreed to grant the public an easement on dry sand to walk along the shore. The Supreme Court held that requiring the owner to grant the public the easement, as a condition for the permit, was an unconstitutional taking of property from the beachfront owner. A public accommodations law similarly takes away a portion of the owner's right to exclude and creates a public easement of access. In so doing, it takes part of the owner's preexisting property rights and grants countervailing property rights to the public.

I do not mean to argue that we should start talking about the right of access to public accommodations as a property right rather than an equality right, and

I certainly do not mean to argue that such laws unconstitutionally take property rights. It may be rhetorically more powerful to use the language of equality than to use the language of property to talk about public accommodation laws. But if we consider the social function of property and ownership, it is crucial to recognize that public accommodations laws dictate significant—even revolutionary—transfers of property rights from business owners to the public and from white persons as a class to African Americans as a class, as well as to other racial and ethnic groups who were historically victimized by discriminatory practices, including Asian Americans, Latinos, Jews, and American Indians.

Public accommodations laws therefore divide ownership rights between store owners and the public. An action that would formerly have constituted a trespass now becomes a privileged entry onto land possessed by another. The tension between the right of exclusion and the right of access relates not only to the question of when a nonowner can enter property possessed by another but also to the question of when an owner can lawfully refuse to transfer her property rights. Public accommodations laws not only grant members of the public a right to enter stores; they also grant a right to purchase goods and services. The owner of an appliance store cannot refuse to sell a refrigerator to a customer because she speaks English with a Mexican accent. A landlord who wants to keep Jews from renting in her building cannot do so legally. An employer who wishes to hire only members of her own race is disempowered from doing so. In all these cases the law requires the owner to engage in a transaction that has the effect of forcibly transferring property rights from the owner to the nonowner.

Property cannot exist as a dynamic social institution if there is no ability to acquire property. If one cannot obtain access to a store in order to purchase property, one cannot become an owner. If an owner can refuse to deal on the basis of race, then the ability of members of that race to become owners has been limited. The Supreme Court has recognized this dilemma in its interpretation of the Civil Rights Act of 1866. That act grants all persons the same rights to contract and to purchase property "as is enjoyed by white citizens."[20] Contracts of sale made between white persons and African Americans became legally enforceable, and testimony about such agreements had to be admitted in court regardless of the race of the claimant—both huge changes from Antebellum law. But the 1866 statute was not originally interpreted as *requiring* owners of public accommodations to contract with customers regardless of their race. In 1968, in *Jones v. Alfred Mayer Co.,*[21] the Supreme Court overturned this long-standing interpretation when it held that the rights to contract and to purchase property enshrined in the Civil Rights Act of 1866 outlawed racially motivated refusals to engage in business dealings. The right to contract and to purchase property, for the first time, meant a correlative duty on private owners not to refuse to sell merely because of the potential buyer's race.

The result of the *Jones* opinion was to acknowledge a fundamental tension within the concepts and social institutions of contract and property. Under one view, ownership entails the right to choose when and to whom to sell property, as well as the right to exclude nonowners from one's property. This view suggests that it constitutes a limitation on property rights when the owner of a store who wishes to exclude a customer on the ground of race is forced to admit the customer, or when her right to choose whether and to whom to sell her property is curtailed by law. Under a competing interpretation, however, property rights are only respected if one has the power to acquire property. To do so, the marketplace must be open for anyone to enter and to conduct business. One who is systematically excluded from much of the marketplace has limited opportunities to acquire property. Civil rights laws promote the free flow of property without regard to race, religion, or sex. But to do so they must impose obligations on business owners to deal with anyone who comes through the door.

Allegiance to a system of private property does not automatically entail acceptance of one viewpoint or the other. The ownership idea may appear to favor the position that the one who owns property should have the right to exclude. In this view, ownership must be limited to achieve equal access to property without regard to race, sex, religion, or other irrelevant factors. But the ownership idea also suggests that nonowners are entitled to become owners and that it is unfair to exclude them from doing so by pernicious discriminatory practices. In this alternative view, the refusal to sell because of race denies property rights to the customer; the right to purchase property requires limiting the exclusionary conduct of the store owner. Choosing between these constructions of property entails making judgments about appropriate forms of social life, and the choice is *internal* to the property system.

The conflict between exclusion and access, like that between freedom of use and security from harm, entails a tension—between an absolute right to exclude and the right of access to property to make purchases, obtain employment and housing, and thereby become part of the property system. Public accommodations laws do not represent a wholesale destruction of the right to exclude. In fact, businesses open to the public generally retain the right to exclude individuals who are not there to transact business or who are disruptive or destructive. They therefore draw a line between the store owner's legitimate exclusionary interests and the public's legitimate interests in access.

Public accommodations laws divide property rights in another way, as well. They distinguish between types of property, such as private homes, where rights of exclusion prevail, and types of property open to the public, such as restaurants, motels, and retail stores, where rights of access prevail. Property is not all of a kind; the social context in which the property operates and the types of uses prevalent there affect the assignment of legal rights and obligations.

The idea that property should be open to the public without regard to race cannot reasonably be considered a minor limitation on property rights. Rather, public accommodations laws constitute a revolution in the understanding of ownership and the relation between property and equality. The federal public accommodations and employment discrimination statute was passed only in 1964, nearly one hundred years after the Civil War. It took a bloody civil rights movement and the assassination of President John F. Kennedy to provide the political support needed to pass the legislation. The extension of federal antidiscrimination law in 1968 to housing had to wait for more agitation and the assassinations of Robert Kennedy and Martin Luther King. Given the protracted struggle and steep sacrifice required of the civil rights movement to achieve these goals, it is difficult to conceive of public accommodations laws as limited and narrow changes to property rights. Rather, when viewed in historical and social context, the change in property rights effectuated by these laws is nothing short of revolutionary.

The idea that property should be open to the public without regard to race is wholly foreign to the understanding of the right of exclusion that prevailed in much of the United States before the 1960s. The rights of property owners no longer encompass the right to exclude people from public accommodations on the basis of race. Rather, the general presumption, both in law and in common understanding, is now that owners who use their property to conduct business thereby waive some portion of their property rights, making the property available for public access without regard to race. The effect of this principle is to transfer a large stick in the bundle of property rights from the owner to the public at large. Home owners, on the other hand, retain their right to exclude, as long as they are not renting or selling their property. They are free to act in a racially discriminatory manner in deciding whom to invite into their homes.

One might say that the difference between a home and a business is that the home owners have significant privacy interests in excluding nonowners from their property, while business owners express more limited privacy interests by issuing a general invitation to the public to enter their property for business purposes. Therefore in the home we allow owners to discriminate on the basis of race. Storekeepers, restaurant owners, employers, and landlords, however, are obligated to make their property available without regard to race. In the home, privacy interests outweigh equality interests, whereas in public accommodations, equality interests trump privacy interests.

Because privacy norms may conflict with equality norms, we identify the types of property where one set of norms prevails over the other. Yet it is an oversimplification and a distortion to declare that property rights prevail in the home and equality rights in places of business. In both cases there is a conflict between two property rights: the right of access and the right to exclude. The owners of private homes retain a general right to exclude nonowners from their premises; the right to exclude prevails over the right of access. However, once an owner opens her property to the public for business purposes, the law requires the property to remain for the public uses to which she has dedicated it; the right of access prevails over the right to exclude.

The rules governing the property system not only must protect the interests of those who already own property, but also must establish legitimate conditions under which nonowners can acquire property rights. The owner of a store that wishes to exclude customers on the basis of race claims a right both to exclude customers from the land and to refuse to sell goods or services to customers as the owner wishes. The customer who claims a right of access seeks a right to enter the property as well as a right to purchase goods or services offered to the public. Just as the right to exclude clashes with the right to have access, so the right to purchase property clashes with the right to refuse to sell. The balance between these competing claims is different in the context of the store and the home. Equality norms, as well as privacy and associational norms, all affect how the balance is drawn and which right takes precedence. But in the end we are presented with a conflict among sticks within the property bundle. The tension is not between property rights and equality rights; the tension is *within* our idea of property itself.

IMMUNITY FROM LOSS AND THE DILEMMA OF FORMALITY

People generally assume that property entails the right to keep the property. Theft strikes at the heart of ownership. Theft is the ultimate disrespect for property. Although public authorities can forcibly take property from citizens, they cannot do so without compensation. Yet consider the doctrine of adverse possession. This long-standing rule of law holds that one who openly and notoriously possesses property belonging to another for a sufficient period of time without the owner's permission acquires title to the property. This extraordinary rule appears to vindicate theft if only the thief can hold onto the property long enough. What principle might conceivably justify it?

Most of the current applications of this rule concern border disputes. One owner mistakenly builds a fence a few feet over the border onto neighboring property. The neighbor whose property is encroached on does not notice the mistake. Both owners believe the border is in a different place than it really is. Most owners do not hire a surveyor every few years to ensure that they have not inadvertently encroached on neighboring property or allowed their neighbor to encroach. Rather, the planting of shrubs and trees, the placement of picnic tables, swing sets, fences, and the like serve to mark de facto borders.

Disputes may erupt when somehow an owner learns that a neighbor has encroached on her property as defined in the legal title. For that owner the news brings a windfall. She had not known that her property extended farther than the fence, and the additional land would be an unexpected benefit. She might finally have a sunny spot for her tomato plants—once her neighbor pulls his fence back to the property line specified in her title. She calls the discrepancy to her neighbor's attention, and he is quite taken aback: he had no idea that his fence encroached on his neighbor's land. He did not mean to encroach on it, but the fence has now been there for thirty years. It was there when he purchased his house, and he had no reason to think it was not on the true boundary. He thinks of the land enclosed by the fence as his property, and, until his neighbor's recent discovery of the error, she had too.

Most people assume that formal documents of title prevail in disputes of this kind. They are mistaken. When someone has visibly occupied a piece of land for a long time, the rules assign ownership rights to the occupier, thereby stripping those rights away from the "true owner" of record. Justice Oliver Wendell Holmes explained the rule poetically in a letter to William James. The adverse possessor—the person who has been occupying the property—has come to "shape his roots to his surroundings, and when the roots have grown to a certain size, cannot be displaced without cutting at his life."[22] Property rights are based partly on formal documents of title, such as written deeds, leases, wills, mortgages, and marriage certificates, and partly on expectations that grow from informal arrangements such as long-standing possession, a course of dealings, oral statements, informal understandings, personal relationships, social practices, and customs of the trade.

When a conflict exists between formal and informal indicators of ownership, a fundamental tension is created. When we are in our planning mode, prescribing rules for conduct, we generally expect people to put all their important transactions in writing, to take care to spell out the agreements they make and the responsibilities they assume. But in the messy real world, people do not read the contracts they sign; they write incomplete or inaccurate statements of the deal as they understand it; they make oral commitments that diverge from formal recitations of the agreement; and they engage in courses of action that diverge from the written contract requirements.[23] And sometimes they just ignore formal promises and assignments of property rights and act in accordance with other norms based on personal relationships or social custom.[24] When we see the results of long-standing acquiescence in informal arrangements that diverge from the formal legal arrangements, it often seems unfair to insist on the formalities. After all, when both parties have acted in ways inconsistent with formal property and contract rights, one might even understand the parties' acquiescence in the informal arrangements as an informal transfer of property rights. Adverse possession may look less like theft by the adverse possessor of the title holder's property and more like abandonment by the true owner of part of her property and possession of the abandoned, unowned land by the neighbor, who thereby interferes with no one's legitimate expectations.

If we are interested in granting owners immunity from loss of their ownership rights without their consent, we are hoping to protect their reasonable expectations while confirming their secured entitlements to what they rightly consider to be their own. Yet it is not clear how to define which expectations are reasonable. Is it reasonable for an owner to rely on long-standing informal borders? Should a reasonable owner pay for a survey every so often? Would a reasonable owner allow someone else to occupy part of her land for fifty years and expect to retain property rights to it? The idea of immunity conceals within it a tension between the norm of protecting the title holder from loss of her rights without her formal consent to a change and the norm of protecting the user's expectations based on long-standing possession without interference from anyone, including the owner of record. Title is sometimes based on formal and sometimes on informal sources, and the concept of property gives us no help at all in formulating a rigid answer to the question of whose immunity rights should be protected in cases like this.

THE POWER TO TRANSFER AND THE ALIENABILITY DILEMMA

Another central entitlement encompassed by ownership is the right to transfer ownership rights by sale or gift. The transfer may even take place after the owner's death if it is stipulated in a valid will. The converse of the right of immunity—the right not to lose ownership rights without one's consent—is the right to transfer ownership rights by selling or giving away all or some of one's entitlements in a particular piece of property.

Although the right to exclude is sometimes characterized as the most basic property right, the power to alienate property—to transfer ownership—is also often identified as one of the core rights associated with the ownership concept. The identification of property with transferability is so close that courts sometimes determine that an interest is not a property interest just because it cannot be transferred. For example, current law allows property acquired during marriage to be equitably distributed between the spouses if they divorce. Some recent cases have involved individuals who worked to put their spouses through graduate school, only to be served with divorce papers shortly after graduation. Some courts have held that the enhanced earning potential embodied in the graduate degree cannot be property that can be distributed on divorce precisely because degrees are not transferable.[25]

However, the right to transfer is not absolute. Antidiscrimination laws require owners of property to sell housing and goods and to employ workers even when they might wish to act differently. The right to sell one's property to whomever one chooses may clash with the right to purchase property without regard to morally irrelevant factors, such as race or disability. An absolute power to determine when to sell would inhibit the ability of individuals to enter into transactions for the purpose of becoming owners.

The bulk of the rules traditionally taught in the property law course in U.S. law schools relate to regulations of property conveyances that are imposed to promote the alienability of property. In a classic example, an owner transfers property to his son, A. The deed says that the property is transferred "to A and the heirs of his body." This conveyance traditionally created a property interest called a "fee tail." The property will be owned by A during his lifetime and, on his death, will pass to his heirs. In England the heir traditionally was the eldest son. The son would, in turn, own the property for his lifetime, and on his death it would pass to *his* oldest son, and so on. The effect of the conveyance was to ensure that subsequent owners could never write a will leaving the property to someone other than the eldest son. The owner, A, could attempt to sell the property, but if he did so the buyer would only get what A owned—a property right for the life of A. When A died, the ownership would automatically pass to A's oldest son. The fee tail disaggregates property ownership by conferring present ownership rights on the grantee, A, and future ownership rights on A's heirs.

The effect of this property interest is to substantially limit the alienability of the property. It will be quite difficult to find a buyer for the property since they will not receive permanent ownership rights, only a "life estate" for the life of A (or A's heir if A has died). Nor can a potential buyer buy the future interests from the future heirs; one cannot tell who will inherit the property until A dies, and even then nothing can be done because one cannot contract with that owner's heirs either. Potential purchasers who might wish to buy for the life of the current owner will certainly not invest in developing such lands or creating new businesses on them. The fee tail is likely to have the effect of taking the property out of the real estate market and leaving ownership of it inside the family. Keeping the property inside the family has two negative effects: it inhibits the autonomy of the current owner and may substantially reduce the value of the land, thereby decreasing social welfare.

Autonomy is affected because the current generation is effectively under the control of the prior generation. If A wanted to sell the land and move to London, he could not do so; he is effectively tied to the land in a manner that resembles feudalism rather than liberal individualism. Allowing him to sell the land and use the proceeds to buy land elsewhere increases his liberty to live where he pleases, do the work he wants to do, and engage in the associations that make his life meaningful. Economic efficiency may be significantly impeded by the fee tail because no one is going to buy the land or develop it for business purposes if they will lose ownership once the current owner dies. Because of this, neither ownership of the property nor its use can easily change. There is no reason to believe that the original use of the property will forever be the use that is most beneficial, either to the current owner or to society as a whole. Because it restrains alienation, the fee tail also prevents property from being put to its most valued use.

In order to allow the current owner to use the property as he sees fit and to allow its transfer to someone who can use it more profitably, the law must step in to consolidate property rights in the current owner. In both England and the United States this occurred through legal devices that allowed the current owner to cut off the interests of future generations and be vested with full ownership rights. Most states in the United States abolished the fee tail in the nineteenth century. In those states, conveyances that purport to create a fee tail will be interpreted as a fee simple, and the owner can sell the property outright, lease it, or leave it to his heirs.

In order to consolidate rights in the current owner, we must limit the ability of the prior owner to disaggregate the rights in the property bundle to create a fee tail. In other words, an owner who wishes to create a fee tail, thereby passing ownership rights from generation to generation until the line runs out, will not be allowed to do so. Contracts and wills that purport to create a fee tail will be regulated by law. An attempt to create a fee tail will fail; the grantee will be treated as a full fee-simple owner of property. Notice that consolidating property rights in the grantee limits the freedom of the grantor to enter into enforceable contracts or grants that create vested property rights in future generations. In this kind of case, freedom of contract clashes with the ownership ideal. In order to vest full ownership rights in the grantee, the grantor's power of disposition must be limited.[26] This limitation produces a conflict not only between contract norms and property norms, but also between property rights. In giving the grantee the right to transfer property, the grantor loses the right to divide up property rights between the son and his heirs to ensure that the property will stay in the family after his son's death.

Parents may want not only to keep land in the family but also to control the future behavior of their children. Sometimes parents leave property to an unmarried child, but if the child later marries, ownership shifts to someone else. Such conveyances used to be common for daughters; they would provide support while the daughter was single, and then the assumption was that her husband would take care of her and she would no longer need the income from the property. This type of conveyance may have the effect of inhibiting the daughter from marrying, since marriage would cause her to lose the property. It also assumes that she neither needs nor is entitled to own property once she marries. Thus the conveyance may interfere with the child's liberty interest in choosing to marry and, if applied to daughters and not sons, may discriminatorily deny property rights on the basis of sex. A choice must be made between the grantor's right to condition future ownership of the land and the grantee's liberty interests in living her life as she pleases without suffering a loss of property rights because of her choices.

Similar tensions arise from many land use agreements. Consider an owner who wishes to sell part of the land on which she makes her home, but only if she can be sure that a factory will not be built on the parcel being sold. The seller can ask the buyer to promise not to build a factory there, and the promise is enforceable under standard contract law. But suppose the buyer later sells the land to another party? The original seller cannot rely on the buyer's promise unless future owners of the land will also be bound by it; otherwise the buyer could sell her parcel tomorrow to someone who means to build a factory. To make sure that no factory is ever placed next to the seller's house, the buyer's promise must "run with the land" to bind all future owners of the burdened parcel.

But what if the original owner later wishes to sell the remainder of her property? Can she assure prospective buyers that a factory will not be built next door? She cannot do so unless a future owner of her property has a right to enforce the land use restriction. Thus the benefit of the covenant, like the burden, must run with the land. A covenant running with the land, then, is a promise restricting land use, made between the owners of two parcels of land, that binds and benefits all future owners of both parcels. The future owners of the benefited parcel can enforce the covenant against future owners of the burdened parcel. Covenants are usually imposed in a deed. They are also common in leases, where they refer not to two parcels of land but to a single parcel when property rights are divided between the tenant's current possessory rights and the landlord's future reversionary rights.

Covenants (or "equitable servitudes") pose difficult dilemmas for those who want to have the government both provide strong protection for property rights and deregulate property. Consider an owner, Mr. Bach, who wishes to buy a home in a quiet neighborhood but also wants an assurance that the adjacent properties will be used for residential purposes. (Let us assume that local zoning ordinances do not afford this protection.) He must therefore acquire two rights: ownership of the lot where his home will be located and control over the use of neighboring lots. The developer of the subdivision, Mr. Mozart, assures him that no factory or store will be constructed on neighboring lots and even includes this promise in his deed to Lot 1. But some weeks later, when Mr. Mozart sells Lot 2 to Mr. Beethoven, he fails to include a restrictive covenant in the deed. Mr. Beethoven promptly applies for a permit to open a restaurant on the property, and the town grants him a business license. What is Mr. Bach's remedy? Since the developer made a promise he did not keep, Mr. Bach could sue him for breach of contract and obtain damages, probably in the form of a cash award. But he cannot obtain injunctive relief against the developer to control what happens on Lot 2, since Mr. Mozart no longer owns that lot. Mr. Bach could seek an injunction to stop Mr. Beethoven from opening a business on the lot; but as Mr. Beethoven has never promised anyone not to do so, under traditional contract law, Mr. Bach is out of luck. If a remedy is going to be available, only property law can accomplish this by imposing a continuing obligation on future owners of Lot 2.

If Mr. Mozart's promise does not run with the land to bind Mr. Beethoven, Mr. Bach will have to contract with every buyer in the neighborhood independently to obtain their agreement not to use their lots for nonresidential purposes. Yet even that precaution will not protect him, for any of those owners can turn around and sell their property the next day to someone else who has not promised anybody anything. A buyer who wishes to open a business may be willing to pay the sellers enough to enable them to pay damages to Mr. Bach for having violated their covenant with him. The only way to ensure that no business goes up on neighboring land without Mr. Bach's consent is to burden Lot 2 and impose the restriction on all future owners of the lot regardless of whether they voluntarily agree to it.

Richard Epstein argues that the solution to this problem is simple. We need only two rules: owners are free to make contracts that restrict land use, and those restrictions are enforceable against future owners who buy with notice of them. The institution of contract then can be used to create mixed property holdings; some owners are given entitlements to control the use of property possessed by others. Property rights are thereby disaggregated, with some rights held by the possessor and some held by the neighbor. Restricted property entitlements determine what sellers can sell and what buyers can buy; you can only sell what you own, and if you do not own the free use entitlement to a restricted lot, the buyer cannot obtain the entitlement from you. A buyer who purchases a restricted lot with notice implicitly agrees to the restriction. Notice is provided by requiring owners to record their deeds with the local government—typically at the registry of deeds or the recording office. If the buyer wishes to purchase an unrestricted lot, she can look elsewhere or she can bargain with the owners of the dominant estates (those benefited by the covenant or those who have the right to enforce it) to waive the restriction.[27]

Epstein's argument assumes that owners, by contract, can impose restrictions on future purchasers who buy with notice of them, whether or not those future buyers agree to the restrictions. It also assumes that property rights can be unbundled or disaggregated as one likes. There are good arguments for allowing servitudes of this kind to be created, but there are also good arguments for limiting them.[28] Allowing property rights to be disaggregated in this way makes it much more difficult for a potential buyer to purchase an unrestricted lot in the neighborhood covered by the restrictive covenant. Indeed, it is practically impossible if the restrictions are part of a common scheme where they are mutually enforceable by all owners in a neighborhood for it will be extremely difficult to get all the other owners to agree to waive their rights. The requirement of unanimity may mean that the restrictions will last beyond the point when the benefit of the covenant outweighs the burden. For this reason the courts have developed doctrines that allow covenants to lapse if a change in conditions decreases their utility or if they impose an undue hardship on the owner of the restricted parcel.

More fundamentally, it is not clear that strong protection for property rights entails allowing an owner to impose servitudes on future owners. Why should a buyer of property be bound by contractual promises made by prior owners? Because enforcing the initial contract limits the contractual and property rights of new buyers, Epstein's solution is arguably backwards. Perhaps full protection of property rights means that current owners should have the liberty to use their property as they see fit unless they agree to restrictions on its use. In this view, enforcing limits on property rights imposed by a prior owner constitutes a violation of property rights rather than protection of them. Similarly, freedom of contract means that parties are bound by promises they make, and they are not bound when they make no promise. If an owner wishes to bind a neighbor who has made no promise, that owner is free to contract with the neighbor but has no right to impose a restriction on an owner who has made no promise of any kind. The problem is that servitudes pose conflicts between the property rights of the owner who wants freedom from a promise she never made and the property rights of the owner who purchased property in reliance on the enforceability of the promise against all future owners in the neighborhood.

In our example Mr. Bach wishes to create by voluntary agreement a particular kind of property right: the right to keep one's neighborhood exclusively residential. To create this entitlement, he must be able to link ownership of one lot with negative easements in neighboring lots (restrictions on the use of someone else's land) that are enforceable against any and all owners of the restricted lots. This bundle of rights requires restricting the free use rights of the neighbors in order to protect the security of the first owner. The law of servitudes poses a conflict between the liberty interests of owners to use their property as they see fit unless they have agreed to the contrary and the security interests of owners who want to use private agreements to limit allowable uses on neighboring land. Which set of interests should prevail? Which property right—the right to free use or the right to security—trumps the other? The law of servitudes binds new owners to promises made by their predecessors in order to provide security to the owners of the benefited parcels and to allow creation of a disaggregated, rebundled property right.

Covenants also create issues relating to the right of access. Consider a developer who builds houses in a residential subdivision with restrictive covenants limiting use to residential purposes. Another covenant creates a home owners association composed of the lot owners; the association has the legal power to enforce the restrictions, as well as the power to approve future sales of the lots in the subdivision.[29] Perhaps the association's consent is required before a sale, or perhaps the association is given a right of first refusal—a right to purchase the property from the seller before it goes on the open market or to match the price offered by others. The association may use these powers to control the identity of future buyers. One might consider this to be a useful and democratic arrangement that gives the community the ability to protect its way of life by limiting ownership to families and excluding fraternities or time-share condominiums. Or one might see it as a disgraceful exclusionary practice that interferes with the liberty interests of sellers and buyers and is prone to misuse to impose racial restrictions. In either case, we again have a tension between the property rights of the present owners and the rights of outsiders wishing to purchase property in the neighborhood.

These cases bring to our attention inherent ambiguities in what it means to have a power to transfer property. We generally assume that the first owner has the power to transfer all or some of her rights. If she owns fifty acres, she can choose to sell five and keep forty-five. She can place conditions on the use of the property, grant entitlements to neighbors to control the use of the land, and retain powers for herself, such as a power to retake the property if the grantee marries. But giving owners the power to disaggregate property rights in these ways may substantially limit or even destroy the ability of grantees to transfer property themselves, as they would not be able to offer prospective buyers a full bundle of rights in the burdened property. We face a tension, in other words, between the power to transfer property on terms chosen by prior owners and the ability of future owners to use the property and transfer it on terms acceptable to them. Once again, deregulation seems not to be an option. Do we regulate current owners by enforcing land use restrictions made long ago, or do we regulate prior owners by preventing them from imposing restrictions far into the future?

The traditional approach to this problem is to appeal to the policy of promoting the alienability of property—that is, the right to transfer ownership.

This policy pervades judicial decisions about property rights and is used to justify rules that have the effect of consolidating rights in the current owner and removing future interests or undue restrictions on use or ownership. For example, abolishing the fee tail ensures that current owners can transfer ownership rights that will persist after the grantor's death rather than devolving to his heirs when he dies. Consolidating rights in the current owner therefore increases the powers of current owners in a way that makes the property more movable on the open market.

But this understanding of the alienability policy misses two things. First, it promotes property rights by limiting the freedom of contract of prior owners. The result is an odd disjunction between principles basic to property and contract. Contract is portrayed as an area of freedom, where individuals can make whatever agreements they like within the bounds of state regulations. Property is presented as an area pervaded by the principle of alienability, which suppresses the tension between freedom of contract and regulation of property to ensure consolidation of rights.

Second, the free contract principle is not limited to the realm of contract. Within property law, the power to transfer property is viewed as a core right. Because owners often want to control future uses of their property, allowing owners to create future interests (such as interests in future heirs) or to impose land use restrictions (such as enforceable servitudes) is likely to encourage them to part with their land. If an owner can ensure that a factory will not be built next to her property, the property's value might well increase and the owner might be encouraged to sell it. Thus the ability to place restrictions on future owners in order to control future use of a property may promote alienability rather than inhibit it. The alienability principle that is at the center of traditional discussions of property law suppresses the paradox that alienability might be encouraged by allowing current owners to impose use restrictions on future owners yet might also be encouraged by freeing future owners from those very restrictions. Not only does the promotion of alienability point us in opposite directions—allowing versus prohibiting restraints on ownership rights—but it also contradicts the basic principle of contract law that owners should be permitted to make whatever arrangements they want concerning the disposition of their property.

However we look at them, the power to transfer property and the policy of promoting alienability embody essential tensions. Those tensions involve matters of principle, and they arise from ambiguities within the meaning of ownership itself.

FIELDS OF TENSION

The ownership concept directs our attention to the relations between owners and things. It directs us to identify an owner and then ask whether that owner's rights should be limited in the public interest. When we consider the actual implementation of property law in the real world, it becomes apparent that each of the core rights associated with ownership contains characteristic internal tensions. When property rights conflict, we must choose between promoting free use of property and protecting security. When owners of property seek to exclude nonowners, we must distinguish between types of property open to the public, where norms of access should prevail, and types where privacy and exclusionary interests should have priority. When someone occupies land whose formal title is held by another person, the law must choose between formal sources of property rights, such as a deed, and informal sources, such as long-term possession or oral agreement, in determining who is the owner. When owners seek to transfer their property, the law must sometimes regulate their transactions to ensure that the immediate buyers and all future owners have sufficient freedom to use the transferred property.

Ownership is a contested concept. Property is a social institution that is fraught with tensions. It resolves but also creates conflict, builds and undermines expectations, promotes and threatens liberty, demands and resists regulation. Whatever stability it can offer comes only from recognizing its own contingency. Whatever repose it can confer comes from limiting its own claims.

Chapter 2 From Title to Entitlement

The problem of defending individual rights is inseparable from the problem of defining them.
—*Jennifer Nedelsky*

The individual human [is] an inherently social being, inevitably dependent on others not only to thrive but even just to survive. This irreducible interdependency means that individuals owe one another obligations, not by virtue of consent alone but as an inherent incident of the human condition.
—*Gregory S. Alexander*

When Janet Lucas Breene and William Lucas bought a condominium in Bismarck, North Dakota, there were no legal restrictions on their ability to lease the unit.[1] The declaration establishing the condominium did grant the condominium association a right of first refusal should the owners ever decide to lease or sell their property. This meant that Breene and Lucas could choose whether to lease their unit, but they could not necessarily choose who their tenant would be. If and when they decided to lease it, the association had the right to assume the lease itself if it wanted to do so. The declaration could be amended by a vote of three-fourths of the members of the condominium association, which was composed of all the owners in the building.

Five years later, the association voted to prohibit unit owners from leasing the units at all, except in cases of special hardship. It is not clear why the restriction was imposed. Perhaps the owners in the building were tired of getting new neighbors every year and hoped that requiring owners to occupy their units would create more stability in the building. Perhaps they thought that renters were likely to be less well-to-do than owners, and they wanted to exclude lower-income people from the building. Perhaps they were fed up with the noisy parties of students from the local college who had rented units.

Whatever the reason, the new policy was not welcome to Breene and Lucas. When they asked for permission to lease their unit, the condominium association denied their request. In response they sued the association, claiming that the condominium declaration did not provide that leasing restrictions could be imposed retroactively on owners who had purchased their units before the restrictions were put into effect. They also argued that state statutes in North Dakota implicitly prohibited this practice by requiring condominium developers to record restrictions before selling the units. Since no restrictions had been placed on their unit before they bought it, Breene and Lucas argued that they owned the right to lease it. They acknowledged that state law and the declaration itself explicitly authorized the association to amend the declaration, but they argued that an amendment instituting a leasing restriction should apply only to future buyers who purchase their units with notice of the restriction.

The association contended that Breene and Lucas were aware when they bought their unit that it was subject to certain controls by the condominium association, including amendment of the declaration. Condominium owners are aware when they buy that each owner has the right to participate, through the association, in the governance of common areas and, to some extent, the use of individual units. The right to a voice in the management of the condominium is one stick in the bundle of rights that goes along with ownership of a unit. By voting on association resolutions, each owner exercises a certain power to limit the rights of all owners, but the limits are reciprocal: a limit imposed on one's neighbors would likewise be imposed on oneself. The condominium association therefore contended that Breene and Lucas were aware that new restrictions might be imposed on them and that they had implicitly agreed to be bound by such restrictions when they bought their condominium.

Breene and Lucas answered that they knew, at the time they bought, that their neighbors had the power to tax them to pay for repair of common areas and to make collective decisions about management and control of such areas. They may even have been aware that the association could impose certain limited controls on use, such as a rule prohibiting the playing of loud music after midnight. Such rules are akin to limitations imposed by nuisance law, preventing owners from engaging in activities that substantially and unreasonably interfere with the neighbors' use or enjoyment of their own property. But Breene and Lucas did not believe that the powers of their neighbors extended to wholesale restrictions on their ability to sell or lease their unit. Such restrictions, they contended, are incompatible with the individual ownership of units that is the mark of the condominium form. The power to regulate is not the power to take core property rights away from the owner, such as the power to lease one's property to others. People who buy with knowledge of such restrictions may of course be in a different position; they implicitly agree to the restrictions when they close on the sale.

Property rights exist on both sides of this dispute. Breene and Lucas own their condominium unit. At the same time, their ownership is subject to limitation by the owners of other units acting through the association; this right to participate in governance accompanies ownership of each unit. The conflict arises here because the parties have, by contract, divided property rights in the condominium units between the unit owner and the condominium association and because neither the agreement nor the state regulatory statute clearly states whether the association may impose retroactive restrictions on leasing. We face a conflict among neighbors, just as we did in the *Friendswood* case. Here, however, the neighbors are more than neighbors; in a condominium structure, the parties have expressly agreed to share powers over the same property.

The condominium declaration formally grants all the owners in the association rights to participate in governing common areas. It may also grant the association the power to pass rules that limit the use of individual units. The parties have disaggregated property rights among the neighbors. This sharing of power over individual units is the result of voluntary agreement rather than state imposition. The parties have used the contractual process to create bundles of rights over property that link ownership of one unit with limited rights to control the use of other units. Rather than consolidating all property rights in a single owner, the condominium arrangement formally grants certain rights of use and control to the unit owner and other rights to the owners acting collectively through the association. Thus each owner in the condominium owns both her own unit and a percentage interest in the condominium association—an interest that gives her the right to participate in governing the use of common areas and may also include the right to limit the activities that occur inside the units themselves.

Although contractually created arrangements are intended to solve disputes among owners before they arise, they may also generate some of the same kinds of disputes found in land use conflicts among neighbors who have not previously agreed to collective management of their property. As in a subdivision, the condominium arrangement generates conflicts between individual unit owners, who seek to use their property as they like, and their neighbors, who wish to control the use of all units to protect their individual or collective property interests. When property rights in the same structure are divided among several parties and the agreement establishing the division is ambiguous, lawmakers must act to define the legal rights of the individuals and their neighbors. In so doing, lawmakers effectively distribute powers and vulnerabilities among the parties. But even when the courts define presumptive property rights, unforeseen conflicts between legitimate property rights held by each party may arise and bring a dispute to court.

One might think that contractual arrangements are the perfect solution to the tensions within property law. After all, if there are competing property claims, one way to resolve them is to let the parties work them out themselves. Private agreements allow the parties to look out for their own interests. Contracts promote individual autonomy and economic efficiency by respecting the freedom of individuals to make the arrangements that are best suited to their needs and circumstances. And yet the resort to contract to resolve tensions among competing property rights utterly fails as a response to the problems created by those tensions. This does not mean that contract has no part to play in solving such problems; allowing parties to create and transfer property rights that suit them is a crucial component of a property system. But it cannot be the whole solution.

Before two parties can enter into a contract, we must define what they own. Otherwise, we cannot determine who is buying and who is selling. In situations involving neighboring owners, for example, we cannot just leave it to the market—that is, rely on private contracting alone—to determine which party should prevail. In the *Friendswood* case, examined in the previous chapter, it would be difficult for the affected parties to reach an agreement without their having a common understanding of whether the Friendswood Company was entitled to withdraw water from beneath its land. And it would be utterly impossible to use contract to resolve such a case if we could not determine who held the title to each parcel of land. Similar problems arise in public accommodations cases, where we need to know whether the law protects an owner's right to exclude or a nonowner's right of access. Adverse possession also presents this problem: Does the adverse possessor have to purchase the land from the title holder of record, or must the title holder purchase the property from the adverse possessor? Contracts cannot be made to exchange property rights if we do not have rules that determine who owns those rights initially.

Even when parties enter into a contract, its provisions may be worded ambiguously or may contradict one another, as in the *Breene* case. When an agreement is ambiguous, what is the court to do? It cannot enforce the agreement if it is not clear what were the terms to which the parties agreed. It can try to divine the "will of the parties," either by reading between the lines of the contract or by gauging the circumstances surrounding its creation, in order to determine how the parties would have resolved the issue if they had thought about it during the contract negotiation. But in many cases such methods would amount to little more than guesswork, and the court often has no choice but to use its own judgment in allocating the right in question.

We might think that if the contracting parties agree on what rights each holds, and if they draw up a detailed contract that expresses their will precisely and anticipates all contingencies, the contract will suffice to resolve future disputes. But not so fast—certain property arrangements, such as the fee tail discussed in the previous chapter, may have the effect of prohibiting owners from using their property as they wish or from transferring the property efficiently in the marketplace. In other words, a policy of complete freedom of contract would authorize owners to create forms of property that would significantly interfere with both autonomy and efficiency. This is one reason why lawmakers sometimes ignore the intent of the parties and limit their freedom to enter into particular contractual relationships or to create particular bundles of property rights. They may also wish to shape the contours of social life to avoid arrangements that violate public policy, such as agreements not to sell property to members of a particular race.

By applying mandatory or regulatory rules, courts and legislators may void certain contractual arrangements as contrary to public policy. In *Breene*, for example, a mandatory rule might make new leasing restrictions retroactively unenforceable. Alternatively, lawmakers may impose certain *compulsory terms* in the agreement. They might require a supermajority vote (such as 75 percent) rather than a simple majority to approve retroactive imposition of major restraints on alienation such as leasing restrictions. In either case the point of a mandatory rule is to limit the freedom of the parties to create or enter into alternative arrangements. Lawmakers often regulate contracts by limiting the kinds of property arrangements that will be respected by the legal system. Such limits are needed to ensure that owners do not create property bundles that violate public policy. Some property arrangements simply cannot be tolerated by the legal system because they interfere with fundamental individual liberties or with the property rights of others.

Property law fulfills two major functions. It creates presumptions about who gets to control particular resources, placing the burden of persuasion on the nonowner to justify an alternative result, and it defines the property interests that it will protect. It accomplishes this through regulatory rules designed to compromise between the goal of allowing individuals to disaggregate property rights and bundle them as they please (the free contract principle) and the goal of consolidating particular bundles of rights in the hands of particular owners (the alienability principle). Both of these functions of property law are achieved by adopting rules that shape the contours of social relations. Whether the rules distribute powers over property, allocate burdens of persuasion, or define the allowable bundles of rights, the law enacts a form of social life. In so doing, it attempts to generate a social environment that places certain kinds of relations out of bounds and creates a space for individual and collective freedom to remake human relations and individual life plans.

When we understand the role that property law plays in managing the tensions within the property concept, it becomes clear that it is impossible to create a precise, logical distinction between government actions that constitute deregulatory recognition of existing property rights and those that constitute regulatory limits on property rights. Rather, most of the law of property could be alternatively characterized as regulatory or deregulatory, depending on how we look at it. The inherent ambiguity about the relation between property and regulation should lead us to adopt another way of talking about the relations between property and power and between owners and the state. Rather than asking whether owners are legitimately subject to regulation in the public interest, it is often more appropriate to ask which set of rules will produce results that best satisfy human needs and desires and that best promote a free society that treats its members with fairness, respect, justice, and common decency.

This new model of property does not make ownership irrelevant, but it puts the concept in its proper place. Property law is about *entitlements and obligations, which shape the contours of social relations.*

PRESUMPTIVE CONTROL AND BURDENS OF PERSUASION

Property law creates presumptions about who gets to control valued resources. The ownership model suggests that ordinarily one person (or entity) controls all rights in a particular piece of property. Once we identify the owner, we can ask whether her rights should be limited because of overriding public interests or values. The burden falls on nonowners to demonstrate that these public policies are sufficiently strong to justify restricting the owner's rights. But when several people have legitimate claims to control various aspects of the same piece of property, the ownership concept may fail us by placing the burden of persuasion on the wrong party.

Instead of mechanically granting presumptive control to the person conventionally denominated the owner, we should choose consciously where to place the burden of persuasion by establishing normative criteria that embody the values we want the law to further. We should focus on the multiple claims that may legitimately be made to control the resource in question and develop an appropriate framework for judging who should have presumptive control over various aspects of the resource.

FREE USE VERSUS SECURITY

My discussion of the *Friendswood* case emphasized that land use conflicts pose a choice between free use claims and claims of rights to security from harm. Who should have the burden of persuasion in such cases? On one hand, we could argue that the right to use one's property as one wishes is the core property right and place the burden on the party wishing to limit free use. This construction suggests that any laws that limit one's use of one's land presumptively violate preexisting property rights. But it ignores the fact that land use disputes arise precisely because there are legally protected property rights on both sides of the conflict. Although we might be justified in sometimes placing the burden on the nonowner to justify limiting the privilege of the owner to use her property as she likes, we cannot mechanically make the same presumption when such uses harm the property interests of other owners. It is just as plausible to argue that the core right in this situation is the right to be free from harm. In fact, Morton Horwitz has argued that at the beginning of the nineteenth century this was indeed the case, in both Great Britain and the United States.[2] The right of property owners to be secure from harm had priority, and the burden was on those who caused harm to justify their actions.

What would our libertarian judge say about this? The deregulatory position seems to suggest that the burden should be on the party seeking to limit liberty by curtailing the free use of property. But the question of which ruling will best promote liberty is not an easy one to answer. According to the classical political theorists, such as Thomas Hobbes and John Locke, the reason we created government in the first place was to enlarge our liberty by establishing collective mechanisms to enhance our security. "If anyone does an act hurtful to others," wrote John Stuart Mill in *On Liberty*, "there is a *prima facie* case for punishing him by law."[3] I feel free to exercise my liberty to walk the streets knowing that the law protects me, to some extent, from violent harm. It affords me this protection by forbidding any person, including me, from assaulting another. It promotes liberty, in other words, by restricting freedom of action. Similarly, I am best able to exercise my property rights when the state prohibits me from interfering in the property rights of my neighbors.

Some kinds of harms so violate individual dignity that we want to place the burden on the party inflicting the harm to justify her actions. For example, when one person causes the death of another, we may want to presume that a wrong has been committed and place the burden on the killer to demonstrate that circumstances did not permit a different course of action. Similarly, when one owner's actions would result in substantial harm to the property of another, we might want to make the party causing such harm explain why her liberty interests should prevail over the security interests of the one whose property is threatened.

Sometimes we may want the burden of persuasion to be on one side and sometimes on the other. The ownership concept cannot tell us which way to go since there are property rights on both sides. Libertarians want to limit infringements on liberty, but they are also in favor of protecting property rights, which may require the state to restrict harmful property uses. By its very nature, property entails restrictions on the liberty of individuals to take what the state has identified as belonging to another. Allocating the burden of persuasion when conflicts arise between free use and security requires a judgment that depends on a host of factors, such as the type of harm at issue, the social value of the harmful conduct, and which use was established first. And in certain cases we may want to acknowledge the underlying tension and operate without any presumption at all, relying instead on a comparative evaluation of the relative merits of the competing claims at issue.

Public Accommodations

Public accommodations laws that prohibit race discrimination in restaurants and other business facilities open to the public appear, according to the ownership model, to limit property rights in order to promote equality. Under this approach we can only justify them by explaining why interests in equality are sufficient to override established property rights. The burden of persuasion rests with the customer who is seeking a right to enter property owned by someone else. But excluding potential customers on the ground of race denies them the legal right to purchase property. An alternative construction of the problem would place the burden of persuasion on the business owner to explain why she should be entitled to exclude the customer.

The ownership model leads us to treat all property as the same. If we define the right to exclude as a core stick in the bundle of ownership rights, then public accommodations laws will be understood as presumptive deprivations of property. If, however, we distinguish between property that is open to the public for business purposes (a public accommodation) from property that is not so open (private property), we may want to alter the burden of persuasion in the two contexts. Privately owned businesses open to the public are in the public world in a way that homes are not. Perhaps the owners of public accommodations should bear the burden of justifying their actions when they exclude members of the public arbitrarily. Exclusion from the marketplace on the basis of race interferes in the ability of those who are excluded to contract to purchase property. Rather than asking the excluded patron to justify her claim to access to property possessed by another, one could view public accommodations laws as remedies available against persons who wrongfully violate the rights of others to contract and purchase property in the marketplace. One might argue that the presumption should be that there is an equality right to participate in the market; actions that limit this right must be justified. The classical ownership concept warps our understanding of the policies involved in the context of public accommodations law. It is morally pernicious, not only because it puts the burden of persuasion on the wrong party but also because it defines a discriminatory exclusion from the market system as a presumptive exercise of protected property rights.

Interpretation of Ambiguous Property Arrangements

When multiple owners are involved in a dispute, the courts are often called upon to allocate property rights among the individuals who own legally protected interests in the property. In such cases judges must interpret ambiguities in the contracts or grants that created or divided up the property rights among the various claimants. When owners have not negotiated a prior agreement about how to handle a contingency, property law steps in to identify those who presumptively can control the entitlement in question. In so doing, the law allocates to other parties the burden of persuading the courts that the usual allocation of entitlements should not be followed.

In the *Breene* case, for example, the owners of a condominium unit claimed a right to transfer possession of the unit by leasing it out. They contended that if there was an ambiguity as to whether restrictive amendments to the condominium association's declaration could be applied to unit owners retroactively, the burden should fall on the association to explain why unit ownership rights should be limited. They claimed that the right to transfer possession of their unit by leasing was a core right in the ownership package they had purchased and thus could not be taken away without their consent. The neighbors, however, might have pointed out that Breene and Lucas implicitly agreed that their use of their unit would be subject to control by the condominium association, of which all owners—including Breene and Lucas—are members. The power to amend the declaration allows the owners as a group, by supermajority vote, to exercise some control over use of the units. The right to vote for such restrictions, and to impose them on all owners, is a core right that inheres in the condominium form and thus belongs to each owner in the building.

One way to resolve such disputes is to try to determine what contractual provision the parties would have made had they anticipated the contingency when they were negotiating the initial contract. This approach, which seeks to effectuate the parties' will on the basis of the available evidence, suggests that the most salient public policy is the promotion of the freedom of individuals to create the property arrangements that best suit their needs. Ideally, such a policy of freedom of contract would protect liberty interests and promote economic efficiency by limiting overbearing government power and safeguarding individual autonomy. Unfortunately in *Breene,* as in many other cases, there is no clear evidence of what the parties intended. We have an ambiguous written agreement. When the ambiguities are too great to make a reasonable reconstruction of the parties' intent, many courts will resolve the dispute by adopting a default rule, which is intended to represent the judge's view of the terms most people entering into such a contract would have adopted, consistent with the contractual language.

Sometimes, however, courts choose to ignore the intent of the parties. They may adopt a default rule that is the opposite of what most people would agree—a so-called penalty default—in order to prompt the parties to negotiate a mutually satisfactory resolution in place of the default at the time they initially contract.[4] Or judges may construct rules by reference to public policies they see as particularly beneficial, such as social justice or social utility. For example, a judge who is suspicious of restraints on alienation of property, such as the leasing restrictions at issue in *Breene,* because they inhibit the autonomy and mobility of unit owners and prevent the efficient transfer of resources to their most highly valued use, may adopt a default rule against finding restraints on alienation enforceable or against enforcing them retroactively. Conversely, if a judge wishes to promote collective governance and owner participation in community affairs, she might adopt a default rule in favor of enforcing whatever restrictions a condominium association enacts.

Another alternative, if the court wishes to affect both values and behavior, is to require the parties to make explicit in the contract negotiations any terms that would allow one side to act in a manner that offends common norms of fair dealing. For example, under current law in most states, a landlord can refuse to renew a lease for almost any reason. (The only exceptions to this rule are imposed by civil rights laws that prohibit discriminatory practices.) Thus a landlord could refuse to renew because the tenant voted for the Democratic candidate for president.[5] We rely on competition among landlords in the marketplace to discourage them from exercising such arbitrary powers.

However, relying on the marketplace may not be fully satisfactory to weed out unfair terms. Prospective tenants may not hear about a landlord's arbitrary action and so would not take it into account when deciding whether to sign a lease. Even if the landlord's propensity for mixing business and politics is well known, other factors—the favorable location of the property or a shortage of rental units in the neighborhood—might keep the market from restraining the outrageous behavior. But if the rules in force required landlords to reveal to tenants that they would not renew the lease unless the tenant supported the landlord's candidate for president, landlords might be effectively deterred from bargaining for such terms. Few landlords would have the audacity to ask for such an outrageous term, no matter how much they would like to have that power. Thus, one might argue that the courts should adopt presumptive contract terms that they think most parties would regard as fair, as a means to induce buyers and sellers to make clear if they have a contrary intention or to induce them to accept the presumptively fair terms.[6]

When parties have used the contractual process to divide ownership rights in the same property among several persons, we again see the conflict within the property and ownership concepts between freedom claims and security claims. Our libertarian judge who favors both property rights and deregulation will have a problem in adjudicating the *Breene* case. Since in a condominium arrangement ownership rights have been divided up among several parties, there is no warrant for assuming that the party who holds the title to the individual unit should prevail. When we are not sure what division of powers was intended, the concept of ownership does us little good. Neither land use conflicts nor complex property arrangements can be sensibly understood or regulated by assuming that all rights in a property reside with the title holder. Ownership involves a bundle of legal entitlements that are seldom held by just one person. Whether by law or by contract, it is almost always the case that more than one person has legally protected interests in controlling certain aspects of a particular property.

When property rights are claimed by both sides in a lawsuit, the court cannot reasonably rule on the basis of appeals to protect property rights and promote deregulation. Both sides claim property rights, and the court must choose one construction of rights over another. Either way, one party will feel that the state has deprived him or her of a preexisting property right. In such cases, neither choice can be reasonably characterized as "deregulatory." Rather, the court should recognize the property rights of all parties and seek to strike a proper balance between them by reference to the ultimate values that support property in the first place, such as justice, liberty, equality, or efficiency. In the *Breene* case, for example, a balance must be achieved between the individual unit owners' interest in free use of their own units and the unit owners' collective security interest in restricting such use. The difficulty in finding an equitable middle ground is evident in the fact that the courts have split over the proper outcome in cases like this. Some, like the North Dakota Supreme Court in the *Breene* case, have chosen to protect unit owners from retroactive restrictions on leasing. Many other courts, however, have interpreted similar condominium declarations and state statutes as authorizing such restrictions.[7]

When the contract does not clearly state which of the parties owns the particular entitlement in dispute, the court must determine who should prevail. To do so, the court must define the package of entitlements that ordinarily belongs to each owner. As we have seen, this is more complicated than it first appears. In order to defend the property rights implicated in the case, the judge must first define them.[8] In so doing, the court allocates presumptions of control and burdens of persuasion. In other words, it engages in regulation.

THE AMBIGUOUS ROLE OF REGULATION

Land Use Regulation

The ownership model suggests that we can define property rights without regard to their social effects and then ask whether or to what extent they should be regulated by government. But when property rights conflict, the relation between property and regulation is not so clear. When interests in free use conflict with interests in security, the ownership model suggests that we see the issue as a conflict between freedom (advanced by deregulation) and security (advanced by regulation). This picture of the relation between owners and the government identifies free use as the core property right, and hence the default position, and views regulation as a regrettable though perhaps necessary interference with freedom for the sake of security. If a conflict over property rights reaches the courts, the ownership model places the burden of persuasion on the owner who wishes to restrict—read "regulate"—someone else's free use of property.

This construction of the problem identifies limits on free actions as regulatory and a refusal to limit land use as deregulatory. This view is based on our conventional understanding of the relation between individuals and the state—that is, the model of *negative liberty.* Individuals are free to do what they want unless the state regulates their conduct to protect the rights of others. Negative liberty connotes freedom from interference by the state. In contrast, positive liberty connotes a right to call on the aid of the state in creating the conditions under which one can effectively exercise one's liberties.

But when we think about government's role in protecting property rights, it is not at all clear that deregulation is always advanced by expanding the realm of negative liberty. After all, a legal system that protects property rights is not the state of nature; law entails the use of state power to protect the rights of owners to control their property. One of the rules of property law is that owners have the right not to have their property destroyed by others. This basic right of possession is protected, not by deregulation, but by the exercise of state power. Trespass and nuisance law delegate to owners the power to call on state officials to prevent others from taking or harming their property. Deregulation might free owners to use their property as they like, but since it would leave them vulnerable to depredation by neighbors, they might soon have no property left to enjoy. Property seems to require regulation.

This second construction is less well understood than the first because it does not fit the negative liberty model of the relation between the individual and the state. It acknowledges that individual claims to liberty are not absolute; as Jeremy Waldron argues, a person can only legitimately claim *"the most extensive liberty of action possible,* compatible with an equal liberty of action for everybody else."[9] Because property rights depend on state action limiting the individual liberty of nonowners to protect the exclusive rights of owners, it makes no sense to conceptualize all government regulations as limitations on property. In fact, many government regulations *protect* property.

For example, suppose a court finds that the actions of the Friendswood Company violate the property rights of its neighbors and therefore can be enjoined. The law now is that the neighbors have a property right that protects them from further actions by Friendswood which undermine the support for their land. Owners like Friendswood now have a duty not to destroy their neighbors' land. Friendswood lobbies for a change in the law: it seeks a state statute that explicitly authorizes owners to withdraw as much water as they like without limit. From the standpoint of negative liberty, such a law may appear deregulatory. After all, it lifts a law that regulated Friendswood's conduct and thereby increases its freedom of action. Such a law, one might think, is liberty-enhancing and therefore deregulatory. From the standpoint of the neighbors, however, the law deprives them of preexisting property rights. It does not increase their liberty but authorizes Friendswood to destroy their property. The state cannot itself destroy their property—by sending state employees to demolish it, for example—without violating the constitutional prohibition on uncompensated takings of property. Similarly, the state cannot deputize a private actor to accomplish the same result. Yet by "deregulating" Friendswood's use of its land, the state has promulgated a rule of law that allows one owner to destroy another owner's property. The neighbors want to be left alone to enjoy their property in peace. But the government has *not* left them alone; it has stripped them of a property right. What to Friendswood looks like a liberty-enhancing, deregulatory statute, to the neighbors looks like a regulatory measure that invades their property rights.

Something very similar to this occurred when the majority of states passed "right-to-farm" statutes in the early 1980s.[10] These statutes were reactions to court decisions that found farms to constitute nuisances when they were located near residential neighborhoods, even though the farms had been established first and the home owners had "come to the nuisance." The courts reasoned that nuisance law required a comparison of the conflicting land uses and a weighing of the harms and benefits of each activity. The fact that the "victims" came to the nuisance was relevant in determining whether it was fair to shut down the farm, but it was not the sole factor, since changes in the neighborhood might turn a lawful use into a nuisance if it began to cause substantial harm to other owners. These court rulings protected the security rights of the neighbors but seemed to threaten to shut down family farms that had been in operation for generations. In response, state legislators passed statutes that granted farm owners the right to operate without regard to nuisance law if they had established their operations first. They thereby elevated the coming-to-the-nuisance doctrine into an absolute (or near-absolute) defense against a nuisance claim by neighbors whose homes were built near an existing farm.

The right-to-farm statutes may have appeared deregulatory from the standpoint of the farm owners, whom they freed from restrictions imposed by nuisance law. On the other hand, they took away from home owners the right to be secure from activity on neighboring land that caused substantial harm to their property interests and whose costs to society arguably outweighed its benefits. Thus from the standpoint of the home owners the right-to-farm statutes were regulatory measures that decreased the value of their property and stripped them of a preexisting property right to obtain an injunction shutting down farm operations that substantially interfered with the use and enjoyment of their property.

The U.S. Supreme Court grappled with the ambiguous relation between property and regulation in *Miller v. Schoene.*[11] The Court considered a Virginia law that required owners of cedar trees infested with cedar-apple rust to destroy their trees. The rust, a fungus, does not seriously harm the host cedars, but it can cause considerable damage to apple trees if it spreads to nearby orchards. Since only spores released during the cedar stage of the fungus's life cycle can infect apple trees, the owners of distressed orchards can be certain that the source of the rust is a cedar. From the standpoint of the cedar owners, the law mandating the destruction of their trees was not only an unwelcome regulation but also a taking of their property. While it might be in the public interest to save the apple industry in the state, it was wrong, in their view, to make the cedar owners bear the cost of the rescue. This wrong was so grave, they contended, that the state had a constitutional duty to compensate them when it mandated the taking of their property to save the property of others. Their argument assumed that the only way the state can take away anyone's property is by regulation. Hence if the state refuses to regulate—if it does nothing—it cannot be held responsible for the apple growers' loss of property when the cedar-apple rust destroys their trees and their livelihood.

The Supreme Court saw it differently. Judge Harlan Fiske Stone wrote for the Court:

> The state was under the necessity of making a choice between the preservation of one class of property and that of the other wherever both existed in dangerous proximity. It would have been none the less a choice if, instead of enacting the present statute, the state, by doing nothing, had permitted serious injury to the apple orchards within its borders to go on unchecked. When forced to such a choice the state does not exceed its constitutional powers by deciding upon the destruction of one class of property in order to save another which, in the judgment of the legislature, is of greater value to the public.[12]

In the *Friendswood* case, as in *Miller v. Schoene,* the state was faced with a choice between protecting Friendswood's freedom to exploit its property and preventing the destruction of everyone else's property in the county. If the existing rule of law favored security from harm over free use, then changing the law to authorize destruction would constitute a regulatory action resulting in the deprivation of property rights. And even if prior law was unclear, Justice Stone's insight suggests that, in cases such as this, we do not face a choice between regulation and deregulation; nor do we face a choice between liberty and property. Rather, because we are constrained to pick one property right over another, we have to choose between alternative regulations.

The relation between property and regulation therefore is paradoxical. In one sense they seem pitted against each other, for regulations limit property rights. But in another sense property rights themselves are forms of regulation, for they grant to individuals the right to call on the power of the state to exclude others from "finite and critical goods" that others need.[13] Thus property regulates nonowners as well as other owners.

Consider the famous *Mount Laurel* decision in which the Supreme Court of New Jersey invalidated a municipal zoning law that prohibited the construction of multifamily housing in the township of Mount Laurel.[14] Since low- and moderate-income families cannot afford to purchase single-family homes on large lots, the zoning law effectively prevented them from living in the town. If many towns passed similar laws, they could collectively zone the poor people of New Jersey out of the suburbs and confine them, by law, to a few cities like Camden, Newark, and Trenton. The court held that such a result would violate the state constitution and required every town to write a zoning law that provided a realistic opportunity for low- and moderate-income housing to be built somewhere in the town.

This was a very unpopular decision among many New Jersey home owners, who saw it as nothing less than an attack on their property rights. Yet consider how odd their reaction is, given the current passion for deregulation. The court's initial ruling did not require anyone to do anything. It did not force anyone to use their land in a way they did not want to use it. Quite the contrary—it lifted certain zoning restrictions that had been imposed by town governments. In effect, it said that if an owner in a town wanted to build low-income housing, the town had to find a place where she would be permitted to do so. The decision thus deregulated many parcels of land in the state. It allowed land uses that had been previously prohibited, and it promoted free use by allowing owners who wished to do so to construct apartment buildings in the suburbs.[15] Yet property owners perceived this deregulatory ruling as an attack on their property rights. They did so because their property derived both its character and its value—or so they thought—from being located in a residential neighborhood with other single-family homes on large lots. The zoning regulation protected the value of their homes, and they understood this quite well. They therefore saw the court decision, and not the zoning regulation, as interfering with their property rights.

At the same time, those who opposed the court's decision did not see themselves as asking for more regulation. What they wanted was protection for their property rights. It did not filter into the public consciousness that the opposition to the court decision represented a rousing appeal to the virtues of regulation as a means of promoting and protecting property. This blindness can only be explained by the ideology of the ownership model, which pretends that any state action that seems to protect property rights must, by definition, be deregulatory. But of course if this is the case, we have traveled far from the model of negative liberty. Property may be threatened by regulation, but it also seems to require it.

Public Accommodations

After the Civil War public accommodations laws were passed in most of the former states of the Confederacy, as well as Massachusetts and Pennsylvania, requiring owners of inns, common carriers (such as trains, ships, and coaches), and places of entertainment to admit patrons without regard to race.[16] To the owners of the affected businesses, these laws seemed to regulate their property rights by limiting their right to exclude—a right traditionally associated with property ownership. In 1875 these Southern public accommodations laws began to be repealed, leaving the choice of whom to serve to the discretion of the owners—a move those owners welcomed as deregulatory. African American customers, however, experienced the repeal of the public accommodations laws differently. For ten years African Americans who had been excluded from public accommodations could obtain damages and sometimes injunctive relief when courts ordered businesses to admit them. But with the repeal of the laws they once again found themselves shunted aside from the mainstream of commerce. If racial prejudice is widespread, the absence of a law or rule forbidding businesses to exclude on the basis of race has the effect of establishing segregated accommodations.

The repeal of the public accommodations laws may have been experienced as deregulatory by businesses, but it was experienced by African Americans as a regulatory move to legalize segregation, because if they entered property without the owner's permission, they would be arrested and thrown in jail. It is true that the decision to segregate was at that point in the hands of private owners, but the movement from a public accommodations regime to a regime of business discretion fundamentally altered social relations. Moreover, the *privilege* to exclude (freedom from sanction for excluding a class of patrons) was supported by a *right* to exclude. A business owner that wished to exclude an African American customer could call on the state, in the form of the police, to drag her off the premises and jail her for trespassing. The owner even could turn to the courts to obtain damages against the trespasser. Although one might characterize this change in the law as a restoration of property rights, it is far from deregulatory. Rather it made the state, through enforcement of trespass laws, an agent for the imposition of racial segregation.

In the 1880s the Southern states began regulating with a vengeance by passing laws requiring businesses either to segregate customers by race or to serve only one race. In 1964 the federal government again reversed the legal situation. Public accommodations laws like the 1964 Civil Rights Act take away the right of businesses to call on the aid of the state for the purpose of excluding customers on the basis of race. Does this represent a regulation of property? Perhaps it does. A law that limits an owner's right to exclude nonowners certainly changes property rights previously recognized at common law and constitutes an exception to the general rule that property owners have a right to exclude nonowners from their property. By requiring owners to allow access, the public accommodations laws regulate property and limit owners' control over it.

Yet this regulation of property is partly effectuated by the state's refusal to intervene to remove African American customers from the premises of a business. If a restaurant owner calls the local police and asks them to remove a patron for trespassing whose only offense is being a different race from the rest of the customers, the police will refuse to do so. The owner may sue the city, arguing that the police violated his property rights, but the court will certainly hold that the city had no duty to help the owner in this way. Enforcement of traditional trespass law would constitute regulation of African American customers, a use of state power to exclude law-abiding patrons from public accommodations at the discretion of the owner. Regulating business owners by requiring them to serve customers without regard to race is deregulatory with regard to those customers whose liberty is enlarged by the removal of restraints on their right of access to public accommodations. A public accommodations law may appear regulatory because it limits the property rights of the business owner, but it also establishes the conditions by which other persons can become owners by deregulating the conduct of previously regulated patrons. Property and regulation may appear antagonistic, but they are also intimately connected.

The Regulatory Ambiguity of Compulsory Terms

Courts and legislatures sometimes limit freedom of contract—that is, the freedom of parties to craft the terms of their agreement—by regulating the division of property rights. In effect, the law either declares certain arrangements void and unenforceable or identifies compulsory terms that cannot be waived by the parties to particular types of property arrangements. In such cases default rules become *compulsory terms.* Rules of law that impose such terms might be called *mandatory* or *regulatory.* Mortgage and anti-eviction laws, for example, set mandatory rules regarding such matters as foreclosure and eviction. The protections of rights created by such laws are enforced even if the contract contains an explicit waiver of those rights. Such *nonwaivable* or *nondisclaimable* terms are imposed for reasons of public policy. Sometimes the purpose of nonwaivable terms is to protect third parties from negative effects arising out of an agreement, such as harm to consumers caused by terms in a contract between two companies that would reduce competition in their industry. But mandatory rules may also be imposed because they are thought necessary to safeguard the legitimate interests of one of the parties to an agreement. In such cases a conflict emerges within property law between preserving freedom of contract and protecting owners' rights.

Consider the following conflict between a landlord and a tenant who signed a one-year lease on an apartment for a set monthly rent. The tenant is a law student who plans to take a summer internship in another city and wishes to sublet the apartment for the summer. The lease prohibits subletting or assigning the leasehold to another person. The tenant finds a friend who is willing to sublet the apartment and approaches the landlord to get a waiver of the no-subletting clause. The landlord refuses. The tenant tells the landlord she is leaving for the summer and has no intention of paying the rent for the period she will be away. In September the landlord sues the tenant for three months' back rent. Does the tenant owe the money to the landlord?

Approximately half the states hold that the tenant does owe the landlord back rent. The agreement did not allow subletting, and by signing it the tenant promised to pay the landlord the rent as it came due in each of the twelve months of the rental period. The landlord had no duty to agree to a sublease. This solution is the one generally understood as deregulatory, because the contract is enforceable in accordance with its terms, and the landlord has no obligations to which she did not voluntarily agree.

The other half of the states, however, have adopted a rule that denies the landlord the right to obtain the back rent, because the landlord refused either to accept the substitute tenant or to look for a replacement herself. In these states the landlord has a "duty to mitigate damages" caused by breach of contract by undertaking reasonable steps to limit the monetary losses caused by the breach. In this context, the landlord has a duty to make reasonable efforts to find a new tenant or to accept a reasonable replacement found by the existing tenant if the landlord wants to be financially protected when the tenant breaches. The tenant is required to reimburse the landlord for the costs of finding a replacement and for the rent covering any period during the search when the apartment was vacant; but the landlord is not entitled "to stand idly by the vacant, abandoned premises and treat them as the property of the tenant and recover full rent, when [the landlord] by reasonable efforts could have avoided" the damages that accrued.[17] The amount of damages the landlord can recover is reduced by the amount of damages the landlord could have avoided had she found a replacement tenant.

The rule concerning mitigation of damages appears to regulate the lease agreement by making the landlord do something she doesn't want to do and never promised to do. But consider more closely. The rule does not require the landlord to do anything. It merely *withholds a remedy* from a landlord who fails to find a replacement tenant or fails to agree to a suitable replacement found by the defaulting tenant. Moreover, the mitigation rule *deregulates* the conduct of the tenant by liberating her to abandon the premises and take the job in another city without the burden of having to pay double rents over the summer. Just as public accommodations law appears deregulatory to previously excluded patrons, the mitigation rule appears deregulatory to tenants, who become free to make agreements *and also free to break them.*

This example demonstrates a fundamental ambiguity in the principle of freedom of contract. Contract law in the United States not only allows people to make contracts; it also enforces those contracts. The formerly Communist countries of Eastern Europe deregulated by allowing their citizens to engage in previously outlawed capitalist relations without interference by the state. American contract law not only allows such relations but even provides remedies that may induce those who make promises to abide by them. Such remedies are clearly regulatory; they protect the expectations of the promisee (the one to whom the promise was made) by creating property rights in those expectations. On the other hand, contract law often provides little or nothing in the way of enforcement of such promises. Contract law generally imposes a duty to mitigate damages on the victim of the breach of contract and limits damages when the victim can find replacement goods or services elsewhere. If a duty to mitigate damages exists, and if the substitute tenant proffered by the defaulting tenant is creditworthy, the landlord will be denied the ability to collect rent from the departing tenant if the landlord unreasonably refuses to accept the substitute tenant or look for another tenant. The states that adopt this approach find that the landlord's legitimate interest in not having to look for a new tenant more than once a year is outweighed by the tenant's liberty interest in moving to take a job elsewhere, so long as the landlord's financial interests remain protected, as they do (at least in theory) under the mitigation rule.

The duty to mitigate damages may appear to regulate the agreement by forcing the landlord to agree to a contract term she would rather not have, but it actually functions to deregulate by granting the parties the liberty to make the agreement and the liberty to break it, at least under these narrowly defined circumstances. By withholding a remedy, the mitigation rule emancipates the tenant from regulation by the state without in any way requiring the landlord to do anything. Of course, the landlord may well be forced to act to protect her economic interests, but this is because the law deregulated the arrangement by giving the parties freedom both to enter such agreements and to breach them.

A system that allowed but did not enforce contracts might be workable. People who breached agreements would get a reputation as breachers. Businesses would spring up that would keep track of such persons and put their names on a list. Breachers would have a hard time finding other people willing to contract with them unless they had cash in hand. Although U.S. contract law purports to enforce contracts, it actually denies remedies for breaches in a variety of situations and hence comes close to the model of a regime in which people are free to make and break promises without interference by the state.

At the same time, refusing to enforce contracts would eventually have the effect of abolishing property law. After all, most property rights have their origin in agreements or transfers of rights. Most land is sold or inherited. Most businesses involve exchanges of capital and labor for compensation. Refusing to enforce contracts that result in production or transfer would be equivalent to refusing to use state power to assign ownership rights or enforce them. On the other hand, not all contracts create enforceable property rights. We usually do not force people to do what they promised to do. Rather, we only require the payment of damages, and often that amount is small. We must therefore distinguish between the kinds of arrangements that confer property rights—where private agreements will be enforced by court order or damage awards intended to induce compliance—and those that will not be enforced or will be enforced only by damages intended to encourage breach by those willing to pay them.

Some compulsory terms, such as the duty to mitigate damages, regulate by withholding legal remedies. Although they seem to limit freedom of contract, they in fact only limit the ability to call on the aid of the state to enforce contracts. In so doing, they actually deregulate. Conversely, other compulsory terms are clearly regulatory in the sense that they rewrite agreements so as to transfer property rights from one contracting party to another. Here is an example. An owner of a parcel of land sells half of it to another person. The buyer agrees to a restraint on alienation: she promises never to sell the property without obtaining the prior consent of the seller. This obligation is contained in the deed of sale and is made both permanent and perpetual—it has no termination point and is intended to last forever. When the seller dies, the right to consent to future sales of the restricted property will pass to the seller's heirs or to a person the seller has appointed by will. The buyer further promises to record the deed with the restriction so that all future buyers of her land will be on notice of it and to include the restriction in the deed of sale whenever she sells the property—with the original grantor's consent, of course. If this consent clause is enforceable, all future buyers of the burdened parcel will have a substantial limitation on their right to control the property. Moreover, because the original contracting parties agreed that the restriction would be perpetual, no future descendant of the grantor has the power to waive or give up the right to consent to sales of the buyer's property. Thus if the original contract is enforceable, the restraint on alienation cannot ever be removed.

If such a restraint on alienation is enforceable, the property rights of the buyer of the burdened land are not absolute, and her powers to control the use and disposition of the property has been severely limited. If we want to secure absolute property rights for future owners of the lot, we have no choice but to regulate the restraint on alienation. One way to do so is simply to declare all the restraint terms void. Or we might enforce the restraint against the present buyer but hold void the clause that burdens the land in perpetuity. Another alternative is to establish a standard of reasonableness and enforce the restraint if it is exercised reasonably and does not unreasonably interfere with the alienability of the property. Whatever strategy is adopted requires a rule of law that regulates the initial grantor's property rights by limiting the conditions that she can place on the sale of the property.

Protecting the absolute property rights of future owners therefore requires us to limit the property rights of prior owners to impose restraints on alienation. In fact, the more rigidly property rights are protected, the more extensive the regulation of property must be. The ownership concept suggests a model of absolute control within clear boundaries, but the more absolute one wants a property right to be, the more the state must regulate the conduct of others to prevent interference with it. Of course, such regulation may infringe on the legally protected property interests of others. Choices must therefore be made about the form that regulation should take, not whether it should be present.

Property and regulation are not opposites; they go hand in hand. Property requires regulation, and regulation, by creating secure expectations, establishes property rights. Conflicts among property rights, and between property rights and other rights, are inevitable. Absolute property rights cannot exist in the real world, because when they conflict, at least one of the rights must give ground. The classical model of property, based on the image of complete control of an object, is a mirage: the closer one examines it, the more it recedes.

A public policy maker who analyzes issues based on the conventional understanding of property would be inclined to defend property rights by getting rid of many regulations that actually protect those rights rather than interfere with them. There is a danger that countries that are attempting to end socialism and are emulating the American market model are basing their public policies on a simplistic ideological fantasy of property rather than the true, complex picture of property under U.S. law. In so doing, they may adopt a form of property that has never existed in the United States and would have had disastrous consequences if it ever had existed. Even the most rudimentary property system requires substantial regulation to answer questions about the allocation and scope of property rights. Jiri Dienstbier, the foreign minister of the former Czechoslovakia, commented in 1990 that creating a market economy—a so-called free market—required the drafting of hundreds of regulatory laws.[18] If anything, he understated the problem.

Regulation and the Romance of Ownership

In my home state of Massachusetts the bank holds the title to my house. I am, in common parlance, a home owner. Yet when you borrow money to buy a house, the bank takes a mortgage on the property. If the "owner" fails to make the mortgage payments when they are due, the bank can foreclose on the property and sell it at auction to recover the remaining debt. Under Massachusetts law this arrangement is effectuated by granting title to the property to the bank and leaving the "owner" with something called an "equity of redemption." According to Massachusetts property law, home owners own nothing. They are merely the beneficiaries of an equitable doctrine, codified in Massachusetts statutes, that grant them rights generally associated with ownership, such as the right to tear down walls and renovate the property, as long as they do not violate obligations in the mortgage agreement to maintain the property's value. Why do we consider the buyer to be the owner when the bank has the formal title? Title and common understandings of ownership diverge here. Possession and control matter more than formal title. Yet at the same time we identify landlords as owners of property even though they, like the bank, are not in physical possession of the leased premises. This difference can partly be explained by the history of the development of landlord-tenant law as opposed to mortgage law. But historical origins are not sufficient to account for the persistence of these popular impressions of ownership.

Consider a landlord who converts an apartment building into a condominium. This means that she sells ownership rights in the units to individual buyers and establishes common ownership of common areas in the building. If a current tenant offers to purchase her unit at fair market value, should the landlord be required to sell to her or should the landlord be free to sell to an outside buyer and evict the tenant? What if the tenant promised to match or even top the highest outside bid? New Jersey and the District of Columbia have statutes that protect some tenants in such situations from eviction by giving them a "right of first refusal."[19] They have the power to purchase their apartments from the landlord in preference to third parties. In a state that did not have such a statute, the landlord would be free to choose to sell an apartment to a third party, even if the existing tenant had been living there, had been paying rent on time for thirty years, and were fully capable of paying the price asked for by the landlord and of matching any higher offers by third parties. Should the landlord have the power to refuse to sell the apartment to the existing tenant? Most states say yes, on the assumption that the landlord is the owner and can choose to sell to whomever she likes, as long as she does not engage in invidious discrimination.

But compare the legal treatment of owners whose property is subject to a mortgage. If a home owner fails to make the mortgage payments due the bank, existing legislation protects the home owner from losing her home if she can make up the payment in a reasonable time or if she can borrow money from another lender (or otherwise obtain the money) and pay off the remaining bank debt. If the bank goes through with the foreclosure and auctions the property, it is entitled by law to the proceeds of the sale up to the amount of the unpaid debt, but any proceeds above that amount belong to the home owner. This policy of mortgage law is intended to protect the bank's financial interest in the property as well as the home owner's personal interest in remaining in her home and her financial interest in retaining ownership of the equity she has built up in the house over the years.[20] In other words, legal protections afforded the bank are limited to its financial interests, even in states that grant it the title to the property. As long as those interests are protected, the borrower is treated as the owner and granted the right to stay in the home and to retain the value of her investment in it.

In the case of rental housing, however, we do not grant the person making her home in the building similar protection from being put out on the street. In part this is because we understand the landlord, not the tenant, to be the owner. But if we focus on interests, it becomes apparent that in many cases the landlord more closely resembles the bank than she does the home owner. The landlord's interests in the property, like the bank's, often are solely economic. If we support the idea that the law should protect home owners' personal interests in staying in their homes as long as the bank's financial interests are protected, it is not clear why we do not similarly protect tenants' personal interests in staying in their homes when they do not conflict with the landlord's financial interest. New Jersey and the District of Columbia have accepted this reasoning and adopted anti-eviction laws that give current tenants the right of first refusal to purchase their units, and that prevent landlords from refusing to sell to tenants who are willing and financially able to buy unless landlords have a valid personal reason for doing so, such as wanting to move into the property themselves.

Mortgage laws are not viewed by the public as oppressive interferences with the rights of owners, but rather are welcomed as protectors of those rights. Yet they regulate the relationship between lender and borrower—between the bank, which holds the title to the mortgaged property, and the home owner, who in reality owns at best a partial bundle of rights in the property. In contrast, a condominium conversion law that grants tenants a right of first refusal is commonly understood to constitute a regulatory law that limits the rights of owners. The ownership model prevents us, however, from seeing that these laws in fact have very similar policy bases.

The real question in these cases is how to understand and regulate the relationship between the parties. If we place a high value on the ability to continue to live in one's home, as mortgage law seems to demonstrate, then long-term tenants should be considered owners of their leaseholds, and their hold on the property should be protected as long as the landlord's interest is purely financial and is also protected. Indeed property lawyers understand leaseholds to constitute recognized property interests and talk about ownership of those interests. Conventional lay usage, however, does not identify tenants as owners, even though they have a clear bundle of entitlements that closely resembles the home owner's bundle. Because in the public's mind they are not owners, tenants have had a heavy burden of persuasion in asserting property rights in their leasehold. But if we are really concerned with protecting interests such as the ability to remain in one's home, we need to rethink property law and the concept of property itself to ensure that we place the burden on the right party. We need to escape the romance of ownership; rather than blindly following conventions about who the owner of a property is, we should focus on the interests asserted by those who claim they should be entitled to control various aspects of the property, and determine, on the basis of appropriate normative criteria, who should have presumptive control of the entitlement in question and who should have the burden of persuading us to shift the entitlement.

THE LEGAL-REALIST APPROACH

I have argued that the ownership model fails us because it obscures important facts about the nature of property and the necessary tasks of property law. It suppresses the tensions that exist within the concept of property and within the institution of property as implemented in law. It suggests that we award presumptive control over property to the person conventionally denominated its owner and place the burden of persuasion on all other claimants to rights in the property—a move that, as we have seen, is not always appropriate. It mischaracterizes the relationship between property and regulation by failing to recognize that government actions conventionally decried as regulatory are often essential to bring property into existence or to establish a form of property that coheres with our sense of which kinds of human relationships are consistent with respect for human dignity in a free and democratic society.

The defects of the classical ownership model require that it be replaced. At the beginning of the twentieth century a group of scholars known as the legal realists proposed that property be viewed as a bundle of identifiable entitlements, each of which should be considered separately to determine its meaning and scope. In the case of a public accommodation, for example, the traditional owner has the exclusive privilege to determine how the property is used—whether to sell appliances or cater weddings or prepare tax returns—but has no right to exclude nonowners, the customers, from the property on the basis of race and other arbitrary criteria. Conversely, a landlord may have the right to exclude trespassers but has no right to enter and use the units rented to tenants.

The legal-realist model recognizes that the sticks in the bundle of rights can be unbundled or disaggregated and distributed among several parties. Rejecting or limiting one right in the bundle has no necessary effect on the other rights. Because the rights accompanying ownership can be disaggregated by law or contract, the concept of ownership becomes blurry. The real question is how to define and allocate the different rights in the bundle.

This view, adopted by such legal realists as Wesley Hohfeld and Arthur Corbin, was enshrined in the American Law Institute's Restatement of Property and formed the basis of Thomas Grey's famous argument that the concept of property has disintegrated and lost its utility as a legal category; what matters are the specific entitlements in the bundle of property rights.[21] The crucial steps are to identify the interests for which individuals seek legal protection and to use policy analysis to adjudicate conflicts among those interests and to determine the appropriate extent of legal protection for each one. Property as a category has no utility except to obfuscate the policy choices that underlie individual rules. Specific entitlements and policy concerns should replace the formalist and conceptualist attempt to imbue the concept of property with operative force in its own right.

Proponents of the legal-realist model recognize the defects of the ownership concept. They acknowledge that rights may conflict and that a resource may have more than one owner. This view is appealing because it requires attention to specific social contexts, disputes, and relations and to relevant values and policies rather than using formalistic arguments to adjudicate those disputes. It rightfully rejects the idea that a simple, all-encompassing theory can neatly answer questions about property law and encourages a more nuanced approach to the subject.

Nonetheless, this model has its defects. It fails to recognize the cultural endurance of the concept of property for both citizens and judges. The ownership idea—for good or for ill—is extremely powerful and affects the way legal and social problems are analyzed. Demonstrating that ownership can be deconstructed does not deprive it of force as an organizing category. It retains its power to create unconscious presumptions about who should win particular disputes by appealing to commonsense assumptions about who the owner is. In addition, it affects the rhetoric of public discourse in ways that limit the creation of alternative solutions to public problems by establishing the presumption that all rights to a given property should be consolidated in a single owner and that those rights are absolute.[22]

We should recognize that property concepts perform a number of rhetorical functions. First, by identifying a particular person as the owner, we commonly presume that that person wins disputes about the property. As we analyze choices among alternative property law rules, it is important to be sensitive to the persistent influence of the ownership concept in the assignment of the burden of persuasion.

Second, the property concept sometimes creates an assumption that certain sets of rights are bundled or consolidated together and must be owned by the same person. This idea is implemented, for example, through rules about estates (allowable bundles of ownership rights) and compulsory contract terms. Sometimes, however, the assumption is that particular rights can be disaggregated, as in landlord-tenant relations. The structure of property doctrine effects presumptions about allowable forms of disaggregation.

Third, calling something a property right often reflects an intuition that the right in question implicates a strong moral claim to immunity from loss by the voluntary action of both private and public actors, and it places a heavy burden on those seeking to circumscribe—read "regulate"—the right. Fourth, it fosters a strong presumption that the right in question is alienable in the marketplace and, conversely, that nonalienable interests do not count as property rights.

Given the continuing force of the classical conception in allocating implicit burdens of persuasion, it is important to bring to consciousness the hidden work of the property idea in setting presumptions such as these. In some cases the presumptions are justified, but in others the imperatives of social justice and efficiency would be better served by challenging such fixed notions. One might begin modestly, working within the classical model, by shifting the presumption to the other party and identifying that party as the owner. Or one might recast the legal problem by describing the situation as one in which legitimate property rights exist on both sides. By reconceptualizing the dispute we can even attempt to alter burdens of persuasion in a direction that more closely accords with our moral intuitions. I do not pretend that this will be easy, but it must be done.[23]

The legal realist wrongly assumes that it is possible to engage in policy analysis without implicit baselines. Conceptions of property distribute burdens of persuasion. Recognizing the role that different conceptions of property play in setting the baselines for analysis is crucial to developing an adequate conceptual vocabulary to understand and address legal disputes about the meaning and structure of rules in property law. When judges cannot figure out how to rule in a dispute between conflicting interests, values, or policies, they often fall back on presumptions and burdens of persuasion. Traditional property law, to a large extent, is about adopting those presumptions and allocating those burdens. Yet in so doing, it obscures the tensions that arise when rights inevitably come into conflict with one another and gets in the way of our addressing them imaginatively and sensibly. We need to reconstruct policy analysis by elucidating the structure of the tensions within the concept of property itself.[24] This, in turn, will help us make better decisions.

CONTINGENCY AND STABILITY

Property rights are not the only important rights, of course. The rights of freedom of speech and religion, the right of privacy in family life, and the right of equality are also considered precious. When a property right comes into conflict with a valued personal right, it must be scaled back to make it compatible with that right. Rather than being absolute, legal rights to control property are restricted to the extent necessary to comport with legitimate obligations to both owners and nonowners. Similarly, the extent of a legal right cannot be fixed without knowing the effect the exercise of that right has on others. The title holder does not, therefore, automatically win a dispute about property. Owners have obligations as well as rights—obligations not to interfere unduly with the rights of others—and choices about the appropriate extent and character of those obligations require us to focus on the social context in which owners exercise their rights.

Property rights are situated in human relations over space and time. In order for everyone's rights to be secure, individuals must have obligations to shape their conduct so as to avoid harming others' interests. Thus the extent of one's liberty to act is contingent on the effect of one's actions on others. To make legal rights stable, people must be obligated to conduct themselves with a view to protecting the interests encompassed by those rights.

Paradoxically, legal rights get their stability partly from their contingency. An action by a property owner may be benign and therefore perfectly lawful in one place and time but harmful and unlawful in another. Pumping water out from under the neighbors' property drew a lawsuit against Friendswood in a region where the aquifer supported the land, but the same action may not have caused legal problems for the company in an area where the aquifer did not lend the surface structural support. A quarry may have caused no injury to its neighbors when the area was sparsely populated, but after developers built dozens of new houses near the quarry, the withdrawal of water had the effect of undermining the foundations of the old homes. Thus the extent of an owner's property rights is partly contingent on the context in which those rights are exercised.

Any right exercised to excess may also violate the rights of others. Putting up Christmas lights on the outside of one's home is usually quite lawful, but it may cross the line if done to excess. One of the farmhouses near where I grew up had a long semicircular driveway. For the holiday season the owner strung thousands of Christmas lights in beautiful shapes—angels, stars, animals. People came from miles around to see the magnificent display. Because the farm was isolated and far from other home owners, the spectacle did not create any harmful effects in the community, although a police officer had to be assigned to manage the heavy traffic on the road. The same activity, however, in a densely populated subdivision might constitute a nuisance because it could clog the narrow streets with cars and prevent the neighbors from having any peace and quiet for weeks. Indeed, a home owner in Louisiana was enjoined from keeping a lavish display of lights that drew an enormous influx of visitors to a residential neighborhood.[25]

The home owners who sued Friendswood claim rights in their homes. They want those rights to be secure and stable. In order to make them stable, the courts must prevent Friendswood from withdrawing water on its land in a manner that causes the home owners' land to sink in on itself and destroy their homes. In other words, the effect of Friendswood's action must be taken into account in determining whether it is within the legitimate scope of the company's ownership rights. Withdrawal of water by Friendswood may be legal until it begins to cause substantial damage to the interests of other land owners in the vicinity. Thus the stability of the home owners' property rights is dependent on the contingency of Friendswood's rights. Friendswood's rights must be contingent on their not being exercised in ways that unduly harm the neighbors. If Friendswood's actions do not harm the neighbors, they are lawful; but if they cause undue harm, they are unlawful. *Stability of a particular property right is achieved only through a conception of property rules that makes other property rights contingent on not interfering with the right we want to make stable.*

We have a paradox. Property rights can be stable only if they are contingent. It is not possible to make them both stable and absolute. Absolute rights can be gained only at the sacrifice of stability. If we want property rights to be stable, we must define them in a manner that allows us to limit the exercise of rights that interferes with core interests we want to make secure. This requires attention to the social and physical context within which property owners operate.

Multiple Models of Property

There are many models for defining and controlling property relations. These models create paradigms that decision makers can follow. Bringing these paradigms to the forefront should help to emphasize and clarify the choices that decision makers face as they set legal rules.[26]

If we broaden our view of property from the stereotypical image of a clearly defined plot of land with a single house where the unique owner lives—the image fostered by the traditional ownership model—it becomes evident that the legal system contains multiple models of property, each one suited to the various social contexts, such as business or family, in which property rights are held. Even within each of social spheres we have multiple models. With respect to family relations, we have multiple models of marital property (including community and separate property models) and alternative models to determine the enforceability of prenuptial agreements and to divide assets in the event of a divorce, children's claims on family assets (such as child support and inheritance), obligations in adulthood to provide care and support for parents, siblings, and other relatives, and real estate ownership rights reserved to married couples, such as tenancy by the entirety. In the area of housing, models of property include individual and joint ownership (tenancy in common, joint tenancy), leasing arrangements, cooperatives, condominiums, subdivisions, home owners associations, ground leases, charitable land trusts, limited equity cooperatives, tribal property (including original Indian title, recognized tribal title and restricted trust allotments), public housing, and government property.

In the business world we have sole proprietorships, general and limited partnerships, close and public (and quasi-public) corporations, and nonprofit organizations.

The classical ownership model is ill-suited to describe or analyze these widely varied property arrangements or the social relations they entail. For example, community property and equitable distribution laws reverse the usual presumption and vest interests in family members without regard to title. Indeed for many kinds of property, title is all but irrelevant in dividing those interests on divorce. Similarly, in corporate law, title is not helpful in adjudicating conflicts between shareholders and managers. Traditionally, corporate law has narrowly circumscribed the rights of shareholders. Although institutional investors have begun to exercise greater control of corporate managers, their ownership rights have been cut back by state laws that authorize managers to consider the interests of constituencies other than shareholders in managing corporate affairs.[27]

Explicitly identifying multiple models of property can help to alter presumptions and shift burdens of persuasion in appropriate directions. Home owners should be presumptively entitled to exclude others from their homes, but owners of public accommodations should be presumptively obligated to allow members of the public to have access to their places of business. We should generally be presumed immune from forcible conscription of our property to serve the needs of others, but we should be presumed to have obligations toward family members that may involve such conscription, as in the case of child support payments.

BUILDING ON NUISANCE DOCTRINE

As we have seen, the ownership model focuses on a single owner with consolidated rights; assumes that formal procedures identify the title holder; fixes entitlements at the historical moment of their creation; defines property by reference to boundaries; confers absolute powers to the owner within those boundaries; focuses on the relation between owners and things; presumes that most uses are self-regarding; prohibits harmful uses; and assumes that the institution of private property affords everyone the opportunity to become an owner without ensuring that anyone can or does become an owner.

The model of property implicit in the nuisance doctrine is fundamentally different from the ownership model. Nuisance law, we should recall, grants remedies when someone uses her property in a manner that causes unreasonable and substantial harm to neighbors by interfering in their use and enjoyment of their own property.[28] The central characteristics of property as modeled by nuisance law allow for compromise between one party's interest in security from harm and the other party's interest in free use. It may help us develop a new model of property.

Multiple owners with disaggregated rights. The nuisance model starts with the assumption that more than one person may have property rights in the same object. In contrast to the presumption that a single owner possesses consolidated rights, the nuisance model presumes that property rights may conflict when many owners use their own property. In such cases, rights must be limited to ensure that the exercise of one right does not unreasonably interfere with the exercise of others. Thus, individual owners may well have the power to restrict the freedom of others to use their own property as they wish. The nuisance model grants one of the sticks in the bundle of rights to neighbors who don't live on the property and don't hold title to it. The effect is to identify multiple persons who have legally protected interests in the same piece of property and therefore have something to say about how it is used. Some of those rights are owned by the person we conventionally call the "owner" (usually, but not always, the one in possession), but others are owned by individuals conventionally thought of as "nonowners." The rights in the property bundle have become disaggregated rather than consolidated in a single person.

Conflicting rights and the need for judgment. The title holder is not the only person with legally protected interests in the property. Others may have legal rights to control various aspects of the property. Moreover, the rights of the parties are not fully allocated by reference to merely formal criteria. The effects of one's use of property, as well as judgments about those effects, are essential to defining the rights of the parties. The focus is not just on the rights of one owner but on those affected by that owner's actions. As Texas Supreme Court Justice Jack Pope, dissenting in the *Friendswood* case, explained: "What we do cannot be understood except in relation to those we touch."[29] Because owners do not live alone but in society with others, and because property rights may conflict—both with other property rights and with personal rights—we cannot sensibly understand or shape property law without attending to the effects of recognizing particular entitlements. Conflicts among property rights cannot reasonably be adjudicated by reference to fixed notions of entitlement or right since the exercise of an entitlement on the legitimate interests of others should affect our willingness to identify a property claim as an enforceable entitlement.

Change over time. The nuisance model recognizes that changing conditions may warrant changes in property rights. Rights are not inexorably fixed at a magic moment in time. In *Friendswood,* for example, withdrawal of small amounts of water does not violate anyone's rights. Even large withdrawals may not harm neighboring owners as long as enough water is left beneath the surface to continue to support neighboring land. But an owner who withdraws large quantities of water over a long period of time may begin to affect the stability of neighboring land. As continued use generates greater harms, a use that began as lawful may become unlawful.

Similarly, an owner's rights may change because other land owners have developed their property in a way that is inconsistent with that owner's use. In *Hadacheck v. Sebastian,* an owner had established a brickyard in the midst of farmland and operated it unmolested for many years.[30] At the time the owner purchased the land, it was outside the borders of the city of Los Angeles and far from any dwellings. But as the city's borders gradually expanded to incorporate the brickyard and surrounding farms, residences were constructed nearby; lawyers would say that the home owners "came to the nuisance." The city passed an ordinance outlawing the operation of a brickyard within city limits. The brickyard owner claimed that this ordinance could not be applied to a preexisting use without violating the constitutional mandate that property cannot be taken for public use without just compensation. The U.S. Supreme Court disagreed. It upheld the power of the city to regulate property use to prevent harm to neighboring owners, and it rejected the idea that a use that was lawful when established must necessarily remain so. "A vested interest cannot be asserted . . . because of conditions once obtaining. . . . To so hold would preclude development and fix a city forever in its primitive conditions. There must be progress, and if in its march private interests are in the way they must yield to the good of the community."[31] Similarly, a lawful use, such as the production of dioxin in a way that allows it to seep into the ground and spread to neighboring property, may become unlawful when scientific discoveries show that it causes cancer. There is no vested property right to commit harm to other persons or property. Protecting individuals from harm is within the legitimate province of the police power by which the states enforce laws.

Boundaries and relationships. Boundaries are not irrelevant in the nuisance model; they determine, after all, who is free to use the land. But they have a different significance. First, the nuisance doctrine presumes that we cannot identify property rights solely by reference to borders. The boundary idea is implicit in Epstein's suggestion that owners have presumptively absolute rights to use their property as they wish, as long as they do not physically invade the property of others. The nuisance model, however, presumes that rights are not absolute within their spheres. An action is not necessarily lawful just because it occurred on one's own land; it is unlawful if it is unreasonable and causes substantial harm to other owners. To determine whether the harm is unreasonable, it is essential to focus on such factors as whether the use is suited to the community, whose use was established first, the gravity of the harm, and the utility of the conduct. Boundaries are relevant but not determinative.

Moreover, boundaries are not simply a mark of separation but of relationship. The ownership model uses the boundary metaphor to separate the space where an owner rules from the space where the owner's rights cease and nonowners take over. Ownership in this conception confers absolute powers within boundaries. The nuisance model recognizes that the boundary is a place of relationship among owners. For each owner to enjoy her property, every owner must take into account the interests of her neighbors, as well as her own interests. The boundaries of property do not separate owners inexorably from others or entitle owners to consider their own interests alone. What we do inside our borders affects those outside.

Boundaries place duties on nonowners to respect the interests of owners in controlling their property, but they also oblige owners to use their property in ways that will not harm the legitimate interests of others. Owners can achieve autonomy only if other owners moderate their actions to accord their interests due respect. Similarly, the autonomy of nonowners depends on owners' moderating their claims to absolute powers over their property. A relationship based on mutual deference and respect is therefore essential to creating the space within which the owner is free to use her own land. The owner is entitled to use her land within her borders, but because the neighbors are similarly entitled, each owner's rights are inherently limited by the rights of others.

Limited rights. From the beginning, the nuisance model presumes that property rights are limited by the legitimate rights of others. Uses that are unreasonable and cause substantial harm exceed the scope of the rights granted the owner. No one has a vested right to commit harm.

Relationships. The focus in the nuisance model is not on the relationship between the owner and the land but on the relationships between owners, and between owners and nonowners. The nuisance doctrine authorizes property uses only to the extent that they are compatible with the legitimate interests of others. It therefore directs our attention to the ways that law structures relations among persons.

Field of tension. Because it assumes that owners possess absolute powers over their property and that most acts are self-regarding, the ownership model construes the harm limitation narrowly. This is convenient, for it presumes that most uses of property will not affect others and therefore suppresses the actual need for regulation. The nuisance model, on the other hand, brings tension to the core of the property concept. Property uses that cause substantial harm may sometimes be reasonable and hence legitimate when judged in the social context of others' interests and actions. By calling attention to the pervasive conflict in property law between free use claims and security claims, the nuisance doctrine restores to the core of the property system the field of tension that the ownership model had bluntly suppressed or marginalized.

ENTITLEMENT

Because it acknowledges the tensions in property law, the nuisance model can be usefully generalized to create a new vocabulary for describing property concepts. When we adopt this new model, our focus shifts from identifying the owner to identifying the conflicting interests of everyone with legitimate claims to rights in the property in question. We might call this new paradigm the *entitlement model.*

The concept of entitlement has been taken by scholars like Robert Nozick to mean fixed rights.[32] In effect, this construction of entitlement fits with the traditional model of ownership, which recognizes absolute rights within rigid boundaries. This view of entitlement does not accord with current usage of the term in public discourse, where entitlements are thought of as rights to receive benefits from government programs such as Head Start and Social Security. Yet such entitlements are subject to change by the political process through legislative reform, redefinition, and even abolition, as has happened to many welfare programs at all levels of government. In this sense they are unlike property rights, which cannot be taken by state action without just compensation.

In modern legal scholarship the concept of entitlement is used to describe any legal right or protected interest. Because legitimate interests often conflict, it is assumed that legal protection for entitlements is not necessarily absolute.

We presume that only one person has title to a piece of property, while several people may have entitlements of various kinds in that property. The entitlement idea may therefore suggest a slimmer bundle of rights than full absolute ownership assumes, and thus it gives a truer picture of contextually defined property rights. Although entitlements are strongly protected legal rights, they are nonetheless subject to limitations to protect the entitlements of others. Hence the concept of entitlement may be better than the concept of title to express the ability of property rights to be secure in certain ways and defeasible in others.

The word *entitlement* therefore contains a useful ambiguity. On one hand, it describes a strong claim to a particular legal right; one who is entitled has a right to be granted title or given the benefit of a particular legal right. It also suggests that those who are so entitled have strong claims to immunity from being deprived of the entitlement. In this sense the entitlement concept has the flavor of the traditional conception of ownership. On the other hand, the word suggests that such rights are defeasible by political action in the public interest, that they may conflict with one another, and that the rules in force must adjust the meaning of particular entitlements in light of their effects on other entitlement holders. Such claims need not be absolute; entitlements must be defended, and they are subject to limitation and change by law.

To determine what entitlements we should have and how they should be distributed, we need to adopt a normative framework. The entitlement model is not intended to serve this purpose. Rather, it is a conceptual structure designed to replace both the ownership model and the bundle-of-rights model in order to better describe the meaning of property and of the choices posed by a private property regime.

The ownership model focuses on the relation between the owner and the thing and between the owner and the state. The owner's control over the property is assumed to be absolute within its borders, and any limitations imposed by the state represent limits on property rights. Whenever the state acts to expand its influence, the realm of property shrinks. The line separating state powers from protected ownership rights can go up and down, but expansion of state power necessarily shrinks the realm of property rights. Expansion of state power is never associated with an expansion of property rights.

In contrast, the entitlement conception assumes that state action is necessary both to create property rights and to adjudicate conflicts among owners and between owners and nonowners. It centers our attention on the interrelations between the state and its citizens, among owners and between owners and nonowners. Instead of presuming that individuals have absolute powers within rigidly defined boundaries, it focuses our attention on rules that shape the contours of relationships. And in contrast to the bundle-of-rights model, the entitlement model incorporates what is powerful about the ownership model—the understanding that property rights imply strong claims to be entitled to control a particular resource.

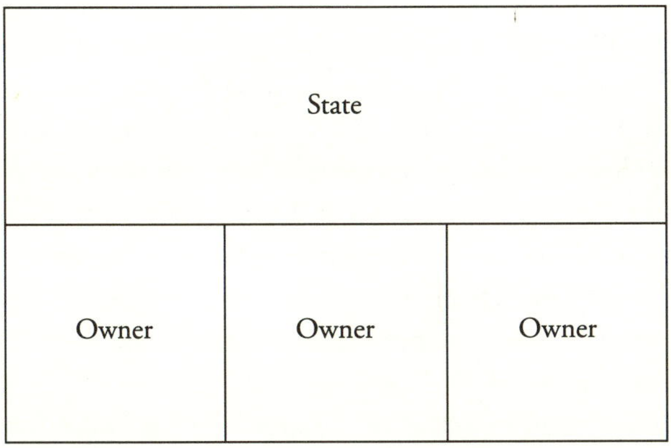

Figure 2.1 Ownership model

In the *Friendswood* case, for example, the entitlement model directs our attention to three relationships: between Friendswood and its neighbors, between Friendswood and the state, and between the neighbors and the state. Protection of Friendswood's property rights may harm the property interests of the neighbors. Moreover, both Friendswood and the neighbors may claim a right to state protection for their respective property rights. Friendswood claims a right to be free from government regulation, while the neighbors claim that Friendswood's exercise of that right constitutes a deprivation of their own property rights. Conversely, the neighbors claim a right to state action limiting

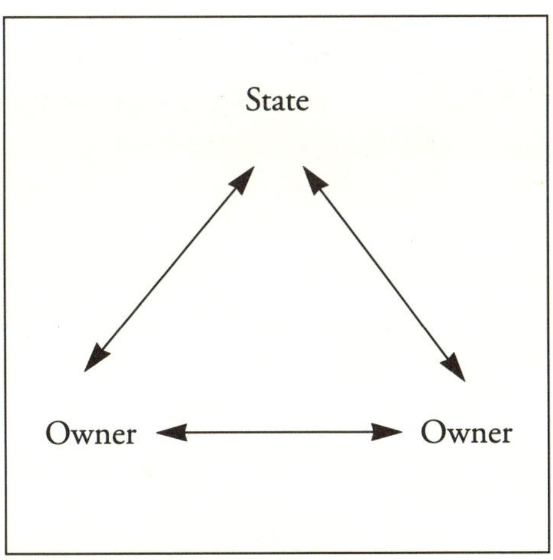

Figure 2.2 Entitlement model

Friendswood's use of its land, while Friendswood claims that such intervention by the state would deprive it of its legitimate property rights.

The entitlement model emphasizes the need for state protection to create and secure property rights against depredation by others and makes the relations between the parties, including the effects of each party's exercise of its entitlement on others, the central concern. Entitlements not only protect individual interests in autonomy and security but also promote social goals, such as economic efficiency, by allocating power between the parties. In assigning presumptive powers of control and burdens of persuasion, property law shapes the contours of social relations.

Because the assertion and exercise of property rights have effects on others, they cannot be absolute. Property rights are inherently shared rather than unitary. For this reason, in cases of genuine conflict, where legitimate interests can be claimed on both sides, resorting to title cannot solve conflicts. Rather than presuming that the person conventionally understood to be the owner should prevail, both the law of property and any acceptable conception of just property arrangements require us to adopt a more nuanced approach. If property law allocates burdens of persuasion, it is up to us to ensure that the burdens are placed on the right person. We tend to expect nonowners to have to justify their claims to place limits on the powers of the owner. But just as often we should require owners to justify uses of their property that limit the freedom of others or impair their security. Sometimes the burden of persuasion cannot be overcome no matter what; racially restrictive covenants should not be enforced no matter how much the parties desire it. What the title holder gets is not a bundle of absolute rights but a bundle of *entitlements.* Those entitlements cannot be defined without attending to their effects on others. Ownership is not a boundary that protects individuals from the obligation to account for the effect of their actions on others. Whatever rights ownership conveys, it cannot go so far.

Chapter 3 Property and Social Relations

If we approach property rights as one of the most important vehicles for structuring relations of power in our society and as a means of expressing the relations of responsibility we want to encourage, we will start off the debate in a useful way.
—*Jennifer Nedelsky*

The whole concept of a boundary depends on relationships: relationships between the two sides drawn by the boundary, and relationships among the people who recognize and affirm the boundary. . . . Once we understand the relationships that are critical to setting and respecting boundaries, we can examine more honestly which boundaries express and promote the kinds of relationships we know and desire.
—*Martha Minow*

Rock Creek Lake is located in the middle of a large ranch in Powell County, Montana. Until 1972 Robert Tavenner was the sole owner of the lake and the land around it, as well as one of the owners of the company that owned and operated the ranch. Beginning in 1922 Tavenner gave permission to various friends, neighbors, and employees of the ranch to build summer homes and cabins around his lake. By

1972 forty cabins had been constructed with a total assessed value of $300,000. The cabins had been built with the ranch owners' consent and possibly their implied invitation.[1]

The arrangement was unusual. Tavenner gave his friends and neighbors the right to build homes on his land without selling or leasing the land to them. He retained title to the land and accepted no money in exchange for the right to build and live on the property. Over decades the residents improved their homes without the benefit of any formal property rights in the land on which the homes sat. At the time they built, all they had was Robert Tavenner's word. That was apparently enough for them.

The houses, some of them quite large, were permanent structures. They were solidly built, sometimes using timber from the ranch and sometimes built with the assistance of the ranch owners. The construction costs were born entirely by the people who had been invited to make their homes there. Why did Tavenner give permission to construct these homes? According to court records, "Reasons given for the ranch owners extending permission include the wish for companionship at the ranch, the help of the cabin owners in protecting the ranch properties, their availability for fire lookout and fire fighting, and their help in maintaining the roads, as well as their friendship and society."[2]

Some of the cabin owners attempted to purchase the land underlying the cabin sites, but Tavenner consistently refused to sell. He feared that sale of the land might transfer with it ownership rights in the lake, which the ranch owners wanted to retain in order to have control of the ranch's water supply.

At first, no written documents of any kind existed to memorialize the understanding of the parties about their relative property rights. After some time, a few of the cabin owners entered into leases with the ranch owners, but these agreements ended by their own terms. For forty years, most of the owners occupied the land without benefit of any formal title or right of any kind. Starting in 1963, however, the cabin owners were asked to and did sign documents entitled "license agreements" drafted by the lawyer for the ranch owners. Tavenner granted the cabin owners a "license for use of the cabin site together with right of access thereto," imposed a fee of six dollars a year, allowed the licensees to erect a structure on the cabin site if approved in advance by the licensor (Tavenner), and provided that the structures should be removed at the termination of the license or they would become the property of the licensor. The license agreements stated that they were personal to the licensee, that they established no landlord-tenant relationship, and that they granted the licensee no power to transfer the license rights by gift, sale, or will. The agreements also explicitly stated that the license could be terminated by either party with thirty days' notice.

Tavenner never terminated any of the licenses between 1922 and 1972, even though after 1963 the written license agreements were breached in numerous ways by the cabin owners without objection from Tavenner. In particular, the cabins were "inherited" and were bought and sold, despite the agreement stating that the cabin owners had no power to do this. Although he was aware of these transfers of ownership rights, Tavenner did nothing to stop them.

In 1969 one of the ranch owners died, and the ranch was put up for sale. On July 21, 1972, Louis Ward, doing business as the Paper Box Company, entered into a contract to buy the ranch, including the lake and the surrounding land. Attached to the purchase and sale agreement was a schedule of the license agreements with the notation "consent of licensees to assignment not required." Toward the end of the negotiations to purchase the ranch, Ward asked Tavenner to terminate the license agreements. Tavenner refused. He later testified that if Ward had insisted on termination as a condition of the sale, the sale would not have gone through. According to Tavenner, Ward agreed to take the ranch "as planned, the cabins and all."[3]

On October 13 Ward notified the cabin owners that he was purchasing the ranch and the lake, including the land on which their cabins sat, and that the transfer of title would take place on December 1. He also sent a notice to all the cabin owners that their licenses would be terminated after the sale date. The notice stated: "The purchaser has examined your license agreement and will construe it according to its literal terms. There have been no oral representations made to anyone with respect to the purchaser's intentions as to this property. You should therefore not assume that you have any rights or privileges other than those arising from your license agreement."[4]

The sale was concluded, and on July 11, 1973, the new owners sent each of the cabin owners a notice of termination of their licenses. On December 20 the cabin owners filed suit against the new owner, who did business as Castle Mountain Ranch, asserting that they had the right to keep their cabins in their current locations permanently. In effect the cabin owners asked the court to declare that although they did not own the land or have a valid leasehold from the owner, they nonetheless owned easements to maintain and use the structures existing on the land. Ward contended, in response, that neither he nor Tavenner had ever granted them easements to occupy the land permanently. Rather, Ward contended that the cabin owners had mere licenses—permissions to enter land owned by another—and that, in accordance with traditional property law, licenses are revocable at will by the land owner. The case, *Rase v. Castle Mountain Ranch,* reached the Montana Supreme Court in 1981.

LAW AND EQUITY

One might think that the case is easy. After all, the formal arrangements are pretty simple. Tavenner was the owner of the land. Owners have the power to exclude nonowners and they have the power to waive this right by inviting nonowners to enter their land. But just as they have the right to grant others permission to enter their land, owners have the power to revoke such permission. This is what happened here. Case closed.

Under the common law, permission to enter property possessed by another is called a *license.* Every day millions of people in the United States enter property of others on the basis of such permissions. Employees entering the workplace, customers entering a store, and students walking across a college campus all are the beneficiaries of licenses.

Owners have the power to revoke licenses at will. If you invite someone to your home for dinner, you have the right to ask them to leave at any time. If they refuse to do so, they are trespassing, and the owner may use reasonable force to throw out the unwanted guest or may call on the police to escort the trespasser off the property.

Licenses must be distinguished from grants of entry rights that are not revocable at the land owner's will, such as leases. A lease agreement that transfers possessory rights to the tenant for a set term cannot be revoked by the landlord unless the tenant breaches a material term of the agreement. Either party can decline to renew the lease, but the agreement is irrevocable while it lasts. Another permanent grant is an affirmative easement, which confers entry rights for a specific purpose. The most common example of an easement is a right-of-way—a right to use a road that cuts through someone else's land. Easements are permanent and irrevocable unless their terms state otherwise. Property lawyers treat easements as "interests in land," for they can be bought and sold in the same manner as title to the property. Easements are created by written agreement and memorialized by a deed that is usually recorded in the registry of deeds to put subsequent owners of the burdened land on notice of the easement.

In the *Castle Mountain Ranch* case, it is clear that the parties did not formally create either a leasehold or an easement at the time the houses were built. The formal arrangements recognized in the 1963 written agreements specified that the cabin owners had no permanent rights but only revocable licenses. Nor did the contract between Tavenner and Ward limit Ward's rights to revoke the licenses. Tavenner did not make it a condition of the sale that Ward would not evict the cabin owners. Thus, when Ward bought the land, he received whatever rights Tavenner owned, and if Tavenner had the right to revoke the licenses, so did Ward.

But did Tavenner have the legal right to revoke the licenses? If the formal arrangements are determinative, the answer is yes. But are they? Ward would argue that they are. Both the written agreements and the prior oral arrangements constitute exercises of Tavenner's right to control access to his land. They did not constitute transfers of possessory rights, as in a lease, or of permanent rights to use the land, as in an easement.

The cabin owners, on the other hand, would assert that the formal arrangements are not determinative. They would point to the parties' in formal arrangements to support their claim to permanent possessory rights. They might claim that they had made an oral contract with Tavenner, at the time the houses were built, that granted them rights to live there in perpetuity. They might maintain that Tavenner's later assurances that the only reason he was refusing to lease or sell the land to them was that he wanted to retain control of the lake and to be able to kick off any cabin owners who were misusing the land—a power he never needed to exercise. In addition to these oral statements, the cabin owners could point to the fact that in more than fifty years Tavenner had never tried to evict anyone from the cabins or to restrict their use in any way—a course of conduct that hardly indicates the kind of temporary license exercised by theater patrons, for example. Finally, the content of the license should give us pause. Tavenner gave permission, not just to come to dinner, but to build houses on his land. It is hard to imagine why a sane person would build a house on someone else's land if she thought the owner might revoke the permission to live there at any time—or why an owner would assume that he could revoke the license after allowing the licensee to build a house on the land.

This case poses a conflict between the formal property arrangements described in the written, revocable license agreement and the informal arrangements established by oral statements and a long course of conduct on the part of Tavenner that strongly suggests a mutual understanding of a more permanent arrangement. The argument for respecting the formal arrangement is based on the formal rules of property law and the statute of frauds, both of which require transfers of permanent interests in real property to be made in writing. On this view the proponent of property rights has no choice but to respect the rights of the owner—in this case Ward, who purchased the property from Tavenner. Neither Ward nor Tavenner made any written promises that grant the cabin owners any legitimate expectation that their right to maintain houses on the land is anything but temporary. The statute of frauds in force in Montana requires all transactions passing title to real property to be in writing, and implicitly declares that any expectations based on a course of conduct are not reasonable bases for asserting legal rights of permanent use.

Could we say that there was a contract between Tavenner and the cabin owners that limited his (and consequently Ward's) right to eject them from the land? If there was an agreement, what were its terms? Was there an agreement by both parties or was there, instead, simply a grant of permission by Tavenner that was acted on by the grantees when they established homes? Does such a grant, with such reliance, constitute a contract at all? If it does, what legal effect does it have? If it does not constitute a contract, does it nonetheless give property rights in the land to the cabin owners? Do the parties' actions over a fifty-year period matter, or should we pay attention only to the intent of the parties? And if intent is the central concern, do we bind the parties by the intentions expressed in the initial oral arrangements or by those revealed in the formal, written agreement?

To find that there was such a contract, we would have to ignore the explicit terms of the grant by Tavenner to the cabin owners, as well as the terms of the written agreements. It turns out that the case for recognizing permanent rights in the cabin owners on the basis of the formal rules of property law is extremely weak. What then is the argument for respecting the informal arrangements between the parties and granting the cabin owners rights greater than those specified in the license agreements? The answer has to do with equity. Property law is composed of not only formal rules but also equitable doctrines under which judges exercise discretion—sometimes substantial discretion—to define and allocate property rights as fairness demands, regardless of who holds the title to the property in dispute.

Equitable doctrines have their origin in England, where the law courts tended to enforce the common law rigidly. Litigants who lost in the common law courts, or who were certain to lose there, started coming to the king's chancellor for relief. The chancellor, often an ecclesiastical official, acted on his conscience and sometimes reached a decision contrary to common law rules. Eventually a parallel court system, the chancery court, developed, along with its own set of rules, known as equity. Thus the law courts promulgated the common law, and the chancery courts promulgated the rules of equity. The normal common law remedy was damages, while the chancery courts acted "on the person" and invented the injunction, a court order requiring someone to do something or to refrain from doing something. Thus, even though the common law denominated someone the owner of a particular piece of property, the equity courts might identify a different person as the owner of "equitable rights" in the property and order the "legal owner" to refrain from using the property in a manner inconsistent with the rights of the equitable owner.

The equity courts, for example, invented the modern law of mortgages.[5] When an owner borrowed money, he would give the lender the deed to his land as security for the debt; the deed was to be returned to the debtor when the debt was paid. Under this arrangement the owner automatically lost title to the land if he could not pay back the loan on the appointed day. The common law courts "construed mortgage transactions strictly and unsympathetically. If the mortgage provided that the mortgagor was to lose his land through defaulting in payment upon a fixed day, then that was that; it mattered nothing that he defaulted by a single day, or that the property was worth infinitely more than the debt."[6] Some owners in this situation approached the chancellor for extra time to pay the debt. The chancellor gave relief to some debtors in difficult circumstances, and by 1625 the equity courts routinely allowed debtors to retain ownership of their land after the contractually specified repayment day if they could repay the debt within a reasonable period of time. In effect, the equity courts ignored the formal terms of the deal in order to protect the ownership interests of the debtor, who had transferred ownership of the property simply for the purpose of securing a debt. As A. W. B. Simpson explains, "The general theory accepted in Chancery from the seventeenth century onwards was that a mortgage, whatever its outward form, was no more than a security for a debt, and that the mortgagee's rights to the land must be so limited in Chancery as to ensure that he obtained a security and no more. . . . The result was that the Chancery freely interfered with mortgage transactions with a complete indifference to the terms agreed by the parties; in no branch of the law was the sanctity of agreement less regarded."[7]

The equity courts also invented a variety of doctrines that created exceptions to the statute of frauds, effectively enforcing informally established expectations in real property. Two of these doctrines are *easement by estoppel* and *constructive trust,* both of which are in force in most of the United States, although their exact contours are unclear. The doctrine of easement by estoppel has been applied in situations almost identical to that of *Rase v. Castle Mountain Ranch.* In the 1906 case *Stoner v. Zucker,*[8] for example, Mr. Stoner had granted Mr. Zucker a license to enter his property to construct a ditch for carrying water. Zucker constructed the ditch at the substantial expense of $7,000. One year later Stoner revoked the license. When Zucker refused to vacate the property, Stoner sued, asserting that "a license in its very nature is a revocable permission [and] that whoever accepts that permission does it with knowledge that the permission may be revoked at any time."[9] The court rejected this argument, concluding instead that "it would be to countenance a fraud upon the part of the licensor if he were allowed, after expenditure of money by the licensees upon the faith of the license, to cut short by revocation the natural term of its continuance and existence."[10] The court concluded that under the doctrine of estoppel the licensor "would not be allowed to do this."[11] Estoppel means that someone is prevented "by his own acts from claiming a right to [the] detriment of [a] party who was entitled to rely on such conduct and has acted accordingly."[12] Where a licensee reasonably expends a substantial amount of money or labor in reasonable reliance on a license, the license becomes irrevocable. "The licensee will have a right of entry upon the lands of the licensor for the purpose of maintaining his structures or, in general, his rights under his license, and the license will continue for so long a time as the nature of it calls for."[13] Under this legal doctrine, the Montana Supreme Court could in *Castle Mountain Ranch* have justified granting permanent easements to the cabin owners on the ground that they had made a substantial investment in improving the land after having received permission from Tavenner to do so.

A constructive trust is "one which is found to exist by operation of law or by 'construction' of the court, regardless of any lack of express agreement between or intent on the part of the parties. When one party has been wrongfully deprived either by mistake, fraud, or some other breach of faith or confidence, of some right, benefit, or title to the property, a court may impose upon the present holder of legal title a constructive trust for the benefit of that party. Thus in order to prevent the unjust enrichment of the legal holder, such person is deemed to hold the property as a trustee for the beneficial use of that party which has been wrongfully deprived of its rights."[14] This is the doctrine that the court seized upon in *Castle Mountain Ranch* because the statute of frauds in effect in Montana contained an explicit exception for constructive trusts.

Invocation of the doctrine of constructive trust did not, however, cleanly resolve the case. The court still had to apply the doctrine, and this meant that it had to decide whether there had been a breach of faith by Tavenner or Ward that wrongfully deprived the cabin owners of a property right. The formal terms of their agreement with Tavenner appeared to give the cabin owners no property rights of any kind in the land. Ward and Castle Mountain Ranch could not be found to have wrongfully deprived the cabin owners of a property right unless Tavenner had conferred such a right on them. To confer property rights on the cabin owners on the basis of the constructive trust doctrine, the court had first to conclude that the property rights involved in the case were not defined solely by the written documents, despite the statute of frauds.

There is therefore a circular quality to the constructive trust doctrine as applied in *Castle Mountain Ranch.* The doctrine states that one may not engage in fraud to deprive another person of a property right. In *Castle Mountain Ranch* the cabin owners had no formal property rights in the land, yet the court determined that the doctrine still applied. The reason is that the doctrine does not merely protect a person's property rights; it *reassigns* rights in a particular piece of property to someone who does not hold formal title. The doctrine does not merely recognize preexisting property rights; it *gives* property rights to "non-owners" when fairness demands. Constructive trusts thus distribute property rights in a manner contrary to formal arrangements and perhaps even contrary to the will of the parties. A court will invoke the doctrine when one of the parties has created in another party legitimate expectations of possessing a property right when the judge believes it would be unfair or inequitable to allow the title holder to act in a manner inconsistent with those expectations. This means, in effect, that the doctrine of constructive trusts recognizes that property rights are founded on legitimate expectations, and that legitimate expectations come, not only from reliance on formal title, but from informal arrangements as well.

In *Castle Mountain Ranch* the court held that Tavenner had no power to grant a revocable license to build homes on his land. Rather, if one grants a right to build a home on one's land, of necessity one grants a permanent (but perhaps not perpetual) easement rather than a revocable license.[15] This result could be justified as an implementation of the actual understanding of the parties, which might diverge from the formal arrangements, or as a regulation of the relationship between the parties, which makes a permanent grant of rights mandatory when an owner gives another person permission to build on the owner's land.

The court chose to ignore the formal arrangements and applied the constructive trust doctrine to force the formal title holder, Ward, to respect the property rights of the informal property holders in keeping their cabins on the land. What rights did they have? The constructive trust doctrine authorizes the court to promote "equity" by defining property rights in a fair manner. The doctrine obviously gives the court a great deal of discretion in defining property rights and in choosing an appropriate remedy. It decided to grant easements but to impose a time limit on them. The majority of the court granted easements lasting only thirteen years. The dissenting judge would have allowed the easements to last for fifty years. Alternatively, the court permitted Ward to buy out the cabin owners if they were willing to sell immediately. Thus Ward could obtain ownership free and clear if he could induce the cabin owners to sell their easements to him.

Application of the constructive trust doctrine did not give a clear answer in the case. Nor was it clear that the doctrine should have been applied here by its own terms, which require a determination that Ward had acted to deprive the cabin owners of a property right to which they were entitled. Since they had no formal property rights of any kind, the doctrine requires a moral judgment that the cabin owners *should* win despite the fact that they do not have title or any other formal legal interest in the land.

Nor would invocation of the doctrine of estoppel have made the case easy to decide. Estoppel, like constructive trust, has its roots in the English chancellor's exercise of his conscience. Equitable doctrines require an exercise of moral judgment. Rather than giving an answer, the doctrine of estoppel would ask a new question: Were the cabin owners entitled to rely on Tavenner's permission to build such that they could reasonably expect permanent rights to keep their cabins on the land and continue to have access to them, even though they had no formal property rights of any kind?

Rase v. Castle Mountain Ranch poses a conflict between formal and informal property arrangements. Should patterns of conduct, or a course of dealing, or understandings suggested in conversations or a relationship between the parties be relevant in allocating property rights or should we enforce rigidly the terms of written grants and agreements? If informal arrangements are relevant, how do we interpret what the informal arrangements were? Are we looking for the understanding of the parties as a proxy to find out what their real agreement was? If so, when do informal arrangements trump formal arrangements? Or should we rather concern ourselves with what appears to be fair and just regardless of what the parties agreed to? What do we do if Tavenner intended the licenses to be revocable but the cabin owners reasonably understood him to be granting them permanent rights?

The legal structure applicable to *Castle Mountain Ranch* is therefore complicated. Formal written agreements clearly make Ward the owner of the land and give him the right to exclude licensees at will upon only thirty days' notice. Yet the rules in force contain equitable doctrines, including estoppel and constructive trust, that may allow or require the court to give preference to other, informal property arrangements. Application of those doctrines is not automatic; they are standards, not rules, requiring the use of considered judgment. How should the court determine whether the circumstances of this case are appropriate to override the formal legal arrangements and allocate property rights based on the informal context? One way is by examining past cases in which these doctrines have been applied. Still, no two cases are identical; although precedents may provide guidance about the meaning and application of the legal standard, they cannot determine the result in a later case. After all, the legal standard being applied requires judgment *in this case* about the justice of the outcome. In addition, a judge seeking to do the right thing must ask whether it is wise to apply these equitable doctrines broadly. What effect will such a ruling have on future cases? Will these doctrines upset understandings that parties have reached on the basis of formal agreements or even encourage fraud by licensees claiming oral statements that were never made?

The prevalent approaches to determining what the rules of property law should be in cases like this are based on rights analysis and efficiency. I want to rehearse briefly the ways in which these approaches might be used to address the case and suggest what is good and what is deficient in these approaches. I will then develop an alternative model for normative debate that focuses on analysis of the relationships central to the case.

RIGHTS AND EFFICIENCY

What is the best language for discussing the question of what property is and whether it is justified? What normative framework should we adopt to debate the wisdom or justice of alternative property regimes? The two reigning approaches among contemporary property scholars are rights and efficiency.[16]

Rights theory, broadly conceived, includes any normative arguments that justify property rules because they are right—because they describe the moral values that should govern the ways in which people behave toward each other in a free and democratic society. It therefore includes considerations of fairness and justice, dignity, autonomy and human flourishing, desert and distributive equity. In its broadest connotation, the language of rights can also encompass the values promoted by communitarians, who emphasize the importance of community life as well as individual rights and argue that individuals have obligations as well as rights. Efficiency theory, on the other hand, uses the language of interests, welfare, and utility to judge the consequences of adopting particular property rules. Its proponents prefer dispassionate economic assessment of the social costs and benefits of various definitions and allocations of property entitlements to the often emotion-laden and contradictory appeals to values and rights. If we are to pursue a utilitarian analysis that considers the consequences of different property regimes for social welfare, is economic efficiency the best way to measure costs and benefits of different property regimes? Are there other ways to measure the relative harms and benefits resulting from different property rules other than market values? Are all values commensurable, so that it would be rational for us to measure them on a single metric such as dollar values? If they are not commensurable, how do we compare incommensurable values? Is there a way to combine the best of justice language and utility language?

Recent discussions of the justifiability of property usually fall into one of two camps: the philosophers who propound rights theory, and the economists who use efficiency theory. Since the two groups do not speak the same language, it is not surprising that each tends to ignore or at best criticize the other's approach. This is unfortunate because both schools have important contributions to make. At the same time there are significant defects in both rights theory and efficiency theory as they are applied by many legal scholars and judges. To better understand property, we need to know what is good and what is deficient in these approaches. They each contain core insights that are valuable. At the same time, I will argue for a new normative framework that considers the role that property law plays in shaping the contours of social relationships. This relational approach will broaden the considerations relevant to law making and will better allow us both to express and to critically analyze our deepest values and commitments.

We can also learn from the way lawyers think about choices of norms. The proponents of rights and efficiency theory miss the boat by ignoring the insights we can gain from the practice of common law adjudication. Legal theorists have tried to fill the gaps or resolve the tensions in property law by resorting to philosophy and economics. But it turns out that philosophers and economists perform their characteristic analyses by making important assumptions about the content of property law. Each discipline, it seems, looks to the others to fill the gaps in its own analysis. The escape to other disciplines to answer the conundrums in one's own discipline is a time-honored practice, but it avoids, rather than solves, the underlying problem. Escape may be attractive when one's own discipline leaves us with unanswered questions, but it is a false attraction.

The ownership model is usually, but not always, associated with rights theory. The theorists who believe that property is a coherent concept typically adopt the model and then justify or criticize it by asking whether individuals have a right to own property. Jeremy Waldron says that rights theory asks whether a particular interest is sufficiently important from a moral point of view that others have a duty to respect it.[17] While this approach has substantial force, it neglects a crucial consideration. The analyst who asks whether an interest should be respected by others is not doing her job if she does not consider the consequences of protecting one person's interest on the people who would be bound to respect it. After all, the goal is to determine whether an interest asserted by one person is sufficiently important from a moral point of view that it places duties on other people to modify their behavior. The recognition of a particular right affects others, either by placing a duty on them to act or not to act in certain ways so as to avoid violating that right, or by making them vulnerable to harmful effects of actions taken by the right holder within the scope of her legal liberty. Rights analysis is therefore incomplete and misleading, from a moral point of view, unless it focuses our attention on the consequences for nonowners of recognizing a property right in a particular owner.

Efficiency theorists, on the other hand, suggest that we adopt rules that will maximize social wealth (maximize the size of the pie) and only then address distributive concerns about how to divide up the pie. They suggest that it is possible to analyze property rights without appealing to considerations of fairness or justice. But any theory of property that evaluates the consequences of alternative rules on social welfare must incorporate assumptions about justice. Moreover, it is misleading and oversimplified to pretend that all questions of justice can be reduced to questions about the distribution of property rights. Efficiency theorists tend to reduce our normative concerns to two questions: efficiency and distribution. But in choosing how to conceptualize and judge property rights and institutions, we are not only deciding how to maximize wealth and how to divide it up. Rather, we are choosing what form of social life we want to have. The question of whether a restaurant owner has the right to exclude customers on the basis of race is not only a question involving the distribution of property rights or maximization of social wealth. It is a question of power and justice. It involves a choice between a model of social relations based on racial caste and one based on racial equality. Unless we relate alternative property rules to consideration of the appropriate and defensible forms of social life, we will not have adequately addressed the question of whether a particular property right or institution is justified.[18]

THE RIGHTS APPROACH

Rights analysis, according to Jeremy Waldron, asks whether a particular interest is sufficiently important from a moral point of view that others have a duty to respect it.[19] The goal is to formulate rules of law that protect interests that deserve protection from the standpoint of fairness or justice. An interest is protected legally because it is right to protect it. It is a commonplace that rights may conflict, and the careful analyst must reexamine rights in the context of those conflicts to redefine them so that they are compatible with one another. The goal is to promote justice and fairness by identifying particular individual rights that demand recognition by others and which promote interests that have a moral backing, such as autonomy, dignity, privacy, equality, liberty, and security, while recognizing that rights end when they conflict with similar rights held by others.

Let us now have a look at how each of the parties in *Castle Mountain Ranch* might state their case for their proposed rule of law on the basis of rights arguments.

The title holder's argument for formality. The issue in the *Castle Mountain Ranch* case, according to the title holder, is simple: Who is the owner of the land? To answer this question, we need look no further than the title. The title is the "formal right of ownership of property."[20] That title is clearly and indisputably held by Ward. Nor is it subject to any encumbrances, recorded or unrecorded. No lease, no easement, no conveyance of a lesser interest in land has passed title to any property right to the cabin owners. All they have is permission to enter the land and perform acts on it. Such permissions are mere licenses, revocable at will by the land owner.

Tavenner, the previous title holder, had never given up any formal property rights to the cabin owners; he had only granted them a general permission to occupy the land. Such licenses are exercises of ownership and are revocable at will. Before selling Ward the land, Tavenner could have granted easements or leases to the cabin owners to protect their interests after the sale. He did not do so. Or he could have sold the land subject to the condition that none of the cabin owners be ejected without cause or their prior consent. Since he did not condition the sale in this way, Tavenner transferred all his rights in the land to Ward.

You keep whatever rights you don't give away. The owner who does not transfer an easement has a right to revoke a temporary permission to use his property. If the cabin owners had wanted to secure the right to occupy the land, they should have bargained and paid for easements or leases. Giving others permission to use your property is an exercise of your property rights, not a waiver of them. No promises were made to them; no one was misled, and no fraud was committed. The licensees have only themselves to blame for failing to secure permanent rights.

No conflicting messages were given. There could be no confusion about the nature of the agreement since it was eventually reduced to writing. No cabin owner sued in 1963 to claim that the license did not represent accurately the rights of the parties. We can therefore assume it represented their understanding of the arrangement. The licensees took a risk, and the court should not protect them from the consequences of their decision not to purchase an easement. It would constitute a wrongful taking of Ward's property rights to make him recognize property rights in the cabin owners that were never created by himself or by his predecessor, Tavenner.

The law provides Ward, as it does all owners, an immunity right to keep whatever rights he has not given away. He can transfer a right if he wishes to do so, on terms chosen by him. He can invite others to enter his property on the terms he chooses. To change a revocable license into an irrevocable easement or long-term lease would take rights from Ward that he never intended to give away. This would be bad enough as applied to Tavenner, but it is worse applied to Ward, who purchased the property in reliance on the record title in the registry of deeds, which identified Tavenner as the full owner of the land and gave no indication of any subordinate property rights in the cabin owners. Ward had a right to rely on the record title, the written contract, and the deed given him by Tavenner, all of which contained no restrictions of any kind. Ward would be unfairly surprised to learn after his purchase that the mere presence of other people on the land meant that Tavenner was not a full owner, that the record title did not mean what it said, and that Tavenner had no legal power to sell the land unencumbered by other property rights.

A title holder such as Ward would argue that equitable doctrines that redefine property rights in a manner different from formal arrangements are unfair because they require owners like Tavenner to give up more rights than they want to give up. Tavenner never intended to grant permanent irrevocable rights when he permitted the cabin owners to use the land. Ward, as purchaser, also has a right to rely on the formal documents of title to determine whether the cabin owners have any existing rights in the land. He should not have to guess from conversations or observation of the land use what the courts will say is a fair arrangement. What is fair is to protect the rights of the owner, and there is no question here that the owner is Ward and that nothing limits his rights to exclude the cabin owners from his land. Applying equitable doctrines in this case and finding in favor of the cabin owners would make everyone's property rights less secure. Any nonowners one has allowed to come on one's land could claim they relied on a conversation or a long-standing pattern of being allowed to enter the land and that they therefore have acquired property rights in the land. Employees who have been at a firm for many years might claim a right to tenure even though their formal contract is at will. Adopting an equitable rule here would have enormous consequences in making property rights of record title holders less secure and less predictable to everyone's detriment.

The cabin owners' argument for informality. The cabin owners would argue that the court should consider not only the formal terms of agreements but also their implicit meaning, as well as the significance of their long-standing course of conduct. The original title holder of the land, Tavenner, conveyed conflicting messages to the licensees. The formal oral arrangement was permission to build cabins without any transfer of ownership rights in the form of an easement or transfer of title and without the creation of a lease arrangement. Eventually reduced to writing, the formal written agreement gave the cabin owners licenses that were revocable on thirty days' notice. But the content of the licenses is permission to invest substantially in building a house on the property. Although no formal property rights were conveyed, the substantive content of the license suggests that the land owner intends not to revoke the permission without a good reason. If Tavenner had ever tried to revoke the licenses without cause, his conduct in extending permission to build would arguably be misleading.

Consider how we would have reacted if Tavenner had given permission to only one person to build a house, stood by and watched her build, and the day the house was done, revoked the license, depriving the builder of any right to reach her house. Surely it would have appeared that Tavenner had misled the builder into trusting that she would have access to the house she built. Allowing substantial investment conveys a message that the land owner is making a good-faith promise that the builder will receive some benefit from her investment and that she will be able to get into her house to enjoy it. Any other interpretation would require the licensee to assume that the licensor was acting in bad faith or in total disregard of the licensee's interests. The court should defer to the actual subjective expectations of the parties rather than the objective expression of them in the formal license.

If the court finds that the expectations of the licensor (the land owner) and the licensee (the builder) differ, it should enforce the expectations of the licensee even if the licensor did not intentionally mislead the licensee. The nonowner (licensee) trusted the owner—because of friendship, neighborliness, or a family relationship, and the owner has no right to abuse that trust by ignoring the licensee's reasonable expectations. Sometimes people may feel hesitant to put things into writing when they involve relationships with neighbors or friends precisely because an insistence on formalities might convey mistrust and chill a warm relationship. It may be embarrassing to ask for something in writing because it would suggest the licensee does not trust the licensor. Consider: Tavenner is giving a great gift to a friend. "Build a house next to my lake and we can spend our summers together. Our kids can play. It will be great." The friend responds: "Can you put that in writing?" It may seem an untrusting response to a generous gift. Given out of friendship, a request for a writing suggests lack of trust in the friendship, a message that may ruin the gift and alter the friendship it implies. It is understandable the licensees did not ask for a writing.

By 1972 Tavenner's long-standing acquiescence in the occupation of his land—in some instances more than fifty years—induced the cabin owners to assume that they would have continued access to it. He induced them not only by the content of his permission ("build a house") but by the long-standing permission. Time matters. Moreover, he gave permission to many people—forty families in all—and never asked any of them to abandon their homes and vacate his property. This course of conduct suggests that property rights have been redistributed. The actual arrangements on the ground, as well as the actual understandings of the parties, differ from the formal arrangements. The owner knows or should know this—and so should the court. The failure to obtain written assurances that the permission would not be revoked is understandable, and to allow revocation would be fundamentally unfair to the licensee and would enable the land owner to commit an injustice, depriving the cabin owners of property rights to which they are entitled.

Nor is this result unfair to the purchaser Ward. Certainly Ward knew the history of the property when he bought it. He could see that forty cabins had been built on the land, and he was put on notice that some of them had been there fifty years. It was unreasonable for him to assume that he could purchase the land free of any obligation to allow the cabin owners the right to get to their cabins.

It is just and proper to recognize the cabin owners' claims even though to do so would mean adopting equitable rules of law that might seem to make property rights somewhat less predictable. In fact, the application of equitable estoppel and constructive trust laws would not make results too unpredictable. A license would become irrevocable only if the licensee reasonably relied on it in making substantial investments in the property. In *Castle Mountain Ranch,* the prior relationship between the parties as friends, family members, or neighbors supports a finding of reasonable reliance. The prior relationship provides added assurance that an agreement between the parties existed to allow the investment. It also suggests a reason why the agreement was not reduced to writing. Even when such a prior relationship does not exist, it is easy to determine when a licensee has invested substantially in reliance on a license. In this case, no one could dispute that building a house meets the substantial investment test. That investment strongly suggests that the licensee believed that the license was not revocable at will. Substantial agreement is likely to exist on the appropriate application of this test; only a small number of cases will present difficult judgment calls. And in those cases it is right for us to sacrifice some measure of predictability to ensure a just result.

Judging Rights

How would a judge who is strongly in favor of protecting property rights view this case? One answer—the simplistic answer—is to protect the rights of the "owner." Who is the owner here? The simple answer is the title holder—Ward. But as we have seen, things are not so simple. The goal of the rights approach is to protect legitimate entitlements. This means that protecting the interest in question is the right thing to do; we are protecting an interest that has a strong moral claim to protection. Ownership is such a claim. But how do we determine who the owner is? Owners have the right to keep their rights or transfer them to someone else. Tavenner, whose ownership of the land surrounding Rock Creek Lake before 1922 is not in dispute, gave others permission to occupy his land. How is the judge to determine whether this act constituted an irrevocable transfer of rights in the land or a mere exercise of a revocable right to admit with a concomitant right to change one's mind and exclude the admittee later?

The problem is that the judge who is strongly in favor of protecting property rights must choose between alternative indicia of ownership. What are the sources of the expectations of the owner? It is not at all obvious that a proponent of property and ownership will identify the title holder as the sole owner here. Even if the judge determines on the basis of formal title that the land was Tavenner's to sell to Ward, the case is not settled. The cabin owners may not own the land, but no one disputes that they own their cabins. They would, for example, almost certainly have the right to remove the cabins and locate them on land the cabin owners *do* own. If they own their cabins, don't they have a right to get to them?

It is not obvious that protection of ownership entails a commitment to look only to formal indicia of ownership. After all, many common oral contracts are enforceable, such as short-term leases. Oral leases constitute transfers of possessory rights; not to enforce them would take property rights from the tenant. An oral agreement allowing construction of a home would seem to include, by its very nature, a transfer of rights of access to the land on which the home is built. Ownership of a home is meaningless if the owner cannot get to it. Permission to build a home perhaps should include rights of some kind in the land.

One might conclude that protection of ownership rights requires the court not to look merely to the formal title but to the actual circumstances on the land. Those circumstances include houses built and owned by persons other than the title holder. The cabin owners obviously built with the expectation that they would have continued access to their homes under circumstances in which the title holder knew they would have that expectation. To allow the current title holder to exclude them from the land would interfere with their property rights as established by permission and long-standing use.

There are arguments one can make for looking only to the formal arrangements. Formal title is easier to determine and arguably therefore may seem to make property rights more secure and certain. But notice that this argument has a counterargument. Formal title does make the *case* simpler; it gives us a clear answer to the question of who will win the lawsuit. But having a clear answer in the lawsuit is not the same as creating secure expectations or correctly defining property rights. Formality, in this case, secures the expectations for the title holder while creating insecurity for the cabin owners. Now one might say that if they want security, they should bargain for formal rights. The question, however, is why they should have to do so. If property is about protecting reasonable expectations, why assume that the only expectations that are reasonable are those based on formal title?

Nothing in the ownership concept or the idea of property rights compels adherence to formality as the only way to identify the legitimate source of property rights in the world. Indeed, in *Castle Mountain Ranch,* mechanical protection of the rights of the title holder of the land may have the effect of totally ignoring the legitimate interests of the cabin owners and denying them their property rights. Similarly, protection of the rights of the title holder conflicts with the rights of the land holders—the cabin owners who are holding the land on which their cabins sit. They are not mere dinner guests; they have been invited to live on the land and to do so, not merely as short-term tenants, but as owners of homes built and paid for by themselves. The concept of ownership does not in any way compel a judge committed to protecting property rights to rule in favor of the "land owner" rather than the cabin owners who claim a legitimate right of access to the land on which their cabins sit. A strong advocate of property rights might be justified in finding that by granting permission to build, Tavenner had created reasonable expectations that could only be met by transferring certain property rights to his licensees. Finding otherwise would violate the licensees' reasonable expectations, and protecting reasonable expectations is what property is all about. Nothing in the ownership concept or the idea of property rights compels us to find the expectations of the cabin owners unreasonable and the expectations of the land owner reasonable. Arguably, the reverse is the case.

Our examination of this case has revealed several problems with rights analysis. First, the concepts of ownership and property do not logically require us to choose formality over informality as the sole method of identifying who holds legal rights in land. Nor does the concept of a property "right" require us to identify legal entitlements as based solely on formal arrangements; such arrangements may be unjust and deny "rights." After all, part of the point of rights theory is to provide a basis for judging whether existing legal arrangements are just. The law, we are told, should protect rights. To argue that rights are based on whatever the law says defines ownership places the formal legal arrangements outside the very considerations of justice by which those arrangements are supposed to be judged. Rather, rights are based on reasonable expectations, and it is a matter of debate what the expectations actually were in this case and whose expectations were reasonable.

Most people assume that property is about ownership and that ownership is defined by the person who has title. But property is also validly understood as an entitlement—a right to which someone is or should be entitled. To say that someone is entitled suggests that she has a right to have title. The one who has formal title may not be the same as the one who, in all justice and fairness, *should* have formal title or at least some stick in the bundle of rights encompassed by full ownership. In other words, we cannot adjudicate a property dispute by making a rule that the owner wins. Which owner? The landlord who is entitled to receive rent or the tenant who is entitled to possess the apartment? The storekeeper who is entitled to sell goods on the premises or the customer who is entitled to enter the store to buy them? To say that the owner wins is circular because the meaning of ownership is exactly what is at question here. What are the proper sources of ownership? What conduct establishes it? What benefits and burdens does it entail? Could there not be two owners here, with property rights divided between the parties, as they are in the case of landlords and tenants?

Rights analysis does not provide a clear way to deal with conflicts of rights. The rights approach starts with individual interests and suggests that we identify interests that are sufficiently important from a moral point of view to demand protection. In the case of *Castle Mountain Ranch* there are strong claims on both sides. Each side has interests that claim our allegiance. In order to judge who should prevail, we need an approach that can allow us to recognize the legitimate interests on both sides and the extent to which they press upon us.

Perhaps we can talk about balancing the legitimate interests of the parties to adjudicate the conflict of rights. The language of balancing has become the standard language in legal opinions today, as well as in law school classes. But the language of balancing sits uncomfortably with the language of rights. We could say that one interest outweighs the other. But why? How have we determined this? What does it mean to say one interest outweighs another? And what does this have to do with rights? Do we say that one claimant wins because her rights outweigh the rights of the other? But why? The language of rights, without more, is conclusory rather than persuasive or argumentative. What we need is a reason for choosing one claimed right over another. Rights language is not very helpful in providing a reason. It has no means by which to persuade us that *it is right* for the owner of record to prevail but can only repeat the circular argument, "Because she's the owner."

One might say that the formal title holder's right presumptively trumps that of the nonowners, who prevail only in exceptional cases. But then the question is why this is not such an exceptional case. Moreover, in *Castle Mountain Ranch* this argument ignores the fact that the cabin owners own their cabins. We have a conflict of rights here, and the reasons of justice and morality that must be given to address this conflict seem to move away from flat assertions of rights to more fluid concerns about fairness and legitimate expectations. We must shift, in other words, to the realm of judgment, of debate, of tragic choices. We cannot say that everyone who thinks about this case carefully will come to the same judgment. It is therefore difficult to claim that the party we want to win should win because they have a claim that rational people in our society cannot reasonably deny.

Rights language purports to eschew consequentialist analysis. It does not ask what the effect of protecting an interest is; it just asks if it is right to protect that interest from a moral point of view. If it is right, then the interest must be protected, and the consequences be damned. But is this position tenable? If we protect the rights of formal title holders, we will create incentives for people in the position of the cabin owners to insist that transactions of this kind be put in writing to protect their interests, thereby formalizing personal relationships. Is that a good thing? Don't people have a right to create and rely on informal relationships? Forcing everyone to put all arrangements in writing arguably deprives them of the right to engage in such relationships. It will make people less "neighborly" and more businesslike. If, on the other hand, we protect the rights of the cabin owners, we may discourage owners like Tavenner from granting informal rights of this kind because they would lose more rights than they intended to give away. They may shy away from engaging in neighborly conduct for fear that allowing neighbors to come onto their property would cause them to lose their rights in it. These effects on neighborliness are quite relevant to determining the appropriate content and contours of property rights.

Careful identification and protection of legitimate interests cannot be accomplished without attention to the consequences of protecting particular interests. By safeguarding the rights of one party today we may create incentives that will lead to depriving others of the ability to enjoy similar rights in the future. If we believe that rights describe important interests that deserve protection, the application of rules that deny those rights in the future cannot be said to unambiguously protect rights.

Rights analysts eschew consequentialist reasoning because they do not want important interests that demand protection as a matter of justice, morality, or fairness to be sacrificed for mere societal interests. They do not want the "rights" of some to be sacrificed for the benefit of others. This impulse is sound, but the inference that we should therefore eschew all analysis of consequences is not sound. Sophisticated rights theorists, like Jeremy Waldron, are well aware of this. Because rights conflict, protecting one interest has consequences for other interests that also deserve protection. Recognizing one person's rights in property may have adverse effects on the rights of one's neighbors, and careful consideration of all the consequences of different ways of adjudicating the conflict of entitlements cannot be avoided if one is interested in making a considered judgment about the moral claims at issue in a case.

Let us acknowledge what is good about the rights approach. It focuses our attention on making judgments about who should win the lawsuit. It forces us to consider what is the right thing to do. It asks us to define property entitlements in a manner that does not ask individuals to bear burdens they should not, in all fairness and justice, have to bear for the good of the community. It asks us to think of a way to explain to the loser why she is losing the lawsuit and to do so in a way that she might accept as reasonable. It asks us to treat individuals as having overwhelming importance, deserving of respect and dignity. Finally, it asks us to consider the obligations we owe each other as human beings. We are not entitled to consider our own interests alone.

The language of rights, justice, and fairness invites us to engage in persuasive moral dialogue. Stripped of its conclusory character, it leads us to attempt to articulate the reasons that support granting legal protection to individual interests. Those reasons, by themselves, are often contradictory. Expectations come from both formal and informal sources, and when those sources lead us in opposite directions, we are led back to narrative. Lawyers in opening statements and at final summation before juries weave compelling narratives about what occurred and how to understand it in order to persuade jurors to accept their side's understanding of what is right and just. In the O. J. Simpson trial, for example, the prosecution presented the facts and in effect asked the jury not to let him get away with murder. The defense raised doubts about the handling of evidence by the Los Angeles Police Department, even suggesting that the police may have planted evidence to incriminate the defendant and in effect asked the jury not to let the police get away with it. The defense also urged that the planting of evidence raised the possibility that all the evidence was planted and that this was enough to raise reasonable doubt and justify acquittal. Both arguments offered stories about what happened—stories with morals. The language of justice asks us to make stories about the relationships between the parties and the shape of the social world in order to judge between conflicting claims. It asks us to engage actively in the judging rather than deferring mechanically to formal signs. This does not mean that informality wins the day. It means that we are concerned with entitlement—a moral claim—and that formal title is only part of the picture.

THE EFFICIENCY APPROACH

The alternative normative approach in current property theory to rights analysis is the efficiency approach. The intent of efficiency analysis is to promote the general welfare or social utility. Rather than reasoning from rights, the efficiency analyst assumes that opinions on rights will always differ. The only noncontroversial goal is to maximize welfare as individuals conceive it. One way to do this is by minimizing costs and maximizing benefits. This does not mean that all costs must be avoided but that the costs and benefits of alternative legal regimes must be compared in order to determine which rule best promotes aggregate welfare. Efficiency analysts measure costs and benefits by reference to the goal of satisfying human preferences. Efficiency analysis purports to eschew moral judgment in favor of giving people what they want. In addition, it assumes that it is both possible and desirable to measure costs and benefits along a single metric, suggesting that multiple values can be aggregated by considering only the magnitude of pleasure or pain that alternative regimes cause individuals.

This approach tends to segregate considerations of distribution from those of efficiency. Efficiency analysis focuses on finding the rules that will maximize the size of the pie; welfare programs can then redistribute the benefits of the pie to achieve distributive goals. Of course, efficiency can be sacrificed to achieve more equal distribution, but the analysis is intended to clarify when and by how much such a sacrifice occurs, especially when the sacrifice may have the effect of making the least well-off person less well off because the size of the pie has so decreased that less is available for everyone.

Efficiency analysis uses market measures to determine the magnitude of costs and benefits. The analyst asks how much individuals are willing and able to pay to obtain particular legal entitlements and what others must offer them to induce them to sell their rights. The hope of the scholars and judges who use this analysis is that market measures help perhaps to quantify the analysis, making it somewhat more determinate. In addition, market measures allow the analyst to take account of the problem of scarcity. To say that someone values an entitlement highly is not helpful if she is unwilling to sacrifice other entitlements to get it. If she is not willing to pay what it costs to obtain the entitlement, this may mean that she values the entitlements she has more than the one she would like to have, or that other people value the entitlement more than she does and are willing and able to pay what it takes to get it.

If the judge in *Castle Mountain Ranch* wanted to promote efficiency, how might the two sides argue their cases?

The title holder's argument for formality. Protection of the interests of formal title holders is arguably efficient for several reasons. First, efficiency is promoted when people can make their own judgments about how to use their property and about when and under what terms to sell it. Facilitating property use and transactions that move property from one user to another who values the property more highly promote social welfare by increasing individual satisfaction. The best way to make sure that property is being held by the person who values it the most is to make the rules of property law clear. People can only use property they own; if they are uncertain who owns property, they will not be sure whether they have the right to use it and will be discouraged from doing so out of fear that it would leave them open to a lawsuit and expose them to financial liability if someone else were to claim ownership on the basis of informal arrangements. Thus, it is crucial to have clear rules about property rights in order to identify who the owner of a particular entitlement is. Clear rules about property rights encourage planning by clarifying who owns those entitlements; thus, property rules should steer away from determinations of fairness or reasonableness and from investigations into the extent of a party's reliance on subjective expectations or custom. Where interests in land are concerned, it is best to encourage people to put things in writing and then to enforce strictly the terms of their agreement. Property use is discouraged if the owner cannot know for sure whether the use is lawful or not, and whether the use will or will not result in financial liability or loss of property rights because of informal reliance by others. Clear rules also cut down on litigation by letting individuals know who will win the lawsuit in advance, thus avoiding the costs of litigation and the uncertainty associated with it.

Property can only travel from an owner who values it less to an owner who values it more if the rules in force facilitate market transfers. But, like use, such transfers are discouraged if the assignment of property rights is uncertain. In this case, application of the doctrines of constructive trust and estoppel, which rest on a subjective determination of reasonable expectations, would impede the transfer of ownership from Tavenner to a buyer like Ward because it would make the assignment of property rights uncertain. This very uncertainty would discourage many prospective buyers from buying either the land or the cabins. People can buy and sell property only if they know what they own and what they do not. If they have to begin their bargaining by negotiating about who owns what, the costs of transacting property sales will go up significantly, discouraging bargains that are to the mutual benefit of both parties. Thus, both property use and bargaining will be promoted by decreasing transaction costs, and the best way to do this is to clarify property rights by reference to formal indicators of ownership, especially the recorded title. Uncertainty about the assignment of property rights is an impediment to sales that will increase social wealth by transferring property from a person who would rather have the money than the property to a person who would rather have the property than the money. Enforcing licenses in accordance with their terms increases predictability and certainty in property rights and so encourages and lowers the cost of transactions.

Reliance on formal title not only clarifies property rights and makes them more predictable but also is more likely to result in allocating property entitlements to the party who values the entitlement the most. If the cabin owners at Rock Creek Lake valued access more highly than the land owner Tavenner valued it, then they should have purchased permanent rights of access from him by offering enough money to induce him to sell or lease the property. If they could not offer him enough to get him to agree, we can conclude that he valued retaining control over the property more than they valued obtaining secure rights.

A further benefit of assuring title holders that the rights they paid for are secure is that if they know they retain the right to revoke licenses, they are more likely to grant them. Adopting legal doctrines that recognize informal indicators of rights would discourage owners from granting licenses because they would worry that they would lose more than they wanted to give up. Protecting the rights of the title holder, by contrast, would encourage neighborly conduct by reassuring owners that if they allow nonowners to hold some of the property sticks, they will not end up dispossessed of the whole bundle. It would increase trust among neighbors by sparing owners from having to face sporadic and unforeseeable loss of their property rights when they allow others to come onto their land. Thus, recognition of formal criteria of ownership encourages transactions by facilitating arrangements that promote the will of the parties. Protection of informally created entitlements will discourage arrangements that benefit all parties and therefore decrease the welfare of everyone.

Finally, because efficiency considerations suggest that we will maximize aggregate welfare if we grant entitlements to the parties who value them most, we need a rule of thumb in such cases about who is likely to value property the most. The easiest rule to apply—and also the most predictable for owners and nonowners alike—is a rule based on formal title. The one most likely to value a particular property right is the one who has purchased it. If access to the land is more valuable to nonowners (the cabin builders), let them purchase permanent rights by buying easements or offering the new land owner enough to induce him to sell. If they cannot offer enough money to induce Ward to sell them rights in the land, then he values the property entitlement in question more than they do and it would be inefficient to grant the cabin owners rights they are unwilling to pay for.

In sum, protection of formal property rights promotes efficiency. First, it assures clarity about who owns which entitlements and ensures that entitlements go to the person who values them most. Clarity gives owners the confidence to use their property in ways that maximize their welfare without concern that their actions may cause them to lose rights they do not intend to waive. It also encourages transactions by decreasing uncertainty about who owns the entitlement in question, thereby facilitating transfer from an owner who values the entitlement less to one who values it more. Second, protection of formal rights is likely to allocate the entitlement to the one who values it the most. Nonowners can prove they value the entitlement more by offering the owner enough money to induce the owner to sell to them.

The cabin owners' argument for informality. Efficiency can be promoted either by lowering the costs of transactions or by granting entitlements to the parties who value them the most. The title holder assumes that the clarity that would result from assigning rights according to formal title would automatically lead to the lowest possible transaction costs. But reference to formal criteria of ownership in all instances of dispute may actually increase those costs. By inducing everyone to put all arrangements in writing in order to ensure that their expectations will be legally protected, insistence on formal title increases the costs of transacting property agreements. It would also discourage cooperation. The result would be that written contracts would become necessary for every single transaction. Why should parties to agreements that are highly unlikely ever to be the subject of a dispute be induced to go to the expense and trouble of putting them in writing? Such a rule would constitute a full employment act for lawyers, but the costs of reducing such understandings to paper outweigh the benefits of increased predictability.

In addition, honoring only the formal terms of agreements would encourage the parties to search for loopholes that might benefit them beyond what they had bargained for or even allow them to back out of implicit deals. To protect themselves from such machinations, each party would add clause upon clause to the written contract in an attempt to anticipate every conceivable contingency that the other might ingeniously use to gain an unfair advantage. The result would be a proliferation of monstrously long contracts, the preparation and interpretation of which would waste private and public resources. The added expense would inflate transaction costs and discourage people from making deals that would increase efficiency and aggregate welfare by transferring entitlements from lower-valued to higher-valued uses.

The cost of transactions may well be lowered by deciding cases by reference to the reasonable expectations that emerge from oral statements, a course of dealings, understandings common to the trade, social custom, and the typical conduct associated with common relationships. Courts should encourage trust in market relationships by enforcing the justified expectations of market actors based on social custom; this is the principle behind the duty of good faith implied by courts in every contract. This is especially true in the context of agreements between neighbors or friends, who typically are uncomfortable having to reduce their mutual understandings to written form. Enforcing actual expectations both lowers the costs of transactions and promotes welfare by satisfying human preferences.

The title holder has argued that formality promotes clarity and discourages litigation. Our society has had a lot of experience with rigid, formal rules of property law. It is not at all clear that they discourage litigation or reduce its costs. In fact, the opposite may be true. When a rigid rule of law promotes a result that many people would view as unfair, someone who has been harmed by the rule has strong incentives to bring a lawsuit to change the rule. She may argue that the rule does not apply in her case, thereby asking the court to narrow the scope of a precedent that created the rule. Or she may argue for an exception to the rule by contending that the policies underlying it are outweighed by competing considerations. Indeed, the more unfair the result required by a rigid rule, the more incentive there is to litigate to create an exception to the rule. In contrast, if the rule in question requires the decision maker to make a judgment about fairness and equity, a judge or jury would be freer to reach a decision in harmony with the community's sense of justice. If the case is one where most people would agree on the reasonable result, the parties are more likely to settle the case and avoid the costs of a lawsuit than if a rigid rule were in place. A reasonableness standard may therefore sometimes be more predictable than one based on formal indicators of ownership, decreasing the costs of both transactions and lawsuits and better approximating the will of the partics.

Efficiency is also maximized by granting the entitlement to the party who is likely to value it the most. The title holder argues that the title holder is likely to value ownership more and that if the licensees wish to prove they value it more, they are free to offer Ward enough money to induce him to sell to them. If he is unwilling to sell at the price they offer, then he is the more highly valued user and it would decrease social welfare to assign property rights to the cabin owners. However, the licensees respond that this argument can easily work in reverse. If Ward really values the property more than they do, let him prove it by offering them enough money to induce them to give up the right to have continued access to their homes. If he cannot induce them to sell, then they value the right more than he does.

In addition, the cabin owners can claim that, although it is true that the formal title holder is likely, in general, to value the entitlement the most (with value measured by willingness and ability to pay), this does not mean we cannot identify particular situations in which the party likely to value the entitlement the most is not the one who has formal title. The cabin owners will argue that this is precisely such a situation. They are the ones likely to value the entitlement in question the most. After having made their homes on the property for fifty years, they have grown attached to it and regard it as their own, despite their lack of formal title. Long-standing acquiescence in these arrangements induced the cabin owners to treat the property as their own. Expectations come not only from formal title but from actual conduct in the world. Because they have come to regard the property as their own, they are likely to value it more than a buyer who has just entered the picture and has not yet made any personal investment in the land. The licensees who invested in reliance on the license are likely to value the entitlement more than the record owner because of their long-term, personal relationship to the land.

Thus, efficiency analysis does not tell us to presume that ownership rights should rest with the title holder. Although licenses ordinarily should be revocable at will, a rule of law that makes them presumptively irrevocable when the land owner induces others to invest substantially in building on the land will not constitute an unpredictable rule of law. It will better protect the reasonable expectations of the parties, grant the entitlements in question to the parties likely to value them the most, and lower the costs of transactions by allowing market participants to rely on conduct and custom rather than expending time and energy to reduce every deal to writing.

Judging Efficiency

Efficiency analysis usefully presses us to consider the consequences of alternative property regimes. It asks us not to rest assured that granting legal protection for an interest will maximize protection for that interest. Regulation has consequences, and not all of them necessarily foster the goals of the original rule. Attention to efficiency reminds us that interests conflict and that protection of one interest necessarily impinges on other interests, sometimes in ways we do not foresee.

On the other hand, efficiency analysis has fundamental drawbacks. First, by suggesting that we measure costs and benefits by market values, it assumes that market prices are accurate proxies for social utility or welfare. But are market prices good ways to measure the costs and benefits of alternative legal rules? Consider the use of market prices to determine whether social welfare would be maximized by granting rights to the purchaser of the formal title to the lakefront property. If Ward were to throw all the cabin owners off the land, what would he do with it? Perhaps Ward would build a resort around the lake. Such a substantial and profitable business would financially benefit him, his patrons, and some local residents by providing new jobs. These acts would in the short term harm the cabin owners, but in the long run the cabin owners might benefit enough financially from the overall improvement in business in town to allow them to build summer homes elsewhere. This analysis suggests that Ward's ability or willingness to offer more money for the land than the cabin owners can or will offer may promote the better economic outcome for the populace in general.

Yet something is missing in this equation. Two costs are not acknowledged: the loss of trust in the community and the loss of a community's way of life. Trust is sacrificed because never again will neighbors rely on each other as the cabin owners relied on Tavenner. From now on, people will put all arrangements in writing. There will be a change, therefore, in the way of life of the community. Increased formality and increased distrust represent a loss of things that are to be treasured and valued. But they are things that do not have a clear market value. How can their value be measured? The creation of a set of social norms in a community is the product of thousands of interactions over many generations. The court, by a wrong decision, could destroy those norms at a stroke. And it would be very expensive (or impossible) to re-create them. Perhaps local citizens would try to ostracize Ward, by refusing to speak to him or to work at his resort. But Ward can look to other towns to provide the staff he needs, by the same sort of advertising that will draw tourists; and if he lives outside the community and has no personal relationships with anyone there, if his only interest is in making a profit, the townspeople's efforts to make him feel unwelcome will be pointless.

Efficiency analysis does not prevent us from counting losses of trust and neighborliness as costs. Indeed, the theory of efficiency is that we consider *all* relevant costs and benefits without moral prejudgment. The point, however, is that market measures draw our attention away from such costs because there is no market for social norms and no market value for trust. Efficiency analysis puts these costs on the periphery; it makes them less salient than they would be if we considered the effects of legal rules in a language that focused on some other measure than fair market value or expected prices. If we base legal rules solely on market measures, we may not count, or may not count adequately, the loss that follows from discarding informally based expectations or other factors that are difficult to quantify.

The second problem with efficiency analysis is that it wrongly assumes that market measures can give us a close approximation of the costs and benefits of different legal regimes so that we can tell which one most maximizes social welfare. But this assumption fails to account for the various sources of indeterminacy that enter into efficiency analysis itself. One source is what is called the offer/asking problem. The amount someone is willing to pay to buy an entitlement (the offer price) is often less than the amount others would have to pay that person to induce her to sell the entitlement if she owned it (the asking price). One reason for this discrepancy is that whoever is assigned the entitlement is richer than she would be without it; if she owns it, she no longer needs to shell out money to purchase it. Another reason is a psychological one. We may value what we have more than what we could have. This is true because spending money to buy an entitlement often hurts more than "spending" it by giving up an opportunity that is offered to us.

Mark Kelman gives several examples:

> A fully rational individual, a professor at a business school, buys a bottle of imported wine for $5. After its value increases, a wine dealer with whom he regularly deals offers him $100 for the bottle of wine. Although he has never purchased a bottle of wine for $100, in fact he has never paid more than $35 for one and would not do so now, the professor drinks the wine rather than sell it.

The professor's offer price is $35, while his asking price is greater than $100.

> A consumer buys a new color television and decides to keep his old black and white set for which he could *realize* $50. If that second television were destroyed, he would not pay $50 for a second television. . . . Again, the $50 of opportunity income is spent on preserving the status quo, keeping the television [giving up the $50 he could get by selling the television] although $50 of received income would not be spent to get to the same substantive two-television state.

The consumer's offer price is zero—he would not pay anything for a second television—but his asking price is greater than $50; he will not sell it for that amount.

> In a survey course of middle-aged male students in a business school cost-benefit course, the students were asked two questions. The first question was: Suppose you have been exposed to a disease that would kill you painlessly in one week. The probability that you have contracted it is .001. There is a vaccine, limited in supply, that will cure you if taken now. How much will you pay [i.e., offer]? You will have thirty years to pay, so problems of raising large lump sums of income are eliminated. The second question was: How much would a person have to offer you [i.e., how much would you ask] to expose yourself to the same disease? There is a .001 chance you will contract it if exposed, and no cure will be available if you contract it.
>
> [If there were no difference between offer and asking prices], the answers to both questions would be roughly the same, although there might be some small divergence insofar as the marginal utility of money declines. The answers, however, differed by *orders of magnitude* for many students; for example, the same student answered that he would pay only $200 for the vaccine, but would demand $50,000 to be exposed to the disease.[21]

If asking prices are likely to be higher than offer prices, we may arrive at conflicting definitions of which allocation of entitlements is efficient or maximizes wealth. For example, if the court recognized Ward, as title holder, to be the owner of all rights in the land, the cabin owners might not be able to offer him enough money to induce him to sell permanent easements to them, since he might make more money by building a resort on the property or otherwise developing it. On the other hand, if the cabin owners won the case, they might choose to keep the ownership rights to their homesteads by a beautiful lake even if Ward offered them far more than market value for the property. So the offer prices of the cabin owners may be lower than their asking prices.

When offer and asking prices diverge, there are at least five alternative measures of efficiency. The *auction* measure asks us to assume that no one owns the entitlement in question. We hold a hypothetical auction to sell the rights. If Ward offers the most, he will be able to eject the cabin owners unless they can offer him enough money to induce him to grant them permanent rights. If the cabin owners win, they will be able to keep their homes where they stand and obtain access to them unless Ward can induce them to sell to him. We consider who would be willing and able to offer more money in such an auction. The auction measure compares offer prices with offer prices. This measure is obviously heavily influenced by the relative wealth of the parties.

The second measure is the reverse auction, in which we compare asking prices rather than offer prices. We ask which party, if they were granted ownership of the entitlement, would ask the most money before they would agree to sell it.

The third measure is the *status quo baseline* or the *formal title presumption.* In this case we presume that Ward has the right to exclude the cabin owners unless they offer him enough to induce him to sell rights to them. We compare the asking price of the formal owner with the offer price of the nonowners who want to redistribute title. This measure generally favors the title holder.

The fourth measure is the reverse of the status quo baseline. We presume that the cabin owners have the right to remain unless Ward can induce them to give up their informally created expectations. This baseline redistributes title from the formal title holder to the informal claimant. We might then call it the *redistribution baseline* since it uses the offer price of the record owner and the asking price of the nonowner. This measure generally favors the "nonowner" by treating informally based expectations as favorably as, or more favorably than, formal ones.

Finally, we could ignore the particular valuations of the parties and ask which result is likely to maximize the *fair market value* of the property—the price the land would likely fetch on the open market. We have to assess the combined fair market values of all the land and cabins. If Ward wins, this value would be the sum of the price he could get for the land and the price the cabin owners could command for their cabins, which they could remove from the land. If the cabin owners prevail, it would be the sum of the fair market values of each homestead (easement plus house) plus the fair market value of the land owned by Ward (which is subject to the easements).

These five different measures may well come out with different answers. Ward probably would win under the auction and status quo baseline measures, but the cabin owners would probably win under the redistribution baseline and reverse auction measures, because Ward's interest is merely financial while the cabin owners may have emotional, personal interests in keeping their ownership rights rather than selling them for what the market would bear.

The fair market value of the property would probably (but not certainly) be greatest if Ward owned the land free and clear of any competing claims since he could develop a profitable business there. At the same time, the cabin owners would probably refuse to sell their rights to him if he offered them the fair market value of their easements. Remember that, at any point in time, most owners value their property above the fair market value. That is why they retain ownership rather than agreeing to sell it. If they valued their land at precisely the fair market value, they would be ready to sell at any time someone offered them the market value. Established home owners don't sell precisely because they have emotional investments in retaining their homes, having a stable place to make a life, and money is not an adequate substitute for having a stable home. Ward, on the other hand, is likely to be interested in buying the property only for economic reasons and therefore is unlikely to offer more than the fair market value for the property.

Thus efficiency analysis is indeterminate here. It cannot provide a clear answer to its own question about maximizing social welfare. In *Castle Mountain Ranch,* criteria other than efficiency must be used to determine which allocation of the disputed entitlement will best serve that purpose. In other words, we need a way to determine which baseline to adopt when the results achieved by each measure differ since each is technically efficient. Efficiency analysis cannot tell us which baseline to adopt since it is based on market values and market values are dependent on defining preexisting property rights. Choosing an appropriate baseline requires a judgment about the proper way to go about analyzing efficiency. For example, one might apply the criterion of fairness. One could then argue that the unfairness of allowing Ward to revoke access before the licensees have recouped their investment suggests using the licensees' asking price rather than their offer price to measure the relative value of entitlements to each of the parties. Assigning the entitlement to the licensees would allow Ward to buy back the entitlement. This arrangement would arguably represent the fairest distribution of the burden of correcting a mistaken allocation of the entitlement. If Ward really values the entitlement more than the licensees do, let him buy them out, as in fact the court in *Castle Mountain Ranch* required. A contrary interpretation, of course, is possible. The point is that efficiency analysis is indeterminate unless we make value judgments about the right (fair, just) way to frame the issue.

The difficulty of predicting how people will respond to alternative possible rules is a second major source of indeterminacy in efficiency analysis. We have seen conflicting predictions about whether the costs of transactions will be greater if the formal title holder wins the case or if the cabin owners win. Speculation about such empirical questions is likely to be based on controversial beliefs and assumptions and is manipulable in practice. The cost of conducting empirical research to determine the social effects of alternative rules and comparing the relative harms and benefits that alternative rules may cause is enormous. So in most cases, instead of clear answers, all we could expect would be educated guesses about the likely consequences of various rules.

A third major source of indeterminacy in efficiency analysis is the debate over whether the most efficient rule is the one that lowers transaction costs the most or the one that grants the entitlement to the party who values it the most.

Courts may assume that the costs of market transactions are usually lower than the costs of lawsuits, in which case they should focus on making property rights clear so that the parties can avoid entitlement disputes and bargain effectively. Or they may assume that once a few well-publicized court decisions establish precedents governing common property disputes, thereby shortening the judicial process and encouraging parties to settle out of court, the costs of market transactions—and the impediments to them—are likely to be greater than the costs of litigation; in that event the courts should focus on choosing legal rules that allocate an entitlement to the party who is likely to value it the most. It is not at all obvious whether the best way to promote efficiency is to lower transaction costs by promulgating clear property rules that encourage bargaining, or to promulgate rules that allow courts to assign entitlements to the parties likely to value them the most.

Finally, it is not at all clear that it is rational to compare the costs and benefits of competing property rules by reference to a single metric. The use of market measures to express harms and benefits suggests that the goal is to determine the magnitude of negative and positive effects and that the character of those effects can be adequately expressed as a matter of magnitude. But it is not at all clear that this is the case. Many values are not adequately expressed by reference to numbers. How much is democracy worth, for example? Are we willing to pay what it costs to hold elections? What are the benefits of electing leaders rather than using heredity or some other selection criterion? Just asking the question seems inappropriate. This is not the way we judge the appropriateness of democracy. Similarly, if the court rules strictly in favor of protecting formal property rights, and the effect is that people in the community act in a less neighborly fashion and are more circumspect about sharing their property with friends, does it really aid our analysis to impose a monetary value on this loss? How do we pick the number? Most economists deal with these difficulties by placing a value of zero on hard-to-quantify costs. But of course, if there is a real loss involved, the one dollar value we know is inaccurate is zero. Even if we try to use market measures, there is no market for social norms; selecting a figure would involve a moral judgment. More fundamentally, it seems either perverse or obtuse to reduce all relevant considerations in a case to numerical or monetary amounts. It seems so wrongheaded that it even appears irrational.

These various forms of indeterminacy mean that efficiency analysis cannot give a clear answer unless it is supplemented by considerations of fairness. Choosing appropriate baselines for analysis is crucial to solving the offer/asking problem. Choosing how to value costs and benefits that do not have market equivalents requires controversial judgments. Placing their value at zero—ignoring them because they cannot be assigned dollar values—is not an answer; such a value choice must be defended. Moreover, the costs and benefits of some interests are not well expressed in terms of how well people's preferences are satisfied; antidiscrimination laws, for example, seem intended to alter or deny the validity of certain preferences. In addition, placing all interests on a single scale and reducing them to a common denominator does violence to the ways in which we value different interests. Of course, denying that a single metric is adequate to compare conflicting interests, goals, and values places us back in the real world, where decisions involve more than merely adding up benefits and subtracting costs and seeing how the math comes out. They require judgment.[22]

Just as rights analysis cannot escape consideration of the effects of protecting certain interests as legal entitlements, efficiency analysis cannot escape the value-laden world of rights, fairness, and justice. Ironically, in judging both rights and efficiency, we are reminded of the necessity of judgment. No formula, no equation, no theory can remove from us the problem of human choice.

RIGHTS AS RELATIONSHIPS

Autonomy and Interdependence

Is it possible to analyze the justice or wisdom of particular legal arrangements or institutional structures in a manner that avoids the pitfalls of both rights and efficiency analysis? The traditional conception of an entitlement or a legal right used by both rights and efficiency theorists is that entitlements function as limits or boundaries around the entitled person which others cannot cross without consent. In fact, the quintessential image of a right is closely related to the conventional conception of property—an owner in a house on land surrounded by a border gets to control what happens within that border and to keep others from stepping into the protected sphere.[23] Duncan Kennedy has described this image as "powers absolute within their spheres."[24] As Jennifer Nedelsky has said, "Rights define boundaries others cannot cross and it is those boundaries, enforced by the law, that ensure individual freedom and autonomy."[25]

Nedelsky has argued that we should reconceive rights as relationships. The boundary metaphor misconceives the basis for autonomy. "What makes autonomy possible is not separation, but relationship."[26] Paradoxical as this may seem, it is nonetheless true. We respect individuals, not by assuming them to be islands unto themselves, but by acknowledging that they best function and achieve their own ends in the context of social relations that support their own abilities to flourish. Individuals achieve autonomy not by complete separation from others but by a combination of independence and dependence.[27] In other words, *interdependence* is the foundational characteristic of free individuals. If this is true, rights are best thought of as rules that shape relationships. If the rules are fair, the relationships promote desirable forms of independence. Thus, the "human interactions to be governed [by law should not be] seen primarily in terms of the clashing of rights and interests, but in terms of the way patterns of relationship can develop and sustain both an enriching collective life and the scope for genuine individual autonomy."[28]

This vision of rights does not do away with the concepts of autonomy or boundaries but reconceptualizes them. Rather than understanding rights as absolute powers within rigidly defined boundaries, we perceive them as socially situated, contingent on their effects on others, and therefore set within the context of relationships involving mutual obligations. Sometimes those obligations require nonowners to leave owners alone, but at times they require owners to exercise their property rights with due respect for the interests of others, including nonowners. Rather than understanding rights and autonomy as "an effort to carve out a sphere into which the collective cannot intrude," we understand that because rights conflict, we must define them partially in terms of the relationships they instantiate. Property law can therefore be seen as "a means of structuring the relations between individuals and the sources of collective power so that autonomy is fostered rather than undermined."[29]

Rights as Relationships

The relational nature of rights was recognized by Wesley Hohfeld in historic law review articles in 1913 and 1917.[30] Rights, according to Hohfeld, actually constitute jural relations. He identified four types of relationships which he described by eight distinct concepts. These eight concepts can be grouped into four pairs of *correlatives* which describe legal relationships from the standpoint of both the one who is entitled and others who are thereby obligated or vulnerable to the effects of the exercise of the entitlement. Any time the state confers an advantage on someone, it necessarily puts someone else at a disadvantage; it makes someone else vulnerable. In *Castle Mountain Ranch,* for example, if the court grants Ward the privilege to use the land under the cabins however he wishes, it implicitly makes the cabin owners vulnerable to dispossession. If it gives the cabin owners a right of access to the land, it must also assign to Ward the duty to allow them access. Whatever the court's decision, by assigning an entitlement, it simultaneously creates a vulnerability or obligation on the part of others.

Hohfeld identifies eight basic legal rights: four primary legal entitlements (rights, privileges, powers, and immunities) and their opposites (no rights, duties, disabilities, and liabilities). *Rights* are claims, enforceable by state power, that others act in a certain manner in relation to the right holder. In contrast, privileges are permissions to act (or to refrain from acting) in a certain manner without being liable for damages to others and without others being able to summon state power to prevent those acts. *Powers* are state-enforced abilities to change legal entitlements held by oneself or others, and *immunities* are protections against having one's own entitlements changed by others. The four negations or opposites of the primary legal entitlements refer to the absence of such entitlements. One has *no-right* if one does not have the power to summon the aid of the state to alter or control the behavior of others. *Duties* refer to the absence of permission to act in a certain manner. *Disabilities* are the absence of power to alter legal entitlements and *liabilities* refer to the absence of immunity from having one's own entitlements changed by others.

The eight terms are arranged in two tables of correlatives and opposites that structure the internal relationships among the different fundamental legal rights.

Hohfeld's concept of "opposites" conveys the message that one must have one or the other but not both of the two opposites. For example, with regard to any class of acts one must either have a right that others act in a certain manner or no-right. Similarly, one must have either a privilege to do certain acts or a duty not to do them.

The concept of correlatives expresses the insight that legal rights are not simply entitlements, but jural relations. Correlatives express a single legal relation from the point of view of each of the two parties. "[If] X has a right against Y that he shall stay off the former's land, the correlative (and equivalent) is that Y is under a duty toward X to stay off the place."[31] If A has a duty toward B, then B has a right against A. If the court determines that Ward has a right to keep the cabin owners off the land, then the cabin owners must have a duty to him to stay

Right	Privilege	Power	Immunity
No-right	Duty	Disability	Liability

Figure 3.1 Jural opposites

Right	Privilege	Power	Immunity
Duty	No-right	Liability	Disability

Figure 3.2 Jural correlatives

off the land. The two expressions are equivalent. Rights are nothing but duties placed on others to act in a certain manner. Similarly, privileges are the correlatives of no-rights. "[W]hereas X has a *right* or *claim* that Y, the other man, should stay off the land, he himself has the *privilege* of entering on the land, or in equivalent words, X does not have a duty to stay off."[32] If A has no duty toward B, A has a privilege to act and B has no right against A. Thus, if A has the privilege to do certain acts or to refrain from doing those acts, B is vulnerable to the effects of A's actions. B cannot summon the aid of the state to prevent A from acting in such a manner no matter how A's actions affect B's interests.

It was commonplace before Hohfeld to note the relationship between rights and duties. Rights place obligations on some persons to act in a certain way toward those who hold the rights. But Hohfeld was the first to popularize the idea that liberties entail relations. A liberty or privilege is the freedom to engage in certain actions without legal sanction. Traditionally, liberties were viewed as "self-regarding" in the sense that they protect the individual from state control but do not describe relations between individuals. Hohfeld emphasized that people who are affected by the free actions of others often complain to the state that those actions cause them harm and therefore should not be allowed. After all, a major purpose of the state is to protect individuals from harm at the hands of others. Allowing an action to occur, despite the harm it causes to the interests of others, creates a kind of relationship. The right bearer is free to act without interference from the state, and others are vulnerable to the effects of those actions; they have no legal right to obtain relief. The one who has the freedom to harm others has power over them.

Similarly, Hohfeld argued that individuals may have the power to alter rights held by themselves, as when a property owner transfers title to another person. He pointed out that if one has the power to sell property, others are "liable" to suffer the effects of the exercise of that power. For instance, when a landlord sells a house to someone other than the tenant, the tenant's lease remains in force for the full term. But when the term is up, the new owner has the power to evict the tenant. Since the landlord has the power to sell the property, the tenant has no power to prevent the landlord from selling it. Moreover, the possibility that the landlord will sell places the tenant at risk that the new owner will want to move into the house herself rather than rent it. Thus the landlord's power to sell places a vulnerability (which Hohfeld called a liability) on the tenant. Similarly, an owner who builds a fence several feet onto the neighboring yard and possesses the property for a long time has the power to take title to the land from the record owner, making the record owner liable to lose her rights if she does not protect them. If, on the other hand, we fixed title in the record owner rather than the adverse possessor, we would confer an "immunity" right on the record owner and a "disability" on the adverse possessor to take rights merely by long-term possession of the property.

Property and Social Relations

Focusing on rights as rules that shape the contours of human relationships changes our approach to property rights in particular. Whether we speak in the language of justice or utility, we will do a better job of understanding our own values and the consequences of alternative property regimes if we direct our attention to the kinds of relationships we want the legal rules to foster or discourage.

Property rights are best understood as legal rules that shape the contours of human relationships regarding control of valuable resources. As Jennifer Nedelsky argues, "what rights in fact do and have always done is construct relationships—of power, of responsibility, of trust, of obligation."[33] Property law creates a setting in which individuals live their lives and interact with others. This setting partly consists of rules requiring individuals to respect the legitimate interests of others in controlling certain portions of the physical world. Other rules are designed to ensure that the property system as a whole functions well, with tolerable efficiency and justice. We should understand property as a social system. It involves not only relations between people and things, but also relationships among people.

What difference would it make to focus on relationships? We have seen how rights and efficiency theorists might analyze the issues in the *Castle Mountain Ranch* case. Those discussions are useful despite their indeterminacy. A judicial opinion concerned with social relations might well address the rights and efficiency arguments rehearsed above. But it might also add something like the following.

The social context in which the conflict arose is crucial to understanding both what occurred and what the appropriate response of the legal system should be. It is evident, both from the relationships between Tavenner and the cabin builders as friends, neighbors, and employer and employees and from the sparse protection that the written agreements accorded to so large an investment as a home that the context involved issues of trust. The cabin builders agreed to contract terms that gave them little security because their personal relationship with Tavenner led them to feel that they were entitled to rely on this relationship in deciding how to act. They trusted him to treat them fairly and not to revoke permission to be on the land the minute the cabins were built. Their personal relationship appears to have inhibited them from demanding greater protection for their interests.

At the same time, it is not clear whether Tavenner exhibited the same trust. After all, the terms of the deal he made appeared to give him dictatorial authority to revoke the permission to build or keep the cabins on the land. Such a broad authority probably was not necessary to protect his legitimate interests. Thus, his insistence on a one-sided arrangement may have injected an air of distrust into the relationship and perhaps signaled to the cabin owners that he might enforce the licenses strictly. Perhaps they were wrong to assume that they would be entitled to permanent rights in the land. On the other hand, the very one-sidedness of the agreement might have been negated by the personal relationship and oral representations of trust and mutual understanding. Although it is evident that the cabin owners trusted Tavenner when they decided to build their cabins despite having no tenure on the land, it is not at all clear that their expectations of permanence were justified.

From Tavenner's point of view, there was nothing amiss in the arrangement. He retained title, and the cabin owners knew this. The formal terms of the licenses were clear, and nothing in the history of the parties' relationship could alter them. But relationships, even those that have lasted for many decades, are subject to change, sometimes suddenly. If the cabin owners, after fifty years of good relations with the land owner and of his acquiescence in their occupancy, thought that their licenses would never end, clearly somehow they misjudged the situation. For when Tavenner sold the land to Ward, he made no attempt to secure their right to stay on the land. It appears, then, that the cabin owners were wrong to trust in the good faith of the land owner.

These alternative interpretations of whether the parties indeed trusted each other and whether that trust was justified are crucial to determining how the law should respond to the crisis occasioned by the sale of the land. This case does not fit the usual model of arm's-length bargaining between strangers. Understanding the case requires us to judge the relative interests of the parties but it also involves understanding and shaping social relations by adopting rules of law that either mirror or promote viable and defensible social relationships.

Understanding the social context enables us better to judge who was taking advantage of whom. In other words, we need to focus on the social relations to determine whether the interests asserted by the parties are legitimate in this situation. If rights shape relationships, we will better understood the field of moral conflict in which the parties are embroiled by taking a sympathetic but critical look at the character of their relationships.

If we adopt a rule of law that protects the reserved rights of the record owner, we may induce people like the cabin owners not to trust their employer, neighbor, or friend in a property transaction like this one. If this happens, they will either refuse to accept neighborly offers or insist on a formal negotiation of terms and a written contract, changing an informal relationship between friends into a formal one. In other words, a relationship based on friendship, trust, and cooperation may be replaced by one based on distrust, clever bargaining, and lawyerly worry about the "loopholes" in the agreement. The overall result is a devaluation of the personal relationship of the parties, changing it from a neighborly arrangement to a business relationship.

But perhaps none of this will occur. Perhaps a change in the governing law will have little effect on actual relations.[34] Even so, the choice of a resolution in this case will affect the advice that lawyers give clients. It may also affect public understandings of proper social relations. Reports about a case such as this are disseminated widely in the local media, especially when many property owners are affected. Even if no systematic change in social behavior occurs, a resolution of the case will suggest, and may even depend on, a particular understanding of the appropriate norms of behavior in this kind of situation. Whatever result ensues will have the effect of shaping our understanding of the legitimate sources of expectations. Protecting the interests of the cabin owners will reinforce the idea that expectations are not based solely on the content of written agreements but may also rest on informal understandings or customary behavior. Protecting the interests of the land owner will reinforce the idea that legal protection will only be extended to those who can produce formal documents certifying their claims and will be withheld from those who do not insist on having their understanding of the deal reduced to writing. In other words, the choice of a legal rule may have effects on social behavior related to property use and transfer.

A change in legal rules will bring about changes in the character of social relations over time, regardless of whether any immediate effects are visible. This in turn will influence public perceptions about what kinds of conduct are allowable and appropriate and what kinds are not. It may even affect beliefs about right and wrong. Changes in Supreme Court doctrine, for example, have had a profound effect on public discussion about affirmative action. Opponents of affirmative action take great comfort from the fact that the Supreme Court has ruled that it is illegal in some cases. These effects are not restricted to popular notions of proper behavior but also show up in people's perceptions of what kinds of legal claims are plausible and which ones are either utopian or perverse.

While it is plausible to claim that owners retain whatever rights they do not give away, it is also important to recognize that the legal rights created by human behavior must be defined with reference to common understandings and considered judgments about which expectations are reasonable. One who invests substantially by building a house on land belonging to another demonstrates a high degree of confidence that access to the house will be assured. In *Castle Mountain Ranch* those expectations were reasonable because the land owner induced the cabin owners to understand the license arrangement to be a mere formality. We should adopt legal rules that acknowledge claims based on reasonable expectations because a society in which they are protected is a better, more secure, more dignified place to live than one in which people are free to betray trusts. If we do not, we will be encouraging people to be distrustful in their dealings not only with strangers but even with friends and neighbors, and we will be licensing them to renege on agreements reached by mutual understanding with the other party whenever it is convenient for them to do so. This rule might introduce some unpredictability to property law, but the result is warranted here because the reliance of the cabin owners is so clear and their investment so substantial.

There is nothing in this revised opinion that could not be expressed in the language of rights or the language of efficiency. Attending to social relations draws our attention to issues that might have been ignored under those approaches. We should ask what it would be like to live in a world where owners were free to act as Tavenner and Ward did, and what it would be like to live in a world where owners were bound to keep the commitments to others that are implicit in their actions. There are legitimate interests on both sides of the *Castle Mountain Ranch* case. Plausible rights and efficiency arguments can be made in support of each party's claim, as can arguments in favor of a compromise (the path actually taken by the court) that would give each side some but not all of what it asked for. But only by examining the social context of the transactions between the parties, and the character of the relationship they had established, are we reminded that the legal rules we choose may have deep and lasting effects on our social world. In order to make decisions and craft rules that will promote social justice, we must consider those consequences. If property shapes social relations, we need to ask ourselves: "In which world would we rather live?"

How might social relations language help us in resolving other land use cases? In the *Friendswood* case we saw that it is not sensible to adjudicate the conflict between the parties as an abstract contest between rights of free use and rights of security. Nor can we mechanically apply rules without regard to their consequences for social relations. The Friendswood company is not just an owner using its own land; its actions, if not checked, will destroy the county around it. The central question is whether its property rights can extend so far. Perhaps they can. After all, if it is the case that the state has created the impression that Friendswood's actions are legally privileged, the community can stop Friendswood from continuing its course of action by taking its property by eminent domain and compensating the company for its lost property rights. In other words, we need to ask whether the burden we would impose on Friendswood by enjoining it from drawing well water is one that it should rightly bear for the good of the community. Conversely, we need to ask whether by relying on the existing rule and giving Friendswood carte blanche to remove as much water as it likes we would be imposing a burden on the neighbors that they should rightly bear for the good of the community. The question becomes one of defining the obligations of members of a community to each other. The choice of a legal rule will shape the social world and should be shaped, in part, by a conscious decision by the law maker about appropriate obligations within social relationships.

Similarly, the dispute between the condominium association and the Breenes involves a choice about the nature of community. What powers do neighbors rightly have over each other? What difference does it make that an individual seems to have consented to extensive control by neighboring owners? Might community controls go too far? Conversely, when is it reasonable for an individual owner to insist on exercising her rights to use her property as she wishes despite the evident objections of her neighbors to a particular use? Which construction of the social relations within the condominium community strikes the right accommodation between individual freedom and collective governance? The choice we make as law makers will alter the nature of the world in which we live.

Perhaps we should defer to the community association on the assumption that if each condominium is allowed to create arrangements that suit their members, prospective residents can choose the community best suited to their lifestyle. On the other hand, some types of community control seem illegitimate even if freely bargained for, either because they wrongly lock parties into arrangements that unduly inhibit their liberty or because they act in a wrongfully exclusionary manner that discriminates against "undesirable" residents.

Whether a property conflict concerns use rights, access to public accommodations, condominium governance, written agreements between landlords and tenants, or informal arrangements between friends and neighbors, we are faced with choosing legal rules that will both respond to and shape social reality. Different rules will distribute power differently, impose obligations differently, shape expectations differently, and order social relations differently. Our choice of a particular property regime alters the social world. It will determine what expectations people have a legal right to expect. It will impose duties and vulnerabilities in a certain pattern. It will make life harder for some people and easier for others. The social world will be different depending on how we shape the law. We will live in a different world. Rights structure relationships and can only be adequately judged if such considerations are brought to the center of our attention.

Chapter 4 Systemic and Distributive Norms

In a capitalist order, one person's proprietary value (or power) is obviously relative to other people's. A constitutional system of proprietary liberty is, therefore, incomplete without attending to the configurations of the values of various people's proprietary liberties. The question of distribution is endemic in the very idea of a constitutional scheme of proprietary liberty.

—Frank Michelman

The propertyless are not only themselves deprived of property. Their inability to recognize freely the property rights of others undermines the rights of those who have property.

—Johan W. G. van der Walt

You are advising the new government of an Eastern European country that has just emerged from communism and is seeking to institute a private property regime. As an advocate of private property, you recommend that the government organize a program to privatize government-owned industries, housing, and farms. Your goal is to create a free and democratic society characterized by individual liberty and a market economy. Imagine your reaction if the prime minister proudly announced to you that the government had privatized all its properties in one day by handing out all the land, buildings, and industry in the country to the ten families who had formed the crux of the aristocracy in the nineteenth century. Those owners were chosen because their families had historic roles of leadership and could be trusted to guide the country out of the darkness of dictatorship and into the bright future of freedom. These new owners are free to do what they want with their property. Everyone is free to make a living without government interference—no more government ownership, no more communism, no more welfare, no more regulation. All the state will do is enforce property and contract rights and protect individuals from personal harm. With the establishment of private property, the prime minister looks forward to joining the free world, where individual initiative and personal responsibility reign—no more coercion, no more oppression, no more government handouts, no more restrictions on liberty. Of course, some kind of court system and police force will be necessary to protect these new rights and to enforce their attendant obligations, but that is a minor detail.

You would think the prime minister had a screw loose. He fundamentally misunderstands the ideals underlying the institution of private property. He seems not to understand what private property is. The concept of private property does not simply mean that property is owned by private individuals rather than the state; it also presumes that there will be many owners—that control over valued resources will be dispersed rather than concentrated. Although private property systems may not entail an absolute right to own things, they at least guarantee everyone the opportunity to become an owner. Moreover, that opportunity must be real rather than hypothetical. Reasonable people may disagree over how many owners is enough, but ten does not even come close.

Widespread distribution of property is virtually a defining characteristic of private property systems—or at least the norms that justify such systems. A country that has handed its resources over to ten families has not created a private property regime; it has created something close to an oligarchy or an aristocracy, even if it separates economic from political power and allows democratic voting for government offices.[1] Undue concentration of ownership not only undermines social equality and individual dignity but also is incompatible with a well-functioning market.

As we have seen, establishing a private property system certainly does not mean letting private owners do anything they want with what they own. The danger of such unfettered freedom is especially acute if ownership is limited to ten families. If the government protects their absolute rights to exclude nonowners, the new owners can condition access to their property on any terms they like. Because the rest of the population has been left propertyless, they are dependent on these new owners for the material resources they will need to survive. They will therefore be vulnerable to the owners' whims. If those owners are free to do what they wish with their property, then liberty will be unequally distributed in this brave new world. The ten owners' right to exclude and the nonowners' dependence on access to the owners' property to satisfy the nonowners' basic needs would allow the owners to rule the nonowners as effectively as any commissar. They could use their monopoly on ownership to freely engage in ethnic discrimination, to deny food and jobs to those who refuse to bow down to them or who refuse to vote for the owners' preferred candidates for public office.

Concentration of ownership, combined with absolute powers of control over property, effectively subjects the bulk of the population to the power of the few. The few owners may be free, but the many nonowners are not. Moreover, such a massive concentration of wealth would come back to haunt those few owners. In South Africa roughly 10 percent of the people own about 80 percent of the land on the basis of apartheid laws that denied the bulk of the population the right to own property simply because of their race.[2] What is the legacy of such a history? I have seen homes owned by white families surrounded by barbed-wire fences and with heavy steel front doors that—from the look of them—would serve better for a prison cell than a family home. I have a friend in New York City, another place where inequality in the distribution of wealth is much in evidence. Her beautiful house in Greenwich Village looks somewhat rundown from the outside, the better to discourage burglars who might covet what is inside. "The propertyless are not only themselves deprived of property," writes Johan van der Walt. "Their inability to recognize freely the property rights of others undermines the rights of those who have property."[3] The failure to ensure widespread ownership of property and equal opportunities to participate in acquiring property can have catastrophic consequences, not only for those shut out of ownership but also for those few who are lucky enough to count themselves as owners.

Property implies a vision of the social world—a vision of many owners, of equal individuals with tolerably equal opportunities to participate in the market economy and hence to exercise autonomy, to experience freedom, and to enjoy material security. From the standpoint of the individual, a property right may appear to be an absolute right to control something; but from the standpoint of society as a whole, private property is a regime and an institutional structure. Modern conceptions of property imply a well-functioning market characterized by fair competition, individual mobility, freedom of contract, and protection for legitimate expectations. To achieve those ends, the rules of property law must take into account, not just individual justice claims, but the ways in which individual claims impinge on each other. Resolution of conflicting claims will establish the social context and institutional structure within which individuals will create relationships within the family, the workplace, and the market.

These thought experiments reveal that property, as we understand it, is not just an individual entitlement but also a system. The *Oxford American Dictionary* defines a system as "a set of connected things or parts that form a whole or work together." What distinguishes systems from other collections of like things is the idea of interconnectedness. A property system is not merely an aggregation of individual entitlements. It is an institutional structure that sets the ground rules for human interaction to ensure that the exercise of entitlements by some can peaceably coexist with like entitlements in others. Private property is not just an entitlement; it is a regime.

I am not yet talking about positive rights to property. Frank Michelman has pointed out that the positive/negative distinction plays a central role in philosophical discussions of property rights. Yet, as he notes, it describes two very different distinctions: positive and negative liberty versus positive and negative rights. *Negative liberty* means "absence of external social constraint on what one does," while one who has *positive liberty*, on the other hand, possesses the means and the ability to engage in "rational self-direction or self-government."[4] Free use claims, as we have seen, are claims to negative liberty, conceived as freedom to manage one's property as one sees fit. Proponents of strong property rights are not in favor of absolute negative liberty; after all, protecting property rights constrains the liberty of those who would seize goods they do not own. Positive liberty suggests that one has the means necessary to exercise one's negative liberties. One of the things that might confer those means are positive rights. *Positive* or *affirmative rights* are entitlements to be granted ownership or control of resources, as through a government welfare program or an inheritance. *Negative rights* are understood as rights to "be left alone in certain respects free of interference by others."[5]

Although these two pairs of positive/negative distinctions are central to philosophical discussions of property, neither one adequately captures what I mean by declaring that property must be understood as a system and not just an individual entitlement. Property rights must be limited to ensure that the exercise of rights by some does not interfere with the ability of others to obtain and exercise similar rights. Property rights must be defined and structured so as to grant legal protection for particular interests while at the same time limiting that protection to ensure an environment in which all people may exercise their rights. Defining the environment within which rights are exercised requires identifying substantive goals by which to judge whether right holders can interact in a manner that results in a defensible distribution of the benefits of those rights.

Contrary, perhaps, to popular belief, this means that one of the purposes of property systems must be to distribute ownership widely. To create conditions in which individuals may enjoy both liberty and property, power has to be decentralized. Decentralization of power is achieved by establishing conditions under which ownership is widespread. And if we want to treat each person as equally entitled to respect—to life, liberty, and the pursuit of happiness—then the system of rules, practices, and institutions should ensure that everyone can become an owner.

Decentralization promotes justice by recognizing the dignity and equal worth of each individual. It promotes the utilitarian goal of maximizing human satisfaction by creating the conditions necessary for economic efficiency and social welfare. These justice and utilitarian goals often go together. They both encompass such ideals as promotion of well-being by ensuring widespread access to the opportunity to own property and by limiting the power of owners to monopolize markets or to exclude others systematically from the property system for illegitimate reasons. Sometimes, of course, they conflict; public policies and property law rules may generate investment and wealth in a manner that leaves a substantial portion of the population in desperate poverty.

Although the idea of private property seems at first to lead inexorably to justification of inequality, the systemic aspects of property remind us that the various reasons we recognized private property in the first place (such as decentralization of power, promotion of individual autonomy, and protection of the ability to obtain material security) require rules that ensure a tolerable level of equality in the distribution of power and material resources. Private property, in other words, is not just a placeholder for nongovernmental ownership. It evokes a vision of a world that values liberty and equality while promoting an appropriate accommodation between freedom of action and security. In this sense, property requires rules of law that ensure a social environment in which individuals can effectively exercise their personal and property rights.

Current scholarly literature tends to reduce the systemic goals of property law to two—efficiency and distribution. Efficiency theorists adopt a utilitarian stance designed to maximize aggregate social welfare by choosing rules that will maximize the ability of individuals to satisfy their preferences. They suggest that we address distributive concerns later, on the assumption that distributive goals often conflict with efficiency goals. If we start by making the economic pie as big as possible, we can figure out later whether fairness and justice require us to redistribute the pieces. In this way we can make everyone better off.

Rights theorists have argued, in contrast, that efficiency is a subordinate goal. The first business of a political or legal theorist is to define the basic ground rules for society that are respectful of human beings as individuals of infinite worth. Economic wealth is meaningless if it is obtained in a manner that denies respect for the equal dignity of individuals. Once fair ground rules are established, we can then do our best to satisfy preferences by promoting economic efficiency.

Each of these schools of thought has useful contributions to make to the construction of property law, but each misses something crucial. By focusing on individual claims, the rights approach may fail to pay adequate attention to the consequences of protecting particular claims as legal entitlements—consequences both for other right holders and for society as a whole. Focusing on the consequences of alternative property regimes might cause us to redefine the rights that should be protected in the first place. Conversely, by focusing on aggregating preferences, the efficiency approach fails to provide room to debate how to define the fair ground rules that constitute the institutional structure of the market.

In addition, both schools of thought tend to deny the complexity of moral judgment by reducing all normative questions to a few basic principles. Some rights theorists, for example, seek to identify a single basic norm that underlies all justice claims. Candidates include treating persons as ends rather than means, fostering equal concern and respect for individuals, promoting human flourishing, and adopting rules that can be universalized or that would be agreed upon in a suitable contracting setting, such as an original position in which each person was under a veil of ignorance about the values and abilities she would have and the social role she would play in the world. Some efficiency theorists attempt to reduce all normative questions to economic efficiency and distributive fairness. Others deny the relevance of distributive questions entirely, arguing that the only goal should be to maximize the well-being of individuals in society by maximizing aggregate satisfaction of preferences.

In contrast, I will argue that an appropriate systemic approach to property, and indeed to all law, will recognize the connection between legal institutions and social relationships and will acknowledge the plurality of values we hold as well as the plurality of ways in which we value things. The rules of property law have a lot to do with creating and maintaining forms of social life. They not only affect individual opportunities and choices but also create patterns of social interaction that are both recognizable and systemic. If a system is a "set of connected things or parts that form a whole or work together," a "set of rules or principles or practices forming a particular philosophy or form of government,"[6] then the rules of property law both protect individual interests and shape the contours of social relations. Those relations may exist at the individual and local level—among neighbors and among family members, between employers and employees, between landlords and tenants—or they may exist at the societywide or global level. Because they shape the contours of relationships, property rules should be conceptualized not only as protecting individual rights (moral claims of individuals) but also as establishing property systems. Property systems form the overall social context in which individuals live. They describe the limits of allowable social relations and channel interaction into certain patterns. Some systems provide for more freedom than others. It is important to remember that the very definition of a property right simultaneously assigns control over some aspect of a resource to someone while denying such control to others. These patterns of control are shaped by property law and help to define a prevailing form of social life with an attendant range of allowable relations.

ENTITLEMENTS AND SYSTEMIC NORMS

The presumption of the conventional ownership model is that property rights are individual rights. The only question is whether, from a moral point of view, we can justify granting individuals exclusive control over scarce and valuable resources needed by others, and if so, how we should allocate control over those resources. This model fails to consider the fact that property rights are exercised by individuals who live not in isolation but in society, among other people. The exercise of property rights by certain individuals may make it more difficult for others to exercise similar rights. The choice of rules has profound effects on the distribution of security and insecurity, freedom and coercion. A person's opportunities in life can be dramatically affected by such choices. If we care about this—and we should—we must learn that the systemic effects of property rights are crucial to defining their meaning and their legitimate scope.

Many existing rules of property law serve systemic goals or promote systemic norms. By this I mean that they are geared, not just to protecting "individual rights" or granting entitlements to parties who value them most, but to creating a social and legal context in which productive and satisfying activities and relations can flourish. Rules promoting systemic norms are geared to creating a well-functioning property system. They are intended to create a social context that affords all individuals the opportunity to pursue happiness.

Some of these rules are intended to promote efficiency. For example, antitrust law was created partly to ensure the existence of a competitive market structure that can both discipline companies and better serve consumers. Other systemic rules aim at ensuring a fair distribution of property. Antidiscrimination laws, for example, ensure that individuals have access to the market without regard to race or other irrelevant factors. Similarly, antitrust law might be intended, not just to ensure an efficient market, but to lower prices for consumers and to protect companies from being unfairly crowded out of the market by monopolistic practices. Still other rules shape social relationships to create a context for human flourishing and dignity by setting minimum standards for human interaction. Such rules include, for example, rules that require landlords who wish to evict defaulting tenants to use judicial proceedings that give the tenants time to find a new place to live rather than just throwing their belongings onto the street and changing the locks on the door. Some of the most important sets of rules in property law serve to ensure that the property system as a whole operates well. Here are some examples of such rules.

The Estates System

A traditional focus of first-year property courses in law schools is the estates system.[7] This system contains rules that limit the kinds of property rights that can be created. It originated in the feudal era and involved rules that mediated the relations between lords and tenants and between the generations. As it developed over time, the estates system served to reform the feudal land system and to prevent its reemergence. It also served to ensure that current generations are not unduly controlled by their great-grandparents. These rules governing future interests and property transfers had the effect of moving power downward from the feudal lord to the actual possessor of the land and from prior generations to current owners. They thereby decentralized and dispersed power over property and made property available to satisfy current needs.

Substantial regulation of property transfers is required to ensure that sellers of land do not load it down with restrictions on use and ownership that will be enforceable far into the future or which cannot be removed when circumstances or needs change. In other words, a system premised on absolute ownership rights must restrict freedom of contract (the power to transfer) to ensure that, most of the time, sellers transfer to buyers most of the interests associated with property ownership. The rules operate partially to decentralize control over property by bundling certain rights together and placing them in the control of the actual possessors (buyers) of the land. The estates system created the "fee simple" form of property ownership. By vesting power in current possessors rather than absentee landlords or deceased grandparents, the fee simple created the closest thing we have to absolute ownership. Thus the rules of the estates system are intended to shape overall social relations in order to promote the dispersal of power over land. This goal has an undeniable distributive basis.[8]

In a previous chapter I discussed the fee tail, a property right that would be inherited by the owner's direct descendants. In England the heir would be the oldest son, and the fee tail was intended to descend to that son's eldest son, and so on, until the line died out. No owner of a fee tail had the power to leave the property by will to anyone other than the direct blood descendants. Moreover, if any owner tried to transfer his interest during his lifetime, the grantee (the buyer) would only own the property during the lifetime of the grantor (the seller). The transfer could not defeat the rights of the grantor's heir(s) who would inherit when the grantor died, even if the land had been previously conveyed to someone else.[9] Nor could current owners attempt to persuade the heirs to waive their rights, because one could not identify a grantor's heirs until the grantor had died, and at that moment ownership would immediately shift to the heirs, so there was nothing to leave by will to someone else. If at any time the direct line ended, whether through a grantee's childlessness or the death of his children, the property would revert to the grantor if he was still alive (as might happen if the fee tail had been created, not in a will, but in a deed transferring the property during the grantor's lifetime). If the grantor was not alive, the property would go to other relatives of the grantor, such as nephews and nieces.

The fee tail was invented to establish and protect family dynasties. If not regulated by law, it could effectively prevent property from being transferred out of the family. If the fee tail were still a common property institution, the current pattern of social life in the United States and the relation between individuals and property would undeniably be quite different from what it is. The fee tail associates land ownership with family membership, assigning certain members to be managers of the property and possibly of the family itself. It suggests the feudal system of land ownership, where lords would keep an estate in the family for generations, establishing it as the center of the family's economic and political power.

The fee tail substantially limits the power of current owners of the property. They cannot easily sell the property or mortgage it to raise cash. They cannot easily change the use of the land, because the form of the fee tail assumes that the property will pass from generation to generation in much the same state as the grantor left it. Demolition of a castle to make way for a factory might well be considered "waste" that would deprive the next generation of its rightful inheritance. The fee tail appears suited to a society of landed dynasties, where property is not treated as real estate that can be transferred easily from one owner to the next or used however the current owner wishes. It is a static form of ownership ill fit for a market economy. If its use were widespread, it would inhibit the development of a vigorous real estate market. If fees tail were common, someone looking to buy a home would be precluded from making an offer on many homes in a given neighborhood, thereby possibly increasing the market price of the scarce properties that remained.

Because the fee tail inhibits the alienability of the property—the ability of the property to transfer freely from seller to buyer in the market—it may interfere with a transfer of ownership that would be to the mutual benefit of all the parties (and others, as well) and would therefore increase aggregate social welfare. In modern efficiency terms, the transaction costs of converting a fee tail to a fee simple interest are high and may prevent an efficient transfer of ownership. Since the heirs cannot be identified until the owner dies, they have no power to waive the rights of future generations; and if no one can be appointed their guardian to do it for them, the transaction costs of converting to fee simple ownership are close to infinite.[10] For this reason the rules of property law in both England and the United States developed in a way that either allowed owners of fee tail interests to cut off future generations and convert to fee simple ownership or abolished the fee tail entirely. In the United States only a few states allow the fee tail to exist, and in those states the interests of future generations can be destroyed by the current owner of the property or her children.

The abolition of the fee tail in most of the United States was achieved by adopting a rule of property law that denies enforcement of the grantor's intent to create a fee tail. If an owner attempts to create a fee tail, the courts will allow the grantee or her children to ignore the restriction and treat the property as her own. This rule of property law serves a number of distinct but related functions. On one hand, it protects individual rights, including the right of current generations to be free to use their property without undue control by prior generations. In this sense the rule promotes liberty interests. Of course, it does so by limiting the liberty of the prior owner, who seeks to restrict the liberty of current owners. The regulatory rule abolishing the fee tail also prevents past owners from controlling what future owners do with their property. In order to create a preference for the liberty interests of the current generation and allow property to be used for current purposes, it cuts off the rights of past and future generations.

At the same time, the rule prohibiting the fee tail serves a variety of systemic purposes. First, it promotes efficiency by allowing property to be transferred in the marketplace to owners who value it most highly. The fee tail had blocked such transfers. Prohibiting the fee tail limited the power of grantors and increased the power of grantees. A rule prohibiting the creation of a certain kind of property right has negative effects on the owner who wishes to create the right. The efficiency determination suggests that the harm that the rule causes such owners by preventing them from creating the right is outweighed by the benefits to future owners who want the property to be freely alienable. In other words, the assumption is that when we compare the costs and benefits of a rule allowing fees tail with the costs and benefits of a rule abolishing them, we will conclude that society as a whole is better off by prohibiting these arrangements.

Second, the abolition of the fee tail not only protects the rights of the current generation of owners but also has an effect on the character of social life. It may limit the prevalence and longevity of family estates and encourage the development of a vigorous real estate market in which land is treated as a commodity whose market value contributes to determining who owns the property and how they use it. Thus abolishing the fee tail not only favors change over stability but also fosters one form of social life (market relations) while suppressing another (family dynasties). It shapes social life to make more of it subject to market norms and less of it subject to family management schemes insulated from market pressures and incentives. Most of the rules of the estates system taught in the basic property course in U.S. law schools share this feature. They protect important individual liberty interests in free use of land and promote systemic norms associated with efficiency concerns as well as concerns about the appropriate contours of social life.

Another example of systemic rules of property law is regulations of grantor consent clauses. Suppose a developer sells homes in a residential subdivision, and in each of the deeds he secures to himself the right to approve future sales. Even after the developer has sold all the lots and no longer owns any land in the community, under the terms of the grantor consent clause written into the deeds, none of the home owners can sell their property without obtaining his consent. The rules in force in the United States generally prohibit this arrangement. A grantor consent clause that allows an absentee developer to block the sale of homes, and that puts no limits on the developer's discretion to consent or refuse consent to the sale, is almost universally held to constitute an "unreasonable restraint on alienation" and will be held void by the courts. The effect of this prohibitory rule is to transfer power from the absentee developer to the home owners in the community.

The estates system defines particular bundles of rights that can be linked to create different kinds of property interests. There are many ways to bundle and unbundle the many specific property entitlements and many ways to distribute the rights among owners. The rules of the estates system place some limits on an owner's ability to disaggregate or unbundle rights at will. It forces some rights to be held together by a single owner while allowing others to be split among several owners.

The rule prohibiting enforcement of the grantor consent clause protects individual interests while promoting systemic functions. It allocates powers over property in a manner that protects the individual autonomy of current owners and invalidates what might be viewed as an oppressive power relationship. In this case the rule takes power away from the developer and gives it to the owners who live on the land. It thus not only protects the rights of the home owners to control their property without unreasonable interference by a prior owner but also has the systemic effect of passing power over property from developers to the residents of the neighborhood. It may therefore decentralize power over property by making it more subject to the control of those who possess it currently. This decentralization is achieved by promulgating and enforcing a *regulatory rule* outlawing a particular package of property rights. In this kind of case, it can be argued, liberty is promoted by regulation, and the property rights of some individuals are protected by limiting the property rights of others.

This decentralization of power has both liberty and efficiency dimensions. It grants liberty to residential owners and promotes the alienability of the land. Grantor consent clauses require the consent of both the grantor and the owner before the property can be sold. As it is more difficult to obtain the consent of two people than one, abolition of the clause removes a transaction cost (an impediment to the transaction), promoting transfer to an owner who values the property more than the current owner, and may therefore increase efficiency.

This analysis does not necessarily mean that the rule abolishing the grantor consent clause is a good one from the standpoint of justice or efficiency. After all, the rule prohibits the developer from transferring property on terms chosen by him and may itself therefore prevent a transfer that is in the mutual interest of the parties. The rule limits the freedom of the developer (and the home owners) who wanted to create such an arrangement. The liberty of current owners to control their neighborhood is protected at the expense of the liberty of the grantor to retain control of the development. There may be legitimate reasons for recognizing developer consent-to-sale provisions. As we have seen, many condominium associations retain a right of first refusal when a unit owner wishes to sell; such rights may allow other unit owners to buy units that go on sale or may allow exclusion of incompatible uses, such as when a buyer intends to use a unit for business purposes. The point is that recognition or nonrecognition of grantor consent clauses or rights of first refusal in condominium associations will have systemic effects on the housing market and the distribution of powers over land, which will implicate concerns about efficiency and about the just contours of social relations. Attending to those systemic concerns is one of the core purposes of property law.

Antidiscrimination Laws

Property is a system because it regulates relations among individuals in a manner that alters the nature of the social world. Although property rights are individual entitlements, the choice of property rules has systemic effects. Until 1948 racially restrictive covenants were common in the United States. These covenants were agreements among land owners to exclude nonwhite buyers or renters from certain neighborhoods. They were widely used to discriminate against African Americans, Jews, Asian Americans, and American Indians. In effect, owners of property promised each other never to allow their property to be occupied or owned by members of particular races. They also sought to prevent any future owners from allowing the property to be so occupied by creating "restricted lots" or "restricted neighborhoods" composed of property that could not lawfully be sold or occupied by members of excluded groups. These covenants became popular after the Supreme Court ruled in *Buchanan v. Warley* in 1917 that it was unconstitutional for municipalities to promulgate local zoning laws that mandated segregation of housing by race.[11]

In 1948 the Supreme Court ruled in the case of *Shelley v. Kraemer* that court enforcement of racially restrictive covenants violated the equal protection clause of the Constitution.[12] Thereafter it was unlawful, not only for a state to prohibit owners from selling or renting real property to a person on the basis of that person's race *(Buchanan),* but also to facilitate segregation by enforcing private contracts among land owners or between buyers and sellers that purported to limit the sale or occupancy of that property by race *(Shelley).* It was not until the Fair Housing Act of 1968, however, that federal law prohibited individual property owners from refusing to sell or rent property because of the race of the buyer or renter.

The question of whether the rules in force require, facilitate, allow, discourage, or prohibit racial discrimination in the housing market may seem a matter of individual rights to dignity, freedom, and security. The legal system protects those interests either by state action prohibiting private conduct that infringes on them or by laws that affirm or delegate powers to individuals to exercise their freedoms. At the same time, these issues obviously concern not only the rights of individuals but also the structure of society as a whole. Different rules will have the effect of establishing different kinds of social relations. They will, in short, have systemic effects.

The segregation laws in the southern United States and the apartheid laws in South Africa did not merely limit individual rights; they created social and economic as well as political regimes. We are used to associating the word *regime* with political systems, such as communist regimes, democratic regimes, and military regimes. But the notion of a regime may also apply to social and economic systems supported or structured by law.

Public accommodations laws require owners of businesses open to the general public to serve customers without regard to race (as well as other factors, such as gender and, in some states, sexual orientation). Yet in addition to protecting the individual rights of all customers to obtain service in restaurants and stores, these laws serve a structural function: they prevent the creation of racially segregated markets. In so doing, they not only protect individual rights but also shape the system of social relations in order to promote a particular market structure—one that creates opportunity for people of all races to participate in the market on an equal basis—and prevent the formation of a society based on fixed racial caste.

Antidiscrimination laws have much in common with the property rules embodied in the estates system. Both sets of rules are intended to combat pernicious social hierarchies and to establish protected legal rights to engage in public commerce on equal terms. A major systemic function of legal rules governing property is to mold the social relations that comprise the market. In the case of antidiscrimination laws, such rules prevent the emergence of a particular form of social life inimical to a free and democratic society. Both the constitutionally required prohibition of enforcement of restrictive covenants and the statutorily imposed duty to serve all members of the public without unjust discrimination reject racial segregation as a form of social life. Even when there is public consensus about the goals that society wishes to achieve, it is not easy to define the kinds of relations that should be promoted and those that should be discouraged. It does mean that attention to such concerns is a crucial part of formulating what property means.

Competition and Intellectual Property

In the mid-1980s Apple Computer created a graphical computer interface that associated the abstract language of directories and codes with pictures of common objects like folders and trash cans.[13] When this interface was incorporated into the operating system of the company's new Macintosh computers, it revolutionized the industry. Consumers without technical knowledge, who had been frightened away from purchasing home computers by the arcane terminology and syntax of MS-DOS, now flocked to the stores. Soon the Microsoft Corporation—whose founder, Bill Gates, had created MS-DOS—followed Apple into the marketplace with a graphical interface called Windows, which ran on top of MS-DOS in personal computers (PCs), Apple's main competition. When the Windows interface, which bore an uncanny resemblance to the Macintosh interface, bit into Apple's share of the market and the profits, Apple sued Microsoft for violation of copyright.

Much as people can claim ownership rights in land and other physical objects, they can assert entitlements to intellectual property—ideas they have come up with and expressed in words, music, pictures, and inventions. Apple claimed the icon-based user interface as its intellectual property and argued that Microsoft had infringed on the company's property rights by using it without permission. Since in Apple's view Microsoft was illicitly reaping astronomical financial rewards from an invention that was not its own, Apple in effect accused Microsoft of theft. Microsoft denied that it had stolen anything and, in its defense, challenged Apple's rights claim. No one, Microsoft argued, could own the idea of using pictures to manage computer files any more than anyone could own the idea of painting a landscape.

The case revolves around a conflict between property and competition. Apple claims a property interest in a creative invention, and Microsoft claims a right to engage freely in competition to provide goods in the marketplace without compensating Apple for the use of its idea. The court's decision in disputes like this will have an enormous impact on the structure of the marketplace and on social relations.

How might a ruling in Apple's favor affect intellectual property law generally? Consider the analogous issue applied to music. If songwriters and composers had property rights in their music commensurate with the rights Apple claims for their interface, hardly a new song could be recorded without the composer's having first secured permission from someone who had already written a piece based on a similar sequence of notes. Western music traditionally has only twelve tones. The combinations are not so endless that one could imagine every composer coming up with a melody and harmonic progression that in no way built on melodic lines and harmonic progressions found in a predecessor's work. The courts might find that an entire genre of music, such as rock or jazz, is beholden to the person who invented its most distinctive characteristics, and that musicians working in that genre bear a legal obligation to the innovator. Indeed, one might say that all modern tonal music owes its existence and underlying structure to Johann Sebastian Bach or to Joseph Haydn or Wolfgang Amadeus Mozart. If one were inclined to do so, one could attempt to engage in detailed descriptions of the musical innovations attributable to each of these composers which is used in much modern music. Rock music, for example, is heavily dependent on the chord progressions and musical structures developed by these composers. If inventors are entitled to be compensated for the use of their inventions, the descendants of those composers might be entitled to royalties every time a piece of rock music is played.The nature of musical composition and the character of musical culture would be quite different if we recognized nearly limitless property rights in musical structures or melodies. Broad or narrow definitions of property in musical, literary, or artistic compositions would have far-reaching effects on the structure of individual speech and the uses of such compositions in social life.[14]

The conflict between property and competition can be understood as a conflict between property rights. The inventor of the graphical user interface system (Apple Computer) and the composer who invented the classical style in music (Haydn) might claim a right to the fruits of their labor.[15] After all, property has its origin, Locke tells us, in a person's "mixing his labor" with objects in the material world. But then other people have a similar right to the fruits of their own labor; if they are able to invent similar but competing products and sell them to the public, they too have a right to the fruits of their labor. The conflict between the norm of free competition and protection of preexisting property rights is a conflict between stability and change, security and freedom, monopoly and competition.

The conflict is manifest in a host of legal issues involving property. Owners of shopping malls often promise in leases to major tenants that the owner will not lease other units to competitors. Thus a McDonald's franchise may obtain a promise from the landlord that she will not rent space in the mall to a competing fast-food chain. If the owner breaches the promise by renting to a competitor, can the franchisee go to court to enforce the promise? In such cases the courts must determine whether the anticompetitive covenant violates public policy by inhibiting the free market and therefore reducing consumer welfare.[16] A decision to void the disputed term of the lease would have consequences beyond the case at hand. A drugstore owner downtown might object if another drugstore opened up in the same block. If the first owner had a property right to benefit from the local market, she might be able to obtain a court order that would in effect limit competition in the neighborhood.

There are fairness and efficiency arguments on both sides of questions like this one. For now, the point to notice is that different solutions to the property/competition dilemma will structure social and economic life in very different ways. These issues, like the others discussed in this chapter, concern not only individual claims of desert but systemic norms about the structure of social and economic life.

Gender

The law in Massachusetts, as in most places in the United States, is that employers are free to hire employees "at will," meaning that the employer can fire the employee at any time for any reason. Some limits exist on the right to terminate employment—such decisions cannot violate the antidiscrimination laws, for example. But in the absence of a promise of continued employment (by a grant of tenure or the like), the employee generally can be fired at will.

In *Upton v. JWP Businessland*[17] a woman who was a single, divorced parent was fired from her job when, because of her need to be with her young son, she refused to work unusually long hours. When she was hired, she was told that the workday went from 8:15 AM to 5:30 PM, with the need to work late one or two days each month. The plaintiff arranged child care accordingly. In fact from the outset the requirements of her job kept her at work until 6:30 or

7:00 PM, and she had to stay even later as the job progressed. In late July 1991 the plaintiff was told that she would have to work until nine or ten o'clock each evening and all day Saturday for at least several months. The plaintiff informed her employer that she would not be able to work such hours because of her responsibilities as a mother. She was discharged two weeks later.[18]

Can an employee be fired for refusing to work overtime because she wants to spend time with her daughter? The Massachusetts Supreme Judicial Court ruled that the employer had the power to fire her since she had been hired at will and had no expectation of job security. The employer was entitled to place any obligations on her that it wished to impose. It also seemed that the employer had the right to demand that she work more than a forty-hour week. The court acknowledged that it had previously adopted a "public policy doctrine" prohibiting the firing of employees who were terminated for "asserting a legal right" (such as filing a workers' compensation claim). The court allowed the employer to fire her, holding that she was not fired because "she did something that public policy strongly encourages (such as serving on a jury)."[19]

Why public policy strongly supports jury service but not child care is something the court did not explain. Perhaps it views parenthood as a private matter and jury duty as a public one. The court explained that "no public purpose is served by the conduct for which the plaintiff asserts she was discharged." In response to her claim that the care and protection of children was a public policy encouraged by Massachusetts law, the court noted that no statute specifically limited the employer's freedom to choose the employee's hours and that in managing a business an employer should not have to worry about a lawsuit every time she insists on a work schedule that is at odds with an "at-will employee's domestic circumstances."[20]

The question of whether employers must accommodate the child care needs of their workers is complicated, and the effects of such regulations are difficult to predict. Nonetheless, it is obvious that the question involves not only the individual rights of the employer and the employee. The answer we give to the question will have systemic effects in structuring both the relations between work and family and relations between men and women. It will also have systemic effects on the distribution of wealth by expanding or limiting the ability of parents to participate in the workplace. Given the fact that women still undertake the bulk of child care work in the United States, the answer we give will also affect the distribution of wealth according to gender.

Legal scholars and judges have often argued that labor provides the legitimate basis of property rights.[21] Some labor theories focus on the moral claims of the producer; others focus on the utility of rewarding productive labor.[22] Both approaches assume that those who labor create property and that their rights over the resources they create are respected by the legal system. This line of argument creates the impression that most property is deserved because it derives from productive labor. Arguments based on first possession also appeal to a labor theory; they conjure up images of long journeys into the wilderness and many hardships in preparing and working the land.[23]

If we think about gender, we may ask with Virginia Woolf: Why it is that women are more likely than men to be poor?[24] Women continue to perform most of the labor in the household. Moreover, they do this work for free or, more accurately, without any direct compensation from the market. Men as a group are heavily dependent on this uncompensated labor, as is the economy in general. In contrast, most of the work traditionally performed by men is monetarily compensated in accordance with the terms of an employment contract or through sales or investments. This social division between uncompensated and compensated labor goes a long way toward answering Woolf's question.[25]

The fact that women undertake most of the labor of caring for children and other family members plays a significant role in perpetuating the correlation between poverty and gender.[26] Women are significantly more likely than men to be poor, especially if they are single and have children.[27] In 1986 the poverty rate for children (20 percent) was almost twice that for adults (11 percent).[28] By 1991, 21.8 percent of children under 18 years of age lived in poverty, as compared to 11.4 percent of adults 18–64 years old and 12.4 percent of adults over 65.[29] The poverty of children is strongly associated with single-parent households. Victor Fuchs notes that "children who live in households without an adult male are extremely likely to be in poverty.[30] Further, there is an enormous difference in the poverty rate for children according to race. In 1986 some 40 percent of African American children lived in households without an adult male, and 70 percent of such children were poor. In contrast, only 12 percent of all white children lived in households without an adult male, and 51 percent of such children were living in poverty.[31] In addition, the 1991 figures show that the overall poverty rate among African American children (45.9 percent) was more than twice the poverty rate for white children (16.8 percent).[32]

In our society the work of taking care of children in the family is not compensated directly. Why do women do this work without compensation? One of the reasons is that gender has historically been a crucial factor in the division of labor. Women are acculturated to see taking care of children and of the home as part of the life they expect for themselves and their family. Men are still acculturated to see their primary responsibilities as being outside the home. The result of this socialization process is that women are more willing than men to work part-time, to interrupt their careers to care for children, to see homemaking as a career in itself, and to accept the "double burden" of work and family obligations.[33] Further, taking care of children is simply not seen as work. Recent workfare legislation directed at women who receive public assistance implicitly assumes that child care does not constitute valuable work. Welfare is regarded as a gratuity rather than an earned salary for parents who do not receive a salary indirectly through the market income of a spouse or partner.

Is labor in the marketplace equally available as a way to accumulate wealth to both sexes and to all races and classes? In a pioneering article Mary Joe Frug explored what she called the hostility of the labor market to working parents.[34] Examination of the gendered relation between work and family has now become a staple of feminist legal scholarship.[35] The fact that women perform most of the work involved in caring for children means that women are systematically disempowered in the marketplace. Because in their prime working years most women, unlike most men, take on the socially necessary task of child care, they cannot devote as single-minded attention to jobs as men can. Because many women work only part-time outside the home for some portion of their earning lives, they do not earn as much money as men who work full-time. Interrupting careers or working part-time interferes with job advancement, which further decreases women's wages relative to those of men. Women tend to bear the double burden of work and family, often with little sympathy or help from their employers and their spouses, and thereby sacrifice career opportunities and higher salaries.

In addition, the historic pattern is that work performed mostly by women is significantly undervalued in the marketplace.[36] Given the importance of education, for example, both to individuals and to the national economy, one might expect that schoolteachers would be accorded salaries closer to those of traditionally well-valued professionals like doctors and lawyers. Yet many schoolteachers are paid relatively low wages.[37] Similarly, nurses have traditionally been paid poorly, relative to their degree of education and the social value of their work. Many people have made comparisons between school administrators and teachers, doctors and nurses, truck drivers and secretaries.

The relation between gender and oppression is not simple, however. Many women in the workforce hire other women to take care of their children while they are at work. Although child care is expensive from the standpoint of the working parent, the wages are often insufficient to meet the needs of the child care worker and rarely reflect the social importance and difficulty of the work she does. Similarly, some women may hire other women to clean their houses. The valuation of this work, the form that personal interaction takes between employers and domestic workers, and the ways that women of different races and ethnicities regard one another may have a crucial bearing on the social construction of both class and racial relations. Elizabeth V. Spelman notes that the failure to consider such relations not only hides from our view the differences among women but also obscures the ways in which some women may participate in perpetuating oppressive social practices.[38]

It becomes apparent that the issue of whether a worker can be fired for refusing to work more than forty hours a week because she wants to be home with her child is not only a question of the relation between her claimed rights and the claimed rights of the employer. The choice of legal rules governing conflicts like this will have systemic effects on the work-family relationship and on relations between women and men and between parents and children. It will determine which forms of social life we encourage and facilitate and which ones we discourage or block.

PROPERTY AND EQUALITY

The Inevitability of Distributive Choices

It is often assumed that private property and inequality go hand in hand. After all, the protection of property rights extends to the rich as well as the poor, and as long as we have a market system of exchange, inequalities are bound to emerge. For this reason, private property systems are necessarily characterized by greater or lesser degrees of inequality. Another common assumption is that redistributive schemes, by their very nature, are unconstitutional takings of private property. In an extreme version of this view, it does not matter that one is taking from the rich to give the poor. Robin Hood was a thief, regardless of his motives and regardless of the unjust ways in which the rich became rich in the first place. That a democratic government, in the name of the people, should offer similar excuses for stealing is all the more reprehensible. Nor can one justify property redistribution by reference to the needs of the poor or their right to become owners. Let the poor get their property by honest labor. Redistribution of property demonstrates contempt for property rights, not respect for them.

The antiredistribution view was championed by the United States Supreme Court in 1915 in *Coppage v. Kansas.*[39] In that case, Justice Mahlon Pitney opined that inequality is a necessary component of a market system that respects both free contract and private property. *Coppage* involved a state statute outlawing "yellow dog" contracts which required employees to promise not to join a union. In striking down the statute, the Supreme Court considered the freedom to make contracts a liberty interest that could not be subject to regulation; hence employer and employee could agree on whatever terms of employment they liked. It did not matter if unequal bargaining power existed between the parties, or if the contract terms were unfair, or if workers had legitimate interests in banding together for mutual support and protection. According to the Court, the employer had no duty to share its property with prospective employees or to grant nonowners, such as employees, access to its property. Interference with the right of the employer to make such agreements as it wished amounted to a taking of the employer's property without just compensation. The fact that employers may exercise their market power to compel employees to agree to unfair terms does not mean that a state may deprive employers of their property rights or may ignore its obligation to protect those rights. In a famous passage from the majority opinion Justice Pitney explained:

> Wherever the right of private property and the right of free contract coexist, each party when contracting is inevitably more or less influenced by the question whether he has much property, or little, or none; for the contract is made to the very end that each may gain something that he needs or desires more urgently than that which he proposes to give in exchange. And, since it is self-evident that, unless all things are held in common, some persons must have more property than others, it is from the nature of things impossible to uphold freedom of contract and the right of private property without at the same time recognizing as legitimate those inequalities of fortune that are the necessary result of the exercise of those rights.[40]

In Pitney's vision, the right of private property includes the right to determine when, and on what terms, nonowners are entitled to enter or use property owned by another. Owners have the power to exclude nonowners as well as to waive their right to exclude; for this reason, employers, as owners of their businesses, have the power to refuse to hire employees or to pay them wages. Conversely, employers may choose the terms on which they will agree to allow employees onto their property, because their immunity rights as owners protect them against being forced to share their property with nonowners. Employers therefore have the freedom to make such agreements as they wish with nonowners such as prospective employees. Any resulting inequalities are necessary consequences of a market system that respects free contract and protects property rights.

The idea which the Court subscribed to in *Coppage,* that there is a necessary link between property and inequality, is false. The institution of private property does entail some level of inequality, but recognition of property and contract does not logically require anyone to accept substantial inequality or to conclude that the rules of property law can and should be shaped without regard to distributive fairness. In fact, the values that justify recognition of private property in the first place also demand concern for distributive fairness and for a substantial level of equality.

Property requires neither that we acquiesce in the inequality it creates, nor that we commit to realizing an impossible ideal of absolute equality, but a willingness to establish a base level of equality that gives every person the ability to enter the property system on terms that are fair and the means necessary to sustain a dignified human life. The pattern of distribution of rights and powers within the property system affects the relative value of those rights to individual owners. Indeed, one cannot understand who has which rights without first uncovering the distributive patterns that legal rules generate.

Every choice between alternative rules of property law will inevitably have distributive effects. Different rules will result in different distributions of rights and wealth and of costs and benefits. Although it may be true that property regimes presuppose some level of inequality, it is not true that questions of distribution are therefore irrelevant in setting the rules that govern conflicts over property. The fact of the matter is that we care about the distribution of the burdens and benefits of property regimes. Indeed, the Supreme Court has adopted a distributive principle as the core test of whether a regulation amounts to a violation of the Fifth Amendment prohibition of government takings of private property for public use without just compensation. The takings clause has been said to "bar Government from forcing some people alone to bear public burdens which, in all fairness and justice, should be borne by the public as a whole."[41] Because any redistribution of the burdens and benefits associated with property ownership and use will affect both efficiency and social justice, judges and legislators must consider the probable distributive effects of new property rules before they create them.

Property is valuable to individuals for many reasons. It promotes individual autonomy by sustaining the basis of an independent, fulfilling human life. It provides a setting for people to develop relationships and to engage in the work of the world. The opportunity to acquire property provides people with incentives to engage in work and thereby increase both their own welfare and that of others. Property therefore promotes both autonomy and social welfare. If we want to make life better for people, then we cannot remain indifferent to the distribution of property that results from the effect of a particular set of rules, or particular applications of rules, on access to that opportunity. Nor is it adequate to engage in post hoc redistribution through taxing people and transferring wealth from the rich to the poor. We need market institutions shaped by property laws that generate a tolerably equal distribution of income in the first place. American culture places a premium on being able to earn a living. A property system that denies some people the chance to participate in the national economy, except as recipients of public charity, strips them of basic human dignity. Increasing the size of the economic pie will not help those who have no means of claiming a piece of it except through redistributive welfare programs.

Some inequality in property distribution is indeed inevitable, but too much inequality deprives the dispossessed of the ability to obtain the benefits the property system offers. Protecting property does not require us to declare property rights to be absolute; indeed, we have seen that absolute property rights are an oxymoron. Regulation of property rights and the property system is essential to create social relations that put ownership and human dignity within everyone's reach.

Some scholars in the field of law and economics have been urging lawmakers to focus on creating rules that enhance efficiency and either put aside distributive considerations till later or even ignore them entirely. Louis Kaplow and Steven Shavell argue that the most efficient way to bring about a desired distribution of wealth is through market mechanisms, followed by a tax and transfer system. They claim that redistribution is less well achieved by manipulation of common law rules or legislative regulation of economic activity because the market's ability to adjust to such legal changes makes it hard to predict their effects on distribution and thus achieves distributive goals obliquely, if at all.[42] Everyone would be better off, in this view, if we adopt rules governing the marketplace that will maximize social wealth and then use redistributive taxation to diminish gross inequities if we are so inclined.

There are many reasons to question this conclusion. First, it adheres to the efficiency model in assuming that market mechanisms always provide the best means of judging the effects of alternative legal regimes. But as our detailed examination of that model in the previous chapter demonstrated, the dollars-and-cents language of efficiency is inadequate to measuring such essential social values as trust and neighborliness. Moreover, the efficiency model takes the status quo as the baseline against which to determine if a particular change in distribution is desirable. In other words, it presumes that the present distribution of property is fair, or at least neutral, and then asks whether the costs to those harmed by the regulation are outweighed by the benefits to those whose interests the regulation protects. Furthermore, this approach takes existing preferences as given and thus fails to consider whether changes in law would change preferences. It is not adequate to presume both the existing distribution of wealth and existing preferences. To determine whether a regulation maximizes social welfare, one needs to consider whether the existing distribution is a fair starting place and whether existing preferences are strongly held or are partly caused by prior preference-structuring laws and therefore malleable. The status quo is partly the result of past discrimination, and preferences for racial segregation or integration have changed dramatically over time. Why should the legal system defer to preferences and divisions of wealth founded in a history of massive racial discrimination rather than participate in changing them in the direction of justice?

Second, the view that distributive issues should be excised from normative argument about property law fails to take into account the systemic effects of legal rules in shaping the contours of social relationships. One of the consequences we must pay attention to when determining whether a set of rules maximizes welfare or responds to human needs is whether it establishes a defensible form of social life. This question necessarily involves something other than the distribution of wealth; it concerns the distribution of opportunities to participate in the market and the character of social relations. Individuals care about whether they have jobs; they feel the difference between getting a welfare check and earning a paycheck. In other words, the distributive effects of different property regimes cannot be completely separated from considerations of efficiency. If opportunities to participate in the market are unequally distributed, and if individuals care about the distribution of opportunity, then the property system may fail to maximize aggregate human satisfaction. The goal of a tolerably just distribution of both economic opportunities and material wealth is a prerequisite for maximizing social welfare. Distributive goals are not ones that we can leave until later.

Third, sometimes two different rules are equally efficient but have very different distributive consequences. In such cases it is possible to make choices between alternative rules of property law without reference to distributive issues only if one willfully blinds oneself to those considerations. How might one choose, for example, whether to impose damages on a factory that pollutes and thereby harms neighboring land. One might conclude that the benefits to society of allowing the factory to operate outweigh the costs and thus refuse to issue an injunction shutting the factory down. But this efficiency determination tells us nothing at all about whether we should impose damages on the company. As long as the company can pay damages to the property owners who were injured by its actions and remain profitable, then we are indifferent, from the standpoint of efficiency, about whether to require the payment of damages.[43] Yet the choice of whether or not to require the polluter to pay damages will have enormous distributive consequences. Either the costs of the factory will be borne by the factory owner and its employees and shareholders through payment of damages, or the costs will be borne by the neighboring property owners who were injured by the pollution.

In deciding whether or not to impose damages on the company, one is necessarily making a distributive choice. One can make such choices by tossing a coin or adopting a presumption against redistribution, but neither of those approaches answers the question of who should bear the cost. The coin toss method substitutes arbitrariness for judgment, and the presumption against redistribution fails to define what would constitute a redistribution. If the prevailing rule of law is that owners must pay damages for pollution, then liberating the owner from this damages rule would constitute a redistribution of wealth from home owners to factories. If the prevailing rule of law is that damages need not be paid, then imposing a damages rules would similarly redistribute property rights. There is simply no way to address this property question without making a distributive judgment.

Fourth, the view that judges should ignore distributive questions is premised on the notion that such considerations belong in the hands of democratically elected legislators, not in the hands of judges. This argument fails to recognize that the legislature will be redistributing from some baseline. Given the strong American ideological commitment to private property, redistribution through the tax system is likely to be difficult to achieve politically. So the baseline is incredibly important. If redistribution is hard to achieve, then an initial unequal distribution is likely to remain so. The opposite is also true: if the initial distribution is more equal, subsequent redistributive schemes are likely to maintain such equalities unless the vast majority of people are made better off by increasing inequality in some way. The result is that the distributive effect of existing rules of property and contract law places the burden of persuasion on those who want to go to the legislature and argue for redistributive policies. As I have noted previously, the burden of persuasion matters, because the starting place is likely to remain the ending place.

In addition, democracy is not only defined by adherence to majority rule but also by protection of individual rights. The majority has been known from time to time to oppress the minority.[44] In many cases we limit majority rule to protect individual rights or to promote social justice. Antidiscrimination laws, for example, are justified whether or not they are politically popular. Democracy, like property, exhibits internal tensions. It would be hard to call a society democratic that had ten owners even if it had an elected legislature, constitutional protection for property rights, and the principle of majority rule. If property institutions structure social life, then the distributive effects of property law shape understandings about settled expectations, and it is not possible to leave all questions of distribution to the legislature. What matters is not just how much wealth there is to distribute, but how it came to be created and who had an opportunity to participate in its creation.

Support for redistributive policies is itself contingent both on what has happened in the past and on current economic conditions. If politics did not enter into the equation, it would probably be true that, once a set of property rules were chosen, one could best achieve a desired redistribution of wealth by a legislative program that directly redistributes property from the haves to the have-nots. Attempting to redistribute wealth systematically by changing the basic rules of property and contract will attain the redistributive goals in a less certain manner. But in the world we live in, if we take political realities into account, tax-and-transfer schemes are likely to have little effect on redressing inequality. This is so for a host of reasons, not the least being that the haves are loathe to give up what they believe they have earned.

Indeed, James K. Galbraith argues that our current situation is one in which some people do very well while inequality increases. In such circumstances one might imagine the haves would be willing to give up some of their newfound wealth to help the have-nots. Galbraith argues that the situation is exactly the reverse; when the haves are doing well, they are likely to conclude that it is possible for anyone to make it on their own. They may thus be less willing to share their wealth with the less fortunate than they would be in circumstances where income and wealth were more equally divided and hence public benefits more equally distributed; under those conditions everyone might imagine that they would benefit from redistributive programs.[45] Given the political constraints on redistributive policies, far greater impacts on distribution might be achieved by adopting policies that would affect the distribution of earnings in the first place.[46]

Finally, as I have argued earlier, distributive questions enter into the very acceptability of property arrangements. In South Africa, after years of government policy that deprived black South Africans of property, the vast majority of the people of South Africa have no property, and a small minority owns most of the land and capital in the country. This gross imbalance is exacerbated by the fact that it was associated with a pernicious racial policy. The inequality of wealth is now politically unacceptable and may promote violence to right it. Owners of all races live in fear of both property and personal crimes. Homes are surrounded by barbed wire, and entryways both outside and inside the houses are blocked by strong metal gates. In such a setting, the property rights of the haves are fundamentally insecure. In other words, property rights have decreased value and cannot fulfill their function of providing for individual autonomy precisely because the old political system failed to spread the wealth. The value of all property rights goes down—even for those who are owners—when too many people are excluded from the system of ownership.

Everyone Should Have Some

John Kenneth Galbraith reports that Robert Montgomery, a professor of economics at the University of Texas, was unpopular with the Texas legislature because of his liberal views. When asked whether he favored private property, he replied, "I do—so strongly that I want everyone in Texas to have some."[47] His answer contains a brilliant and inescapable insight into the nature of property. Property law and property rights have an inexorable distributive component. Jeremy Waldron explains that "people need private property for the development and exercise of their liberty; that is why it is wrong to take all of a person's private property away from him, and that is why it is wrong that some individuals should have had no private property at all."[48]

Most property analysts suggest that property rights can be legitimately limited by other ideals, such as equality and liberty, or that common law understandings of property can be legitimately regulated by administrative and legislative action. Their perspectives, though useful, obfuscate a basic fact: both property theory and our historical practice of property law contain principles that promote the norms of decentralization and distributive justice within the concept and institution of property itself. Once we recognize this, it makes no sense to argue that property rights must always be limited to achieve distributive justice. Private property systems always contain within them a partial system of distributive justice, and the prevailing norms of private property, as it has operated in the United States, have always contained a tension between protecting the rights of title holders (however defined) and shaping property rules to ensure widespread access to the system by which such titles are acquired.

The classical view concentrates on protecting those who have property. It addresses the conditions under which people acquire property but does not include the premise that such conditions must be structured so that everyone has the right to acquire it. It focuses on individual owners and the actions they have to take to acquire property rights, which will then be defended by the state.[49] It assumes that the distribution of property is a consequence of the voluntary actions of individuals rather than a decision by the state. Property law does nothing more than protect property rights gained through individual action. Distributional questions, in this conception, are foreign to property as a system. If the community is unhappy with the distribution of property that emerges from individual actions, it is free to redistribute property through the tax system. Such a move would constitute the first time the government got involved in determining the distribution of property; before such adjustments in the tax code, distribution was privately determined by individuals acting in their own interest. Governmental compulsion is absent from this property acquisition process. No public policy decisions need to be made about property distribution for such a system to work.

This view is fundamentally mistaken. It is both normatively deficient and descriptively flawed. It distorts our understanding of private property as a social and legal institution. The distortions apply both to property theory and to historical practice of property law in the United States.

John Locke's theory of private property is the source of the classical conception of property as well as basis for the historical model championed by Robert Nozick.[50] It has been monumentally influential in the history of the United States as a justificatory scheme.[51] Locke justified property by arguing that individuals who took actions to mix their labor with natural resources thereby became entitled to be protected in controlling the fruits of their labor. This entitlement was based both on the moral claim of rights and on the utilitarian ground that legal protection for property justly produced or possessed through labor promoted useful work and increased social welfare. Locke qualified this theory by the significant proviso that labor creates property rights "at least where there is enough and as good left in common for others.[52]

Jeremy Waldron has characterized Locke's argument as a theory of "special rights."[53] Property rights are premised on individual actions. No general right to own property emerges from this kind of theory. One has a right to own property only if one undertakes the actions needed to generate a legitimate claim. Waldron has made two crucial criticisms of special rights theories. First, it is not clear why the actions of an individual can impose any legitimate obligations on others who have agreed neither to that individual's course of action nor to the rules of the game that define what actions create enforceable property rights. Second, there is no reason to believe that individual actions should have a binding moral effect on others if those actions inhibit or prevent others from taking similar actions.

To some extent, Waldron's twin critiques restate, in a more precise form, the Lockean proviso. Property rights can only be justified if their creation and exercise do not wrongly deprive others of similar rights. Waldron took the proviso one step further, however, and argued that it undermines Locke's theory itself. Possession of unowned land cannot be justified, in Locke's view, if it leaves others out of the system by which property can be acquired. Property rights initially could not be justified, Waldron points out, merely by appealing to actions taken by individuals. Rather, one has to go back one step further, to the social contract itself, to determine whether free and rational individuals would accept a system that would leave them with nothing.

From this perspective, the Lockean proviso looms large.[54] The very legitimacy of a property system depends on the effect of conferring property rights on individuals and allowing those individuals to assert those rights against others. As Frank Michelman has explained, one person's "proprietary value is obviously relative to other people's."[55] A constitutional system of "proprietary liberty" is therefore incomplete without attending to the "configurations of the values of various people's proprietary liberties."[56] The question of distribution is "endemic in the very idea of a constitutional scheme of proprietary liberty."[57] A system of private property not only protects the rights of those who have acquired resources but also ensures the conditions that enable individuals to acquire those resources.

In place of Locke's special-rights theory, Waldron proposes a theory that embraces property as a "general right." The classical source of this view is Hegel, who argued that property is legitimately considered to be a right because the control of property is essential to allow an individual to exercise free will in the world. Individual liberty is impossible without a place to act and without material resources to manipulate in creating a life. Waldron notes that if property is useful because of its intimate connection with the ability of the individual to exercise free will, then we cannot say that it is proper to be indifferent to the fact that some individuals have no property. If they have no property, they cannot exercise their will; if they cannot exercise their will, they are not free. If property is a general rather than a special right, we cannot remain indifferent to the distribution of property as it emerges through history in the practical affairs of people.

Law professors often pass on to their students a parable, drawn from Hobbes and Locke, that illustrates the origins of property. A farmer plants corn and tends the crop for months; at the last moment, just when the farmer is about to harvest it, an interloper comes and takes the corn by force. It is to avoid such problems that we created government and the institution of private property. These institutions serve the utilitarian purpose of granting us sufficient security so that we will be willing to plant, rather than being deterred from planting by the fear that our labor will come to naught when others take from us what we have created. Property also grants us a stable realm in which we can establish a home and live our lives on our own terms, with dignity; it gives us a place to be and thus protects our security and our liberty.

Those who own no property have no place where they are entitled to be. As Waldron notes, "Everything that is done has to be done somewhere. No one is free to perform an action unless there is somewhere he is free to perform it."[58] If nonowners, such as homeless people, are denied the ability to sleep on public property, and if private owners are entitled to exclude nonowners from their property, then it is as if we had made it illegal for homeless people to sleep. But if we created the institution of private property to protect individual autonomy and to ensure a measure of stability and security as an inducement to labor and investment, then we contradict our own ideals if we structure our property system in a way that denies nonowners the ability to obtain access to property needed to sustain human life and dignity.

This ineluctable distributive component of private property has pervaded the historical practice and social understanding of property in the United States. Simply put, a private property system, in the modern world, requires more than one owner. This was not always so, however. The state of New Jersey, where I grew up, was originally owned by two men, Sir George Carteret and John Lord Berkeley; the commonwealth of Pennsylvania was originally owned by William Penn, and several other colonies were similarly proprietary.[59] (This, of course, ignores the prior claims of American Indian nations who never agreed to such claims.) Nonetheless, under modern understandings of what it means to create a private property system, multiple owners is close to a definitional component of a private property system. In the modern view, a private property system—in order to count as a private property system—requires some dispersal of property ownership.

This conception is not only suggested by the political theory justifying private property but is also embedded in U.S. history. In the nineteenth century, the United States adopted a practice of transferring public lands to private citizens through homestead laws, which were designed to spread ownership of land widely across the population.[60] These policies were premised on the idea that property was not a special right but a general right; everyone had the right to own some.

This policy had a pernicious aspect to it. Where did the United States get the land to give out to white settlers? It took the land from American Indian nations. How were those seizures justified? From the beginning, English colonists justified conquest and displacement of American Indians by arguing that the native nations had more property than they needed, were misusing it by not developing it properly, and had a moral obligation to share it with the Europeans who needed access to it.[61] Locke himself attempted to characterize America as a vast unclaimed territory free for settlement by industrious Europeans. His theory, in conjunction with the colonial justifications for conquest, rationalized a massive redistribution of property from American Indian nations to the colonial powers, then to the United States and its white citizens. Both the conquest of Indian nations and the homestead laws defy the typical characterization of nineteenth-century American law as opposed to redistribution of property.

Property and Time

The image of ownership and contract in Justice Pitney's vision is consistent with the libertarian views of Robert Nozick and Richard Epstein.[62] In Nozick's theory, presented in *Anarchy, State, and Utopia,* property rights can be understood and regulated with two simple principles: a principle of justice in initial acquisition and a principle of just transfer.[63] Epstein suggests a similar approach in his recent work.[64] Property rights initially acquired at a particular moment in time by a legitimate method are fully in the control of the owner. That owner has no duty to share his property with others. The principle of transfer allows that owner to voluntarily convey ownership to another person partially or wholly. This principle includes the right to make whatever agreements the owner wishes in terms of leasing, employment, sale, transfer by will, and so on. It also allows the owner to grant conditional access to the owner's property, and it includes the principle of free contract, by which individuals can make whatever agreements they like with others. Under this scheme, property that is properly acquired is fully owned by the owner and cannot be taken by another person or the government without the owner's consent. The state may be able to take the property for limited public purposes, such as constructing roads, but can only do so if compensation is paid to the owner for the loss of ownership rights. Regulations of property use are strongly disfavored; they are only allowable to the extent necessary to protect the property interests of others.

The ownership model, as described by Nozick, depends on a particular conception of the relation between property and time. Nozick characterizes his system as a *historical* model of property rather than a *patterned* model.[65] The historical model, in his view, rests on the assumption that property rights are acquired and fixed at particular moments in time. We might call them magic moments. At these magic moments, property rights are created or allocated to a particular owner. Initially, property rights are acquired by labor or by possession of unowned resources. Subsequently, those rights can be transferred to others. The principle of transfer implies that rights can be acquired by purchase or contract, as well as initially through labor or possession. It also includes the right to leave one's property at death by will to whomsoever the owner may choose.

Nozick contrasts this historical model with a patterned model, which assumes that the resulting distribution of property rights matters from a moral point of view. A proponent of a patterned model might object if the historical process of acquisition and transfer results in a grossly unequal distribution of property; she would therefore justify redistribution to create a situation of greater equality. A historical model, in contrast, according to Nozick, favors whatever distribution happens to emerge from the process of fair acquisition and free transfer. In effect, Nozick identifies the process of acquisition and transfer as the core meaning of property. Any actions that take property rights fairly acquired through the processes of creation or transfer and redistributes them, by definition, interferes with property rights and constitutes a wrongful deprivation. When accomplished by government action, through regulation, taxation, or otherwise, redistribution constitutes a form of oppression interfering with individual rights of property and liberty.

Nozick's model has two significant defects. First, he assumes no tensions within the concept of property or within private property systems. He sees no tensions between competing sources of property rights, such as informal and formal sources of rights. He sees none between competing principles of initial acquisition, such as rewarding labor and protecting first possession. Nor does he see any tensions within the principle of transfer, such as those involved in the law of restraints on alienation. If no such tensions exist, one might posit a simple model of acquisition and transfer such as he proposed. But once we recognize the tensions that emerge as we try to define property rights in practice, it becomes impossible to implement a simple scheme of protecting property rights justly created or acquired. We must look to other criteria, of either fairness or utility, to adjudicate tensions within the property concept itself.

Second, Nozick's historical model of property assumes that acts that happen in history fix property rights inexorably. In addition to ignoring conflicts or tensions within property institutions, Nozick presumes that rights must be fixed without regard to consequences. In other words, he fails to address the problem of conflicts among rights that emerge over time. He seeks to fix rights without regard to their effects and without regard to whether the protection of rights has the effect of preventing others from obtaining similar rights. This model makes no distinction between the acquisition of property by a settler staking out land in an unowned wilderness and the inability of a homeless person today to engage in similar acts of possession. The current unavailability of land for such a person is irrelevant; the initial acquisition of property was justified, and so the current inability of others to exercise similar rights is of no consequence.

It has been the central purpose of this book to explain the inadequacy of Nozick's simplistic conception of property. The most obvious flaw of that conception is its failure to recognize the extent to which ownership rights conflict and therefore require government regulation to determine which of several competing property rights is to prevail. It fails to recognize that property rights may conflict with personal rights. The simplistic ownership model grossly understates the extent to which the exercise of property rights affects the legitimate interests of other owners and nonowners.

The historical model of property is more properly understood as an antihistorical model. It presumes that property rights are fixed at magic moments—the moments of acquisition and transfer—and that subsequent events have no effects on the scope of those property rights. This image is antihistorical in the sense that it presumes that the context in which property rights are exercised over time is a matter of no interest. This presumes that the exercise of property rights by owners generally will be self-regarding, having little or no effect on the legitimate property or personal interests of others. I have argued that this assumption is false. The exercise of property rights has consequences. It is irrational to define the extent of property rights without reference to whether their exercise impinges on the rights of others. Ignoring the tensions that arise between competing rights plunges the theorist into self-contradiction. If the point of protecting property is to protect preexisting rights, one cannot register indifference if the exercise of a property right has the effect of impinging on the right of another.

In contrast, I have argued, time is crucial in defining property.[66] Time is not composed of a few magic moments; rather, time is a continuing phenomenon. Property rights are exercised over time. The legitimacy of the exercise of a property right depends on the consequences of exercising the right. Those consequences are historical events; they take place in time. Thus, the time that matters is not only the magic moments of acquisition and transfer. Rather, what matters are the continuing moments in which property rights are exercised. The tensions that are a necessary component of the institution of private property affect not only choices about initial acquisition and transfer but also the proper moral and legal response to exercises of rights as they happen over time. One can only pretend indifference to the effects of exercising property rights if one blinds oneself to the ways in which the actions of some persons affect the ability of others to engage in similar actions.

This is the answer to Nozick's famous Wilt Chamberlain example.[67] Nozick argued, in the mid-1970s, that the voluntary transactions of the thousands of individuals who pay to see Chamberlain play basketball justify the concentration of property in the hands of the star center and prevent outside interference with his use of the property justly acquired. The reason it may be legitimate to limit the amount of property Chamberlain owns, or to limit his powers over the property he owns, is that the failure to so regulate his ownership rights may have the effect of giving him too much power over other people. That concentration of power changes the context within which others find themselves in a way that may prevent them from exercising the same rights that he exercised. Property rights mean something different when the context changes; what in one context appears to be legitimate individual use of resources appears, in another context, to be illegitimate control of other persons that prevents them from similarly developing their individual life plans or from acquiring similar rights themselves. This is the lesson of the *Friendswood* case.

Two conclusions follow from this analysis. First, property rights will differ depending on the context within which they are exercised and the effects they have on other actors; and second, they must be redefined over time to prevent the illegitimate concentration of power in ways that keep individuals from participating in the market system on fair and equal terms. Once we understand property as operating in history, it becomes clearer that we cannot inexorably fix in advance the meaning or allocation of property. If property rights are valued because they are related to individual liberty or the ability of an individual to pursue happiness, then it matters when gross inequalities of property affect the ability of the dispossessed to enter the system and become owners themselves.

Property and Politics

Market enthusiasts argue that government regulation is almost always counterproductive. Rather than helping its intended beneficiaries, regulation generally harms them by interfering in the ability of the free market to work its magic by reallocating resources in an efficient manner. This is especially the case when regulations impose compulsory terms in contracts, because those terms necessarily prevent the parties from reaching the deal they would have voluntarily adopted in the absence of the mandatory legislation. Requiring employers to give early notice of plant closings or to grant workers greater severance benefits, for example, will simply force employers to compensate by decreasing other benefits, such as wages. The result will be a trade-off of different benefits that is less appealing to workers than the package they would have voluntarily adopted if the government had left them alone to maximize their own welfare.[68]

This argument assumes that the original distribution of investment capital and human capital is sufficiently equal and just to conclude that market participants are able to get what they are willing to pay for. If, as I believe, the existing distribution of economic benefits is not just, then the results of private contracting may reflect, not the voluntary arrangement that maximizes the joint interests of both parties, but the imposition of exploitative terms by the more powerful party on the more vulnerable one. The question is not whether the parties get what they are willing to pay for, but whether each party has sufficient bargaining power to obtain just terms from the contractual relationship. If they do not have such power, there is no reason to conclude that compulsory terms necessarily leave the parties worse off in their own terms. Rather than interfering with the preferences of private actors by limiting their contractual freedom, imposition of compulsory terms in contracts often respects the preferences of those who benefit from the statute by giving them what they want but do not have enough bargaining power to get in the private market.

An objection to this argument is that, even if it is true that workers have insufficient bargaining power and therefore get inadequate compensation and benefits, they are still the best judges of what trade-offs to make. Compulsory terms force employers to cut back on other benefits; this in turn forces employees to accept a different mix of benefits than those to which they would otherwise have agreed, thereby making them worse off in their own terms. But if it is true that compulsory terms necessarily hurt their intended beneficiaries, why do labor unions lobby for legislation that guarantees minimum terms in employment contracts? Why do they lobby to increase the minimum wage? Is it sensible to argue that regulations override workers' preferences when workers support and lobby for the legislation?

One response often given to this question is to suggest that workers irrationally think compulsory terms legislation will give them something for nothing; they falsely believe that employers will not respond to minimum standards legislation by cutting back on other benefits. Market valuations are more rational than political valuations because they force actors to take into account the problem of scarce resources and to determine how much they are willing to pay for a particular entitlement. Political choices are inferior because they mask such considerations.

On the other hand, we might argue the opposite: political preferences are rational because they are based on considered judgments about justice and the contours of appropriate and supportable social arrangements. Market judgments, in contrast, are irrationally biased by the need to pay for each entitlement. Imagine, for example, that workers had no protection against being beaten on the job; they might very well agree to work without job security in order to obtain the right not to be beaten. The point is that there are some things that should simply not have to be bargained for but are owed to each person as a matter of common decency. To put it bluntly, slaves should not have to pay for their freedom. To ask whether slaves really value freedom by asking whether they are willing to buy it may result in an answer that they do not so value their freedom; but that answer does not take into account their inability to afford to pay for their freedom. In contrast, a political choice is not wrongly influenced by such considerations.

Neither of these arguments is completely correct, but neither is completely wrong either. People behave differently and exhibit different preferences depending on the social role they assume. They may want different things depending on whether they are acting as consumers or as citizens.[69] Both political and market understandings of our interests have their place and are legitimate expressions of human life. It is not the case that one kind of preference can be identified as real and the other as distorted; they are both real and they are both distorted by the narrowness (or broadness) of the perspective within which they were developed. Neither way of thinking can be permanently treated as superior to the other for all purposes.

Regulations often help people get what they want by shaping the contours of relations that comprise the market system to achieve a form of social life that can be supported as just. We take these relations for granted. As an extreme example, consider the institution of slavery. One might argue that a free market system that is antipaternalistic and is protective of individual liberty would not balk at enforcing slave contracts by which one individual, freely and upon full disclosure of the consequences, agreed to become the slave of another. After all, who are we to interfere in such a private choice? But the truth of the matter is that we rarely hear such an argument proposed seriously. The question is: Why not?

A woman falls into a deep pit filled with poisonous snakes. A passerby sees her precarious situation. A ladder is nearby, and the passerby offers to lower it into the pit if the woman will agree to sacrifice her first-born child. The woman agrees and is able to climb out of the pit. We do not enforce the contract. Why not?[70]

In a presidential election year, a poor woman agrees to sell her vote to the highest bidder so that she can better provide for her family. We do not enforce the contract. Why not?

The answer in all three cases is partly that the morally repugnant nature of the contract causes us to reject the view that rational people would freely agree to such terms. We therefore can conclude that the contracts were coerced rather than voluntary. But I believe we would reach the same conclusion even if we thought that the agreements were voluntary. Slavery, human sacrifice, and the buying and selling of votes for political office are beyond the pale. Such human relations are excluded from the vision of the market and from democratic governance as they are conceived of by their supporters; protection against them is not something one should have to bargain for, as it is owed to every human being.

This crucial insight applies not only to such wild hypothetical problems as slavery, human sacrifice, and the sale of public offices, but to mundane examples as well. Employers have no right to discriminate on the basis of race, sex, or disability. Landlords have no right to throw tenants out on the street with no notice, even if those tenants wrongfully stopped paying rent. The landlords must give notice, go to court, and possibly give the tenants time to find a new place to live and to move their belongings.

Many of the legal rules that affect the market are of this type. There is substantial room for freedom to develop alternative forms of human relations without having government dictate the terms of association. But there are also bounds to what is acceptable; that is why minimum standards legislation is necessary. Legal rules structure the contours of the relationships within which bargaining occurs. It is in fact impossible for such bargaining to occur without legal rules in place setting the ground rules or the baselines from which bargains are made. It is not enough to suggest that private ordering should answer this question; the problem is to identify the legal structure that will define the outer contours of these bargaining relationships. Legal rules shape the contours of the social relations that comprise the form of social life to which we are committed. Those rules do not interfere with individual liberty; rather, they establish liberty by giving all persons a safe environment within which to live. Such rules do not paternalistically deprive individuals of autonomy; rather, by requiring everyone to treat fellow citizens with common decency, they assure each person the ability to exercise autonomy.

Chapter 5 Reparation

If all the money in all the Swiss banks were turned over, it would not bring back the life of one Jewish child. But the money is a symbol. It is part of the story. If you suppress any part of the story, it comes back later, with force and violence.
—*Elie Wiesel*

In the beginning, the Jewish mystics tell us, God was everywhere. When God made the world, God needed to open up a place for it. God withdrew from part of the universe to make an empty space, the *challal panui,* in which the world could be created. In order to create this new space, God set a part of God's own light in heavenly vessels. But God cannot be contained in a vessel and when the world was born, these vessels shattered into billions of pieces, scattering the light of God into billions of tiny sparks. The world that God created whole was fractured. Those sparks became human souls whose job it is to repair the myriad broken places in the world. It is our task, the human task, to repair the world—*tikkun olam*—to rebuild those vessels and knit the world together again, not all at once, but piece by piece. It is slow work.

On New Year's Day in 1923, a sixteen-year-old Florida woman named Fannie Taylor claimed that she had been raped by a black man. The claim was later believed to be false, the real culprit being her white lover. But her accusation led to a mob riot in which whites completely destroyed the town of Rosewood, which was inhabited almost entirely by African American families. The mob killed at least eight and perhaps up to forty men and burned all houses owned by African Americans. The sole house not burned was owned by a white merchant, who sheltered some women and children and saved them from the mob. Other women and children hid in a swamp for twenty-four hours before being rescued by white rail workers on a train that passed through. Seventy years later the story once again came to light in a series of newspaper reports by the journalist Gary Moore.[1] It was later made into a documentary film by Alan Lipke *(Rosewood Reborn)* and a feature film *(Rosewood)* by John Singleton.

After Moore's reports, the few remaining survivors, who had been children at the time of the incidents and were now in their eighties and nineties, petitioned the Florida legislature for compensation, and a bill was passed in 1994 awarding them (as well as the descendants of survivors who had since passed away) around $2 million. The law also provided for an investigator to determine what happened and for the establishment of an educational fund for survivors and their families. The legislation acknowledged the role the state played in the disaster: "Whereas, the Rosewood Massacre was a unique tragedy in Florida's history in that the State and local government officials were on notice of the serious racial conflict in Rosewood during the entire week of January 1, 1923, and had sufficient time and opportunity to act to prevent the tragedy, and nonetheless failed to act to prevent the tragedy; an entire town was destroyed and its residents killed or fled, never to return; and the State and local government officials thereafter failed to reasonably investigate the matter, failed to bring the perpetrators to justice and failed to secure the area for the safe return of the displaced residents . . . the State of Florida recognizes an equitable obligation to redress the injuries sustained as a result of the destruction of Rosewood, Florida."[2]

Reparations for gross injustices done to individuals and groups often include efforts to make up for illegal seizures of property. Governments may compensate survivors and their descendants for wrongful takings of land by paying damages. A prominent example is the Indian Claims Commission Act of 1946, which provided for payments to American Indian nations whose land had been seized without compensation or for less than fair value.[3] Governments may also attempt to restore seized property to its rightful owners, as Germany, the Czech Republic, and Hungary have done in the case of property confiscated by the Nazis and by Communist regimes shortly after World War II.[4] Recent court decisions have repatriated stolen objects, such as American Indian human remains and funerary objects held by museums and art objects taken by the Nazi government from both Jews and non-Jews. Swiss banks have agreed to make payments to compensate the families of European Jews who had deposited money in Switzerland to keep it from being confiscated by Nazi Germany, but whose account numbers perished with them in the gas chambers. Reparation may also mean compensation for wrongs committed against persons and for destruction of property, as in the Rosewood case and the 1988 federal legislation providing $20,000 in compensation to each Japanese American unjustly interned in camps during World War II.[5]

Reparation of injustice presents a number of dilemmas.[6] Some involve relations between the wronged group and others; some have to do with problems within the group demanding reparation. Reparation includes three separate practices: *restitution,* or return of property; *reparations,* damages in the form of monetary compensation for personal or property losses; and *repair,* the object of commissions appointed by offending nations to discover the truth about their own misdeeds, war crimes tribunals to prosecute human rights abuses, and affirmative action to redress the imbalance in access to valued resources. Examples of repair are the South African Truth Commission, the Bosnian War Crimes Tribunal, and land redistribution schemes in South Africa.

All three forms of reparation contribute to the task of mending the world. The original cannot be re-created; the shattered vessel cannot be unshattered. But it can be mended—perhaps returned to a condition close to the one it was in when violence was done to it. Or perhaps not. The thing cannot be what it was because it is a thing that was broken and repaired and not something that is free from such trauma. It has a history; it has known loss. No response can ever be adequate, yet not to respond may be more inadequate still.

SOVEREIGNTY AND PROPERTY

On October 18, 1987, thirty-six members of the Missisquoi Abenaki Tribe were arrested by officials of the state of Vermont for fishing without a license.[7] In an amazing turn of events Judge Joseph J. Wolchik found that the federal government, the only entity with the lawful power to extinguish Indian title, had never extinguished Abenaki title to the tribe's traditional lands in Vermont, including the land on which the defendants had been fishing.[8] The state of Vermont therefore had no jurisdiction over them, and Judge Wolchik dismissed the charges against them.[9] The ruling was momentous, for it placed in doubt the title to every parcel of land in the state. It was appealed to the Vermont Supreme Court, which overturned it in June 1992 by unanimous decision in the case of *State v. Elliott.*[10] The court ruled, in an opinion written by Justice James Morse, that the Abenakis had lost their original property rights to their lands in Vermont by the "increasing weight of history."[11]

At stake in this case was no less than the legitimacy of the sovereignty of the United States and the claims of non-Indians to ownership of lands gained through conquest. The central issues concerned establishing the current consequences of ancient wrongs and determining what wrongs are too ancient to remedy. The different resolutions of the case by the trial court and the Vermont Supreme Court not only reflect different constructions of property but once again reveal core tensions within our property system and within the concept of property itself.

Judge Wolchik took a relatively formal approach to property rights. He focused on Congress's failure to extinguish the Abenakis' uncontested title to the Vermont lands. He interpreted federal Indian law by reference to long-standing presumptions used in adjudicating disputes over tribal ownership. A federal statute first passed in 1834 places the burden of persuasion squarely on the party challenging tribal title: "In all trials about the right of property in which an Indian may be a party on one side, and a white person on the other, the burden of persuasion shall rest upon the white person, whenever the Indian shall make out a presumption of title in himself from the fact of previous possession or ownership."[12] If any doubt exists, this presumption places ownership in the hands of the tribe. Moreover, the U.S. Supreme Court has declared time and again that extinguishment of Indian title requires a sovereign act of Congress,[13] and it has warned that "an extinguishment cannot be lightly implied in view of the avowed solicitude of the United States for the welfare of its Indian wards."[14] In the 1985 case *County of Oneida v. Oneida Indian Nation,* the Court reaffirmed that "congressional intent to extinguish Indian title must be 'plain and unambiguous,' and will not be 'lightly implied.'"[15] It further noted that "relying on the strong policy of the United States 'from the beginning to respect the Indian right of occupancy,' . . . it '[c]ertainly' would require 'plain and unambiguous action to deprive the [Indians] of the benefits of that policy.'"[16] Finding no formal abrogation of tribal rights, Judge Wolchik ruled that the Abenaki title remained valid.

In contrast, Justice Morse and the Vermont Supreme Court seriously considered and were swayed by informal evidence, namely the historical circumstances surrounding the creation of the state of Vermont and its admission to the Union in 1791. It was on the basis of this context that they concluded that Congress had intended to divest the Abenakis of their title, even though it had never formally done so and had never voiced its intentions in so many words. "An historical event," Justice Morse wrote, "although insufficient by itself to establish an extinguishment, may contribute to a finding of extinguishment when analyzed together with other events."[17] Formal action by Congress is required but ambiguities must be judged in light of the context of congressional action. "Moreover, a century-long course of conduct may demonstrate extinguishment, even though the exact date on which Indian title is extinguished is difficult to determine."[18] Presumptions, in other words, can be overcome, not only by clear language in formal documents, but also by common understandings of the social meaning of a course of conduct.

In its opinion the Vermont Supreme Court gives three reasons in support of its conclusion that the Abenaki claim was extinguished. First, it suggests, but stops short of affirming, that Abenaki title had been extinguished when the Republic of Vermont broke away from New York State in 1777 following a military rebellion.[19] Then it argues that Abenaki title was certainly extinguished when Congress admitted Vermont to the Union in 1791.[20] And lest a doubt linger, it declares that any embers of an Abenaki claim to title had been stamped out under the increasing weight of history.[21]

In 1761 the British crown, in an attempt to prevent wars with Indian nations in America, issued a "Royal Instruction" to its colonial governors prohibiting them from granting Indian lands to white settlers without the king's consent. The 1761 Royal Instruction further required non-Indians who had settled on such lands without a grant to remove themselves from Indian country immediately. Two years later the Proclamation of 1763 reiterated the prohibitions contained in the Royal Instruction. At that time, Vermont did not exist as a separate colony. The region was claimed by both New York and New Hampshire.

On August 17, 1763, New Hampshire governor Benning Wentworth, in clear violation of the 1761 instruction, made grants of land occupied by Abenakis in what is now Vermont, on condition that the grantees actually settle there. The governor of New York, Cadwallader Colden, reacting swiftly to New Hampshire's move to fortify its claim to the region by establishing facts on the ground, granting to New Yorkers the same lands Wentworth had just granted to New Hampshirites.

The crown responded to the incendiary actions of its royal governors by issuing a Privy Council order in 1764 that set the boundary between New York and New Hampshire at the Connecticut River and put the Wentworth Grants (and all the territory that later became Vermont) firmly within the borders of New York. The order hardly mattered to the New Hampshire claimants, who defied the New York authorities and the British crown by refusing to quit the lands. In 1767 the crown issued another Privy Council order prohibiting the New York governor from making any land grants in the disputed area until the crown could decide the matter, but it failed to follow up the order with action. In 1769 New York attempted to eject the New Hampshire claimants by ejectment suits. Their response was to revolt. Between 1770 and 1775 the Green Mountain Boys, led by Ethan Allen, fought the New Yorkers who were attempting to claim lands in Vermont. In 1777 Vermont declared its independence from New York and established itself as a republic. Its declaration of independence asserted sovereignty over the lands that had been granted by Governor Wentworth.

After ratification of the federal Constitution in 1789, Congress passed the first in a series of Trade and Intercourse Acts in 1790, one year before Vermont became a state.[22] Among other things, the acts reaffirmed the policy the British had established restricting grants of Indian lands by prohibiting anyone from settling on Indian land without the permission of the federal government. In addition, the acts provided that title to tribal lands could be acquired only by the federal government, not by a state or a private person.

A crucial question is whether the establishment of the Republic of Vermont in 1777 extinguished Abenaki title. It might be argued that the republic broke away from New York in order to protect the property claims of the settlers who based their title on the Wentworth Grants. It would then be inconsistent with this historical fact to conclude that those claims were invalid simply because the Abenaki title had never been formally extinguished by either the crown or by the Republic of Vermont itself.

The Vermont Supreme Court did not hold in *Elliott* that the Wentworth Grants, which were illegal under British law, by themselves extinguished Abenaki title.[23] But it does suggest that the Republic of Vermont may have extinguished the Abenaki title by its resolute action in defense of the grants. The court refused to decide whether in 1777 Vermont achieved sovereignty as a separate nation with the power to extinguish Indian title. Rather, it viewed the period of the republic (1777–91) as a stage in a long historical process by which Indian title was extinguished within the state. According to the court, the crucial point is that the Wentworth Grants were conditioned on settlement. Since those rights could vest only if the grantee settled on the land, they were inconsistent with Indian retention of occupancy rights.

There are several problems with the court's reasoning. First, the Wentworth Grants clearly violated British law at the time those grants were made. It is therefore unclear how one can conclude that they provide a lawful root of title unless one determines that Vermont achieved sovereignty under international law.

Second, the court suggests, but does not conclude, that the Wentworth Grants were not unlawful. The opinion states, for example, "While the Crown may have declared the grants invalid based on a lack of jurisdictional authority in this particular governor, the sovereign's intent to allow British appropriation of the area was not in question."[24] The court argues that it is appropriate to ignore the Royal Instruction of 1761 and the Proclamation of 1763. Somehow, they were "paper tigers," not meant to be enforced.[25] It further asserts that the Privy Council orders of 1764 and 1767 were intended to "pacify the two British jurisdictions, not protect Native Americans."[26] It may be true that the purpose of the 1761 and 1763 edicts was to prevent wars with Indian nations whose territory was being invaded by British subjects rather than to protect Indian rights. Yet it is also true that they clearly delineated the circumstances under which lawful title to Indian lands could be created. The fact that non-Indians continuously invaded Indian lands with impunity may demonstrate that the Proclamation of 1763 was not vigorously enforced, but it does not make that proclamation invalid or in any way strip it of legal authority.[27]

Third, if the Vermont Supreme Court is correct in asserting that the Republic of Vermont was established not only to protect New Hampshire land claimants against New York claimants but also to vest full title to the claimants without regard to Indian rights, Vermont would be the only state to have dispossessed Indians without any regard whatsoever for their rights in the land. It is an uncontested principle of federal Indian law that so-called ultimate or fee title to tribal lands is held by the United States, while the tribes retain a title or right of occupancy.[28] A grant of the fee interest by the federal government does not extinguish the tribal title, which can only be extinguished by a separate act of Congress. Moreover, the consistent policy of Great Britain and, after independence, the United States, was to prevent non-Indian settlement on Indian land until a treaty had been concluded with the Indian nation that had title. When non-Indians illegally occupied Indian land, the United States sometimes responded by ejecting the squatters; in other instances the squatters were given full property rights, but only after the land was obtained from the relevant Indian nation by treaty. The Vermont Supreme Court was unwilling to take the drastic step of interpreting the Vermont republic's declaration of independence as being less respectful of Indian rights than the laws of Great Britain and the United States were. It therefore described the declaration and the republican period before admission to the Union in 1791 as merely one factor that led it to determine that Indian title had been extinguished. By its reasoning the Vermont Supreme Court sends a peculiar message to the state's Abenaki citizens. Holding that validation of the Wentworth Grants requires extinguishment of the Abenaki title tells the Abenaki Nation that the State of Vermont was established to protect the property rights of all Vermonters except themselves.

By failing to assign to the Republic of Vermont clear responsibility for having extinguished the Abenaki title, the Vermont Supreme Court attempted to displace blame onto the United States for the injustice of denying Abenaki claims when it admitted Vermont to the Union in 1791.[29] It hoped thereby to suggest that Vermont was no different from the rest of the states in its treatment of Indians and that any injustice present at its creation was no different than the injustices committed by other governments. Yet in implicating the U.S. government in the extinguishment of the Abenaki title, the court misapplied federal Indian law. Its attempt to shift the blame cannot succeed. The responsibility for extinguishing the title rests with the Vermont Supreme Court itself, and it occurred, not in 1777 or 1791, but in 1992 with its decision in *State v. Elliott.*

The court suggests that the Abenaki title was extinguished when Vermont was admitted to the Union in 1791.[30] It notes that Congress was aware that the Wentworth Grants were contingent on actual settlement and asked Vermont to confirm in writing that the condition had indeed been met. This request, Justice Morse asserted in the published opinion, demonstrates that Congress approved of the Wentworth Grants and understood that they were contingent on settlement. Justice Morse argued that Congress therefore regarded Vermont's admission to the Union as an act that would implicitly extinguish the tribal title to those lands.

This reasoning is incompatible with long-standing precedent, established canons of construction in federal Indian law, prevailing standards for a finding of extinguishment, and the consistent policy of the United States. Canons of construction in federal Indian law require a clear and unambiguous statement that Congress intended to extinguish original Indian title.[31] The mere fact that Congress was aware of the Wentworth Grants and the fact that they would vest only upon settlement does not come close to meeting that test. Throughout the period in question—and to the present day—the law was that the conveyance of the fee title to the federal government did not by itself extinguish Indian title. Conditioning title on settlement was a common practice. In the nineteenth century it was often used by the United States to ensure that land grants went to people who would establish their homes and farms there rather than to land speculators.[32] It thus represented a policy choice about which non-Indian claimants would be given priority rights in land and does not tell us anything about the conditions under which Indian title of occupancy was extinguished.

Moreover, congressional acts that explicitly dealt with federal policy toward Indian nations indicate that at the time Vermont was admitted to the Union, the United States was eager to protect Indian nations from deprivation of their property without a prior treaty. The Trade and Intercourse Act of 1790, which prohibited settlement in the absence of a treaty with the affected Indian tribes, reflects a fear of inciting Indians to make war against the militarily weak and economically depleted federal state.[33] The Constitution, adopted only a year earlier, had centralized power over Indian affairs in the federal government, thereby depriving the states of the ability to take tribal property without federal consent.[34] Since the Abenakis never abandoned their lands in Vermont and had waged five separate wars against the British,[35] it would be extremely odd to find the United States so indifferent to Abenaki claims as the Vermont Supreme Court suggests.

Yet even if somehow it is arguable that Congress intended to extinguish Abenaki title by affirming land grants that were conditional on settlement, this intent is far from "plain and unambiguous."[36] By considering the circumstances of Vermont's admission to be adequate evidence of congressional intent to extinguish Abenaki title, the Vermont Supreme Court fails to respect established burdens of proof that implement fundamental federal policies aimed at limiting the power of state governments to confiscate Indian lands. The supremacy clause in article 6 of the Constitution, as well as the policy of protecting Indian rights, requires that they be taken seriously.

The Vermont Supreme Court was well aware that Vermont's 1777 declaration of independence and the establishment of Vermont statehood in 1791 were insufficient, either severally or jointly, to demonstrate a clear intent to extinguish the Abenaki title. It therefore viewed those events as a portion of the cumulative evidence of congressional intent to extinguish Abenaki title over time. That evidence is established, in the court's view, by the "increasing weight of history."[37] Actual settlement of lands in Vermont by non-Indians and the persistent failure of the United States to act to protect Abenaki claims confirmed the Court's intuition that Congress had intended to extinguish Abenaki title when it admitted Vermont to the Union.

OWNERSHIP VERSUS ENTITLEMENT

In *State v. Elliott* the Vermont Supreme Court acknowledged that extinguishment of Indian title requires an unequivocal act of Congress. How then could the court conclude that the Abenaki title had been extinguished in the absence of any congressional action that even mentioned the Abenaki claims? How could it determine that the property rights of some of its citizens had been casually lost when Vermont was admitted to the Union? How could the court conclude that the Abenaki title was lost when the Abenakis were never conquered and Congress failed to negotiate a treaty or otherwise deal with their property rights in any explicit way? How could it, in good conscience, tell its Abenaki citizens that the Republic of Vermont was established for the purpose of protecting the property rights of all Vermonters except themselves?

The result in *Elliott* reveals two important tendencies in the ownership model of property. One of them has to do with the gravitational pull of either/or thinking, which fails to recognize that various middle positions or accommodations are possible. The Vermont Supreme Court appears to assume that if it recognized the legitimate claims of the Abenakis, the logical corollary would be to deny the property rights of all non-Indian residents of Vermont.[38] Identifying with the state of Vermont and its non-Indian inhabitants, the court assumed that dispossessing them would be wrong because they had legitimately relied on state grants and on the public recording system in establishing homes and businesses. "The New Hampshire grantees ardently relied upon their rights to the land by virtue of the grants, and their assertion of dominion over the area inspired Vermont's revolt against New York and its stance as an independent republic. In short, the relevant focus is on what Vermonters intended to do with the land, not what hindsight discloses Governor Wentworth was authorized to do with it."[39] If it would be unjust to dispossess non-Indian claimants now, the court assumed, it must follow that conquest had happened at some point in the past. Exactly when is not important; what matters is that it took place. If no date can be determined, then it must be found in the "increasing weight of history."

Even if one concludes that it would be unjust or unlawful to dispossess current non-Indian residents in Vermont, it is a logical error to infer that the original inhabitants must therefore have been lawfully deprived of their property rights. One wrong does not make another wrong right. Two just claims may exist and conflict with each other; it may be unjust to dispossess current residents, and it may also have been unjust to dispossess the Abenakis.

This either/or reasoning misconstrues the character of property rights. It presumes that the relevant question is "Who is the owner?" and that once that owner is identified, others' claims have no legal standing. Ruling that the Abenakis had never been lawfully divested of their title would not automatically entitle them to oust the current residents of Vermont or even to collect rent from them. This conflict between justifiable property claims might have been resolved more justly through careful examination of equitable alternatives.

The Vermont Supreme Court failed to recognize that the most appropriate resolution to the case might have been a negotiated settlement. If the court had acknowledged that the Abenakis had never been lawfully deprived of their title to the tribe's Vermont lands, the United States, as holder of the fee title, could have negotiated an agreement with the tribe that would compensate them for their loss by some combination of money and land, as it did in the case of the Passamaquoddy and Penobscot nations in Maine and the natives in Alaska. In other words, the United States could have concluded a treaty with the Missisquoi Abenaki Nation. This way of resolving the conflict would have recognized property rights and sovereignty on both sides.

There was yet another option for deciding *Elliott* fairly that the court did not consider. Rather than making a broad ruling that wipes out all of one party's rights claims, it might have ruled more narrowly and done less damage to the losing side—if only it could have seen past the ownership question. The Abenakis were not claiming a right to dispossess non-Indian Vermonters or to charge them rent. All they wanted was to be allowed to fish on public property without a state license, a privilege that by itself would have little or no impact on private property rights in the state. It is hard to see why this narrow rights claim, based in a title that had never been lawfully extinguished, could not be granted. Since the case only involved this narrow issue, the court could have deferred consideration of what to do if the Abenakis ever claimed more extensive rights in the land. It was only the all-or-nothing view of ownership propounded by the absolutist model that prevented the court from considering this solution.

Second, although the ownership model has enormous power and, in my view, substantially affected the outcome of the case, its application in *Elliott* reveals its fundamental internal tensions. The Vermont Supreme Court's ruling was based on careful consideration of the intent of the individuals who founded the Republic of Vermont, the negotiations between Vermont and the Congress at the time of Vermont's admission to the Union, and the subsequent conduct of the non-Indian Vermonters, as well as the conduct of state and federal officials. All this informal evidence is used to assign title to the lands in Vermont to non-Indians. Given the uncontested prior title of the Abenakis to their lands, a formal approach to property—one based on title rather than possession—would have left ownership with the tribe. No formal document plainly and unambiguously strips the Abenakis of their property rights, and both the title conception of property and existing rules of law require title to remain with the tribe unless Congress expressly takes it away.

It is odd in this case that formal title and formal procedures for transferring title played so small a role. The same seems true about American attitudes concerning land ownership generally. We are sure that current non-Indian titles are valid, no matter what happened in the past. We assume that it simply must be the case that tribal title was lawfully extinguished, at some point, in some way. We hope that this was accomplished formally and according to the letter of the law, but if not, so be it. The expectations of non-Indian owners are such that they believe their title is unimpeachable, no matter what the formal inadequacies of the process by which title was transferred. The case demonstrates, in other words, that title is not the only—or the most powerful—determinant of our conceptions about property. Rather, our sense of propriety seems to play as great a role as title in adjudicating disputes about ownership and public conceptions of entitlement.

DILEMMAS OF REPARATION

Justice and Victimization

Does reparation right a wrong by restoring justice, or does it create further victimization of the oppressed group? Consider the recent attempts by Jews to get Swiss banks to trace and restore, with interest, the accounts of European Jews who had deposited cash, securities, and valuables there for safekeeping during the Nazi era but did not survive to reclaim them. The banks came up with one excuse after another for not finding and revealing the depositors' names and account numbers. Advocates for the dispossessed Jews and their heirs suggested that the Swiss try harder. They pointed out that over the decades the banks had made astronomical profits by investing the principle and accumulated interest from the accounts without concern that the depositors would ever cash them out, and that the bankers' pleas about the sacredness of confidentiality were hollow.

On one hand, acknowledgment and restoration of monies wrongfully held may serve the legitimate purposes of doing justice, returning property to its rightful owners, and establishing in memory the wrong that was done and had been hidden so successfully by so many for so long. Restoration makes those who committed the wrong treat those they harmed as people, as human beings with rights, including the right to own property and to have their property restored to them when it is wrongfully expropriated. To insist that Swiss bankers restore what they have wrongfully and deceitfully taken is to combat the myth that it is the Jews who are deceitful moneylenders who steal other people's property. The act of restoration is an acknowledgment that Jews earned their property honestly, that it rightfully belongs to them, and that it is as worthy of protection as the property of non-Jews. Moreover, by calling the Swiss banks to account, Jews break out of the passive associations with victimhood and become agents of their own fate, as well as the agents of change in Switzerland by having exposed the so-called neutral policy of privacy for bank accounts as an aid to theft and by having forced a reassessment of the ambiguous Swiss role in World War II.

On the other hand, Jews worry aloud that this campaign recalls stereotypes of Jews as money-grubbers who have stashed fortunes in secret bank accounts and now want nothing more than to sit and count their money—as if money could restore the dead or make up for the loss of Jewish lives. Pressing a claim to the money of one's deceased relatives may suggest to non-Jews that all they mean to us, all that we can acknowledge of them now, is a lost inheritance. Thus the demand for restoration may revive the very thing that restoration is supposed to combat.

A similar mixed reaction has attended calls by African Americans for the federal and state governments to make reparations to them for slavery and other injuries and indignities that have been visited on them by the United States. Some see them as righteous demands for recognition of past injustice—demands to be taken seriously and to be treated as human beings. Others, however, view them as signs of a refusal to grow up and acknowledge that one has it in one's own power to make a life in a world that (supposedly) no longer engages in discrimination.[40] The debate over affirmative action has degenerated into a standoff; calls to repair the current effects of past injustice are met with derisory denials that continuing injustice exists and assertions that the problems of African Americans today are now purely of their own making. Here, as in the Jewish case, the demand for justice may re-create conditions that reinforce stereotypes of the oppressed minority as inferior to the majority.

Redress and Reconstruction

In countries that are attempting to move beyond a terrible past, the demand for reparation is most insistent and at the same time almost impossible to fulfill. The greater the injustice, the harder it is to mend the broken vessel; the longer the passage of time, the more impossible it becomes to right the wrong without committing new wrongs. These are two lessons of the *Elliott* case—the Abenaki Indians' attempt to repair the injustices done to them—and others like it.

The passage of time, the "increasing weight of history" that pressed down on the interests of the Abenakis, has an effect on reparations for all American Indian nations. The process by which they were deprived of lands was often illegal and unjust. Land was taken by people and governments that had no legal or moral right to take it. Land was taken with inadequate compensation. Yet so much time has passed since the wrongful deprivations that new legitimate claims—new property rights—have been established by the occupiers of the wrongfully taken land. Righting the wrong not only would require the redistribution of millions of acres of land but would unjustly inflict suffering on a different population—the people who have lived on the land for a century or more. The same dilemma arises in Germany and the countries it occupied during World War II, where Jews and other persecuted peoples were deprived of their property. A woman returning to Berlin to claim rights to her grandparents' house may seek to evict families who have made their home on the property for fifty years and who have no other place to go.

Accommodations between the wrongs of the past and the needs of the present can be explosive. The new South African constitution protects the property rights of the white minority while allowing for, and in some cases requiring, restitution or reparations for lost property and past violations of human rights. This accommodation may have been necessary to allow the transition from minority to majority rule to occur without civil war. It creates a problem, however. How can South Africa compensate the victims of apartheid while respecting the property rights of the white minority—rights founded on expropriation of black lands when they were nationalized by South Africa in the 1930s? A similar dilemma exists in the United States with respect to the property of Indian nations.

The problem of restitution and justice not only concerns conflicts between the goal of righting past wrongs while avoiding present injustice. It may not be possible to provide compensation for all past injustices without wrecking current and future economic prospects. The needs of the Eastern European countries and of South Africa, for example, may prevent the government from raising money from the minority that benefited from the prior regime in order to restore rights to the majority or compensate them for the loss. The needs of the present to create a new economy, a new life, may be incompatible with full restoration of wrongfully taken lives, liberties, and properties.

On one hand, the passage of time works in favor of reparations, because the more time passes, the easier it gets for the current generation to acknowledge the wrong done by its forebears without viewing themselves as personally responsible. On the other hand, for that very reason, the current generation may not feel responsible for the wrongs of prior generations. Moreover, after a period of time new rights arise. The wrongful taking of American Indian lands leaves in its wake a hundred years of property rights established in non-Indian families. When new rights arise over time, the ability to redress old wrongs seems to dwindle or even disappear, especially if the goal is restitution or repossession.

Vindication and Renewal

For years the Sioux Nation litigated against the United States to establish that the taking of their lands had been in violation of solemn treaties. When at last the tribe prevailed and obtained a large (although still inadequate) damages judgment, the tribe no longer wanted the money. It had come to feel that accepting the money would amount to giving up any hope that the land would ever be returned. Yet the land had special spiritual significance, and since much of it is owned by the federal government, it could in fact be returned. In December 1970 President Richard Nixon signed legislation returning to the Pueblo people a lake they held sacred. The Sioux have continued to refuse to accept the money awarded to them after the hard-fought judicial battle, instead pressing for return of the Black Hills in South Dakota. The money sits in a government account collecting interest. It cannot be used by the United States and cannot be accepted by the Sioux.

The Indian Claims Commission Act of 1946 was intended to end all claims by Indian Nations against the United States. It has not succeeded. Indeed in some ways it has had the opposite of the intended effect. By vindicating past claims, it has created an invigorated sense of entitlement. The process of acknowledgment and reparation fuels demands for perfect justice, for the repair of all. Rather than establishing finality, reparation may renew a sense of loss and thereby renew claims for restoration of sovereignty and property. "You broke the treaties in the past; comply with them now." Debate ensues about the continued viability and meaning of those treaties—those past accommodations—and whether vindication of them requires further readjustment of the relationship. Are accounts settled, or is the task of repair unending? Do reparations provide a sense of relief, or do they merely fuel insatiable demands—demands to repair what cannot be repaired, to restore what was, to convert a broken, hastily repaired thing into a new, unbroken thing, a longing that cannot, by definition, be fulfilled.

Often the stated goal of governments in paying reparations is to put the issue to rest, to end the claims, to let everyone get on with their lives. But the inevitably partial nature of the compensation—its inevitable injustice and the inevitable backlash of those who feel they are being made responsible for the sins of others—means the issue will not go away. Reparations may vindicate one people's sense that a wrong was done to them while creating a sense in those who make reparations that they themselves have now been wronged. In addition, views about what constitutes an adequate response may change over time, as we saw happen with the Sioux Nation's demands for reparation for loss of the Black Hills. The money awarded by the courts, which the Sioux now feel they cannot accept, sits in a trust fund held by a government that is unwilling to return an inch of their land. The award did nothing to end the conflict between the Sioux Nation and the United States. If anything, it heightened the Sioux's sense of the inadequacy of the response.

The Character and Scale of Harm

Another paradox is evident. The more serious the harm, the more we need a societal response; but the more we need a societal response, the more inadequate the response will be. In the case of Rosewood, what moved the legislators was not the terrible loss of life but the loss of property. Property can be valued; it can be assessed. Compensation can seem adequate or at least appropriate. For horrors of a more personal nature, money seems not only inadequate but insulting. When Germany was considering making reparations to Israel in the 1950s, a huge debate ensued among Holocaust survivors. Some argued that Israel should never accept blood money, while others demanded that Germany pay.

The scale of suffering creates similar dilemmas. Rosewood was a discrete event, so it seemed conceivable to assign a dollar amount to damages; $2 million was within the capacity of the state of Florida to pay. What amount would be adequate to demonstrate a commitment to overcome the legacy of slavery? If one seriously considered a reparations bill for the descendants of slaves, what amount of compensation would be enough? What form of response would be fitting?

The scale of the harm overwhelms us. At the same time, although no amount of money or penance can ever seem to compensate for such massive harms as slavery and genocide, large wrongs demand a response. Reparations have been paid for the Holocaust and for takings of Indian lands. Restitution of some land has been authorized under the new South African constitution. In addition, large wrongs may make governments feel compelled to account for old events when there is a change in government, as occurred in Germany and South Africa, or after national traumas, as when U.S. participation in the war against Nazi Germany led to passage of the Indian Claims Commission Act and the desegregation of the military.

But if massive wrongs demand a response, they also make it nearly impossible to conceive of adequate reparations. When harms reach into every level of society, as they did in Eastern Europe under the Communist regimes, it might be best to adopt pragmatic policies that push the economy forward rather to look backward and adopt compensatory policies that might wreck it. They might also be discriminatory, in that reparations might be made only to certain groups, when practically all citizens feel they were victims of oppressive rule.

THE HOPELESS DEMANDS OF JUSTICE

Compensation can never compensate. Compensation granted to American Indian nations for unlawful takings of their lands did not fully compensate for the value of the lost lands. Compensation for loss of land or property does not right the wrong, nor does it undo the present consequences of the loss. More fundamentally, many injustices against Indian nations were not vindicated. Some takings of land were never counted as illegal, such as the division of tribal lands into lots and their assignment to individual owners. A provision in the Indian Claims Commission Act for damages for any breach of trust or good faith was interpreted so narrowly by the courts that it was rendered meaningless.

We are left with the hopeless demands of justice. They are impossible to fulfill. We cannot undo what was done or even adequately acknowledge what has happened, much less compensate for it. And yet, they are demands. Like justice, these hopeless demands for reparation press on us despite the futility of attempts to fulfill them. The impossibility of doing justice does not leave us free to escape responsibility. Rather, it makes a claim on us not to forget. This is why memory is so important. Elie Wiesel recounts a Jewish tale whose moral is that "God created human beings because God loves stories." The demand to tell the story, and to show that we understand it by taking it seriously enough to engage in reparative acts, impels us to treat the past as a present force, never to turn away complacently and always to face forthrightly the present effects of past injustice.

Our task is the endless one of repairing the broken vessels. It is the human task; it cannot end. Jews are called by the name of Israel, the name given to Jacob after he had wrestled with a messenger of God. The work of human life, the work of justice in human societies, is not to restore the world to a prior state of unity. It is to acknowledge that the world has been shattered, to remember how the shattering happened and what one's role in it was, and to act—to mend the damage and to rebuild human relationships. The repair of the world requires continuing engagement and responsibility. Satisfaction comes not with the knowledge that one has righted a wrong and put the past to rest but with the structuring and restructuring of life. The broken vessels of God cannot be fully repaired in this life, and yet the work of repair, of *complete* repair, is the very meaning of life. We live this paradox.

Chapter 6 Expectations and Obligations

The paradox of the human situation . . . yields no resolution.
—*Avivah Gottlieb Zornberg*

We will have to find new ways of comprehending and responding to our responsibilities. . . . The puzzle of a nonsubmerged selfhood amidst connective responsibility cannot be solved by walls of rights. We need to take our traditional concepts like property and ask what patterns of relationship among people and the material world we want, what patterns seem true to both integrity and integration. Those questions do not necessarily preclude a concept of property, but they imply a focus not on limits but on forms of interaction and responsibility for their consequences.
—*Jennifer Nedelsky*

Aaron Feuerstein is the owner of Malden Mills, a textile company in Lawrence, Massachusetts. When three of his nine buildings were destroyed by fire just before Christmas in 1995, Feuerstein not only announced that he would rebuild but promised to pay his workers their wages for the next month (at $1.5 million a week) even though he was not legally required to do so. He also promised to attempt to rehire all of them and to help those he could not rehire by retraining them for new jobs. And he assured them they would each receive their expected $275 Christmas bonus.[1] "Grown men cried" when he told the workers his plans, "and in the several languages of the largely immigrant workforce—Portuguese, Spanish, Québecois—prayers of thanksgiving were said."[2] To the public as well, Feuerstein's reaction to the disaster seemed nothing short of astonishing.

Feuerstein made good on his promises—he actually continued to pay wages after the first month, for as long as he could afford—and was haled as a hero by his employees and by public officials.[3] Coverage of his deeds abounded in the media. He was the subject of articles in *Time* and *Newsweek* and was interviewed on television. The secretary of labor, Robert Reich, lauded Feuerstein for having set an example for other corporate leaders to follow.[4] Editorialists praised him, and religious leaders spoke approvingly of his actions in their sermons. He was invited to sit next to the first lady, Hillary Clinton, when the president delivered the State of the Union address to Congress.[5]

Feuerstein's actions took people by surprise because most employers who face financial difficulties do not treat their workers anywhere near as humanely. In recent years corporations have downsized with abandon, laying off thousands of long-time employees to bolster the bottom line. Corporate executives and managers have felt an obligation only to their companies' shareholders, who they have assumed, rightly or wrongly, care only about the value of their stocks and not about the welfare of the workers or the effect of layoffs and plant closings on the communities in which the companies operate.[6] Companies have treated workers as if they were not part of a common enterprise—almost as if they were strangers.

Feuerstein acted differently. He seemed not to regard his workers as servants beholden to him for their livelihood, but as equals. When asked if he considered his employees to be his partners, Feuerstein responded "yes" but then gently corrected the questioner: "I am *their* partner."[7] He owned the company and could have done whatever he wanted with it. He was entitled, by law, to consider his own interests alone, and yet he did not do so. Instead, he felt obligated to his employees and to his community. An owner acted out of a sense of obligation. How odd. Ownership and obligation do not seem to have much to do with each other. Doesn't being an owner mean that you get to do whatever you want with what you own? Owners have rights, not obligations, don't they? Yet, strangely, Feuerstein felt an obligation, *as an owner,* to manage his property in a way that attended to the needs and expectations of others.

Cynics might doubt that Feuerstein's actions derived from a sense of obligation. They might say that bailing out the workforce was a smart business ploy. It garnered him a lot of positive publicity and served to advertise Polartec, a synthetic fabric his company had created.[8] By 1998 the factory had been rebuilt, almost all the workers had been rehired, and the company was doing well.[9] Polartec was wildly popular. Yet later that year, when demand for the company's products sagged, Feuerstein went ahead and laid off workers.

There is no denying that Feuerstein is in business to make money. He himself has readily acknowledged his belief that loyalty to employees is "in the long run the most profitable way to behave."[10] Jeff Bowman, the business manager of Malden Mills, explained in a radio interview that treating workers well helps the company by fostering loyalty and high morale, which in turn encourage employees to work hard.[11]

But Feuerstein's actions after the fire in Lawrence were not motivated by economic considerations alone. At the time he made the decision to rebuild, it was not at all clear that this would be a wise decision financially. When asked why he did not simply close the business and retire, letting the jobs move elsewhere, perhaps overseas, Feuerstein's answer was surprisingly simple: "Because it wouldn't be right."[12] Fourteen months later, as he faced the difficulties of rebuilding, Feuerstein recalled what he had thought that night. "The workers are depending upon me. The community is depending upon me. My customers are depending upon me. And my family."[13] He explained his actions by referring to a Talmudic maxim, "Where there are no men, be a man."[14]

One might understand his response to the crisis as a form of charity. He gave to others of his own resources when he had no legal obligation to do so. But Feuerstein did not act out of a sense of charity, and he was not praised for being charitable. He was praised, not for giving money to needy strangers, but for acting honorably in his relationship with his own employees. They were not the recipients of the kindness of a stranger; rather, Feuerstein acknowledged that he had benefited from his relationship with his workers and that, in some sense, *he owed this to them.* He also felt a sense of responsibility to the city of Lawrence, where he was a major employer. "There was no way I was going to take about 3,000 people and throw them in the street. There was no way I was going to send the city of Lawrence into economic oblivion."[15] Rather than acting out of charity, Feuerstein acted to fulfill a felt obligation. What was extraordinary to his workers and the public was not just his financial generosity but his perception of his own obligations both to people with whom he had formed a long-term relationship and to the community in which he lived. Those obligations were not free-floating; they were not impulses to do good for other persons generally. They were obligations that attached to Feuerstein's role as employer; they grew out of his status as an owner.

The sense of obligation does not make Feuerstein's life easy. He finds his obligations to be complicated. They sometimes pull him in opposite directions. After rebuilding, he felt it necessary to close an unprofitable part of his business in order to ensure economic success. Three hundred workers lost their jobs. "What can I do? It's not always pleasant in life," Feuerstein said in an interview. "To stand for anything, we have to financially succeed."[16] Even though he believed he was doing the right thing, he took these actions only with "great personal regret."[17] Moreover, he did not discard his workers like so much machinery; he promised that he would make every effort to rehire all the displaced workers within two years. He provided an unusually generous package of benefits for those who lost their jobs, including extended health benefits, an extra month's pay, job retraining, and job placement assistance.[18] His commitment to the economic success of the business and to his personal economic interests coexists with a commitment to include the workers in his field of vision and to manage his company with their interests in mind, as well as his own.

Why did Feuerstein feel obligated to his employees and to his community? The answer has a lot to do with his religious convictions. As an Orthodox Jew, he believes that it is morally right for him to treat the people with whom he formed a long-term contractual relationship honorably and decently. He also believes that the world of business is not removed from the world of morality, that being a good businessman and being a good person are not incompatible goals. To reach those goals, Feuerstein is prepared to conduct his business in a way that attends to the needs of others, and not himself alone.

Feuerstein's fame suggested both a longing for this kind of commitment to workers and an implicit criticism of companies that have acted without regard for their workforce. One might suppose that Feuerstein's hero status might prompt other corporate executives to follow his lead. Yet they do not. The fact that his actions were so unusual bothers Feuerstein. To him, it is not only a puzzle but a scandal. "My celebrity," he said, "is a poor reflection of the values of today."[19]

Why haven't other companies followed Feuerstein's example? His actions garnered good publicity and may have even helped the company. Why don't others do the same? The answer has something to do with perceptions about the rights of property owners and with the law of property itself. Most large companies take the form of corporations, not sole proprietorships. We think of them as being owned by their shareholders; managers therefore have a duty to put the shareholders' interests first. Existing law not only does not encourage employers to act as Feuerstein did but may actually prohibit them from responding as he did. If the president of a publicly owned company had followed Feuerstein's example, he might well have faced a lawsuit by disgruntled shareholders claiming that he was not maximizing the value of their shares and thus was acting in contradiction to his fiduciary duties to them as owners of the corporation.[20] Paying money to workers that the company had no legal duty to pay them would take cash out of the pockets of the shareholders, as Feuerstein himself acknowledged.[21]

The Feuerstein story unveils a deep ambivalence about the meaning of private property. On one hand, many people value the kind of commitment shown by Feuerstein to his workers. The outpouring of support and affection for Feuerstein was extraordinary. Part of the reason for the reaction can be found in recent history. The takeover craze in the 1980s and early 1990s, in which smaller companies were swallowed up by larger ones, led to a spate of layoffs. Every week one would read the reports that one thousand, three thousand, forty thousand workers had been sacked. Feuerstein's expression of loyalty to his employees was a welcome contrast.

In response to the mass layoffs associated with takeovers, many states changed their corporate laws, adopting so-called stakeholder or corporate constituency statutes that allow corporate managers to consider the interests of workers and the communities in which the corporations operate in making policy decisions, rather than the interests of the shareholders alone.[22] These statutes demonstrate discomfort with the idea that corporations have no responsibility toward their workers other than to make payroll, and none to the surrounding communities besides paying their tax bill. They also demonstrate a willingness sometimes to use law to promote such responsibilities. By permitting corporate managers to take the interests of workers and communities into account, the stakeholder laws altered property rights. Feuerstein seemed to be acting on the moral and policy judgments that supported the stakeholder laws.

On the other hand, despite the admiration for Feuerstein, we remain, as a nation, firmly committed to managerial prerogatives, among which is the power to hire and fire workers at will. Only if an employer has contractually agreed to tenure or some other form of job security is there any limit on that power.[23] The stakeholder laws do not require companies to attend to the interests of workers.[24] Moreover, despite the implication that corporations should serve the interests of constituencies other than shareholders, courts still presume that shareholders' interests prevail if they are in direct conflict with the interests of other stakeholders, such as workers. Despite the stakeholder laws, shareholders are still viewed as owners of corporations, and in any contest between shareholders and workers the shareholders will prevail. This means that the interests of workers count only so long as they are consistent with shareholder interests. Although Feuerstein's actions were popular, and may have been consistent with the policies underlying the recently enacted stakeholder laws, courts would be reluctant to sanction such actions if undertaken by managers of publicly held corporations unless it could be shown that they ultimately would benefit shareholders. Moreover, if governors or legislators were to propose that corporations be required to act as Feuerstein did, businesses would rise up in arms against them, arguing that such regulatory measures would inhibit investment and interfere with corporate property rights. Resistance would be substantial to any regulatory law that would limit the discretion of corporations to channel their profits as they please.

The Feuerstein story demonstrates that people long for owners who act honorably and recognize obligations to those who are vulnerable to their decisions. They value work and want some amount of stability for workers who invest their lives in a particular enterprise, and they believe that the world would be a better place if such actions were commonplace. At the same time, any attempt to mandate such actions will be resisted on the grounds that such regulations interfere with the liberty of business owners to manage their property as they please and would inhibit business investment so as to make everyone worse off; mobility of both capital and labor is a crucial ingredient of economic efficiency and social welfare.

The traditional way to approach this dilemma is to ask whether regulation of owners is warranted by sufficiently compelling public interests and whether regulation will actually benefit those it is intended to help. I have argued that this kind of dilemma is best understood as a conflict within the property system itself, rather than as a conflict between property and regulation. If property is about justified expectations, it is important to recognize that expectations exist on both sides of the employer-employee relationship. Feuerstein may be an owner and therefore has the first word about how to manage his property. At the same time, he is not acting alone, but has enlisted the help of thousands of people to build a factory, to assemble fabrics, and to serve customers. He has left his home, ventured forth into the world, and begun a common enterprise.

His actions have induced thousands of other people to rely on the company for their livelihoods. They have expectations growing out of their relationship with him. Some of their expectations are justified by considerations of justice and welfare and may be sufficiently compelling to protect as property rights themselves.

Are those expectations sufficient to create obligations? Who is obligated, and in what ways? Some obligations might legitimately be placed on Feuerstein himself. Perhaps employers should not be entitled to fire employees without just cause; perhaps employees should be entitled to sit on corporate boards of directors. Perhaps, too, employees should have a right of first refusal to purchase a factory for its fair market value if the employer plans to close it. Other obligations might legitimately rest on society as a whole. We might, for example, want to use tax dollars to support unemployment compensation, retraining, and relocation assistance for displaced workers, and to grant incentives to businesses to create jobs in areas of high unemployment. Cities might use their powers of eminent domain to take closed factories and then transfer them to buyers who will commit to creating jobs in the community. The definition and elaboration of those entitlements and obligations will in large measure determine the kind of world we will inhabit and the kind of life we will have.

THE PARADOXES OF PROPERTY

A property claim is a claim to own, to control, to master, to *rule* a part of the world. But owners do not live alone, and we no longer like the sound of monarchy. Because property rights may conflict—both with other property rights and with personal rights—we cannot sensibly understand or shape property law without attending to the effects of recognizing a particular individual entitlement. As a judge on the Texas Supreme Court observed in the *Friendswood* case, "What we do cannot be understood except in relation to those we touch."[25] When we consider those we touch, we see that the institution of property involves internal tensions.

Property, understood as absolute control over one's own, is self-defeating. If there were no limits on one's ability to use one's property, one could use it to destroy the property of others. Because others have property rights too, protection of property requires limits on property rights to ensure that one's legal rights are compatible with the rights of others. Property—the paragon of absoluteness, the quintessential example of complete control—is inherently limited.

Property, then, is a paradox.[26] We invite owners to use their property for their own purposes, in their own manner, and at a time of their own choosing. The ability to control one's property can promote human dignity, individual fulfillment, and social welfare. Yet the various tensions embedded in the property system require us to impose obligations on owners—obligations to use their property in a manner that is not inimical to the legitimate interests of others. Entitlement initially appears to abhor obligation, yet on reflection we can see that it requires it. Indeed, it is the tension between ownership and obligation that is the essence of property.

The first definition of the word *paradox* in *The American College Dictionary* is, "a statement or proposition seemingly self-contradictory or absurd, and yet explicable as expressing a truth." The second definition, however, is, "a self-contradictory and false proposition."[27] These definitions of *paradox* present us with a paradox. Does the word describe an apparently self-contradictory proposition that is really true or a truly self-contradictory proposition that is therefore false? Paradoxes present a puzzle. They describe a set of assertions that, considered individually, appear to be true but which, taken together, seem to contradict one another. To solve the puzzle, we first must establish whether the individual propositions are indeed all true or whether at least one of them is false. If we can discover a way to reconcile the contradiction, we may conclude that the propositions are indeed true. In the world of law, we reconcile seemingly contradictory precedents based on seemingly contradictory rules by narrowing the rules so that one rule does not contradict another.

Resolving paradoxes in this way may create a new paradox. For if we conclude that the propositions are impossible to reconcile, we may then also conclude that one of the contradictory statements must be false. But why do we assume this? Why do we assume that contradiction is necessarily false? The model of science suggests to us that two contradictory factual assertions about the world cannot be true. But is this model appropriate when we deal with moral matters? Is it appropriate when we are dealing with a social or legal practice like property?

What if it turns out that the social practice we are studying has been explained and justified by contradictory principles, contradictory moral impulses, contradictory policies, and contradictory practices? We would like to make the contradiction go away, but to do so we must conclude that some portion of our practices and values is wrong and should be discarded. What if we are unwilling to jettison either of two contradictory principles, both of which we hold dear? We generally assume that in every situation there is a right thing to do, and yet many moral dilemmas require us to choose between alternatives that are partly good and partly bad. Each alternative requires us to do something we should, as morally conscious persons, regret.

The paradox is that sometimes the best way to express our values and our social and legal practices is by adopting what seem to be contradictory principles, even though we cannot now, and perhaps never will, be able to reconcile them fully. The truth of our moral situation may sometimes require us to stop trying to reconcile a contradiction. As Martha Nussbaum notes, "If we were such that we could in a crisis dissociate ourselves from one commitment because it clashed with another, we would be less good. Goodness itself, then, insists that there should be no further or more revisionary solving."[28] What if the truth is that our deepest values are in fact contradictory and yet we continue to accept them, without a clear answer to the skeptic who tells us that we must give up one of our commitments? Perhaps this is what the first definition of paradox actually means: seemingly contradictory propositions that are nonetheless true, not because they are really consistent with each other, but *precisely because they are contradictory*—precisely because contradiction is something characteristic of the subject matter under study.

Aristotle began his *Nichomachean Ethics* by noting, "Our discussion will be adequate if it has as much clarity as the subject matter allows." Ethics, the study of the good life, generates "much variety and fluctuation in men's judgments," and it is sometimes the case that people suffer from the "recognized good things in life," as when "men . . . come to grief through wealth, or as a result of their courage. . . . It is therefore sufficient when speaking on such a subject and with such premises to indicate the truth roughly and in outline, and when speaking about things which are no more than approximately true and with like premises to arrive at conclusions of the same character."[29]

The most fundamental paradox of property is that we may best understand it by exploring the tensions—the contradictions—within it. Within the concept, the norm, and the social and legal practice described by the word *property* we may find tension at its core. The coherence that the concept has may be best expressed by those tensions; what is coherent about the concept may be that it expresses fundamental human dilemmas—dilemmas we resolve in different ways at different times. This does not mean that these dilemmas can never be resolved, or that we cannot act or cannot give reasons to justify the way we respond to moral dilemmas. It means that our current moral commitments demand that we continue to believe in values that urge us in opposite directions when it comes time to act. If this is true, perhaps a clear understanding of property requires us to accept, embrace, and explore those tensions. As Nussbaum concludes, "Consistency in conflict is bought at the price of self-deception."[30]

We try to make our practices and our values consistent, but we discover, time and again, that our moral commitments force us to make choices we wish we did not have to make, and no amount of fancy theorizing will suffice to make us feel that we clearly understand the right thing to do and that we can prove the rectitude of our choice to anyone who will listen. Some things excite controversy. Perhaps property is such a concept and practice. If property promotes human values, perhaps it is a mistake to think that it can be fixed in place forever rather than forever contested. As Aristotle notes, "It is the part of an educated man to expect precision in any branch of science only in so far as the nature of the subject allows."[31] We may ask ourselves why we ever expected property to be so removed from human life that it would not exhibit the dilemmas characteristic of us, especially those we observe in our moral and political life. The ultimate paradox is that we may discover, as we study property, that it contains propositions that not only seem contradictory but are truly contradictory—and yet remain true.

This does not mean that we cannot make intelligent, considered choices among alternative property regimes. Nor does it mean that we cannot give reasons—even persuasive reasons—for one construction of property law over another. It means that context matters. We may want, for example, to argue that home owners should have the absolute power to determine whom they will invite into their homes for dinner, but that restaurant owners should not be allowed to exclude customers arbitrarily because of their race. We might say that privacy and associational concerns prevail over equality norms in the home, while the opposite is true for public accommodations. Explaining why this is so is not an easy thing. We have no formula, no theory, no procedure for reaching a decision that would guarantee agreement on this construction of property rights. Until 1964 it was not universally accepted in the United States that equality norms trump associational norms in restaurants. It is important to recognize and confront directly the fact that the choice between exclusivity claims and access claims involves a fundamental choice about social life. We have a lot to say about the relationship between certain forms of social life and norms of justice and welfare. On some issues we may even have a general consensus that is morally justified. What we do not have is a concept of private property that is self-executing and which preserves us from the need to make moral judgments about the appropriate definition, allocation, and distribution of powers over property.

PROGRESSIVE STRATEGIES

Critics of the absolutist conception of property have adopted a variety of strategies to make their case. One approach is to argue for regulation of property in the public interest. This strategy accepts the core image of property as ownership but defends limitations on property rights to promote interests such as a fair distribution of wealth, prevention of environmental harms, or protection from unequal bargaining power. A second strategy, adopted by the legal realists in the first half of the twentieth century, is to conceptualize property as a bundle of distinct entitlements and then to ignore the property concept as outdated. This approach does not get rid of ownership as a concept; it merely asks us to talk about ownership of particular entitlements rather than ownership of the entire bundle. Although it helps in disentangling the ownership bundle, it does not free us from its sway, and it does nothing to alter the conscious or unconscious burdens of persuasion comprised by the traditional ownership concept.

A third strategy, championed by Margaret Jane Radin, distinguishes between types of property that are legitimately commodified and those that should not be commodified at all, such as body parts, or which should be only incompletely commodified, such as the family home.[32] Alternatively, Gregory Alexander argues that property and property law have been viewed as serving both a commodity function and a "proprietarian" function.[33] Property as commodity regards property as a realm of market exchange where things are valued because of their ability to satisfy private preferences. Property as propriety sees ownership as serving public purposes of supporting a proper and just social order.

These critical approaches to property limit the effect of the traditional model either by identifying limits to ownership rights or by referring to alternative conceptions of property that may compete with the commodity concept. They rest on distinctions between ownership and regulation, personal and fungible property, commodified and noncommodified or incompletely commodified property, commodity and propriety. They are compatible with the social relations model I have developed here. There are, however, two major shifts in emphasis in my approach.

First, rather than understanding these tensions as external to the traditional model of property, I see them as contained *within* the traditional model. Ownership, commodity, market exchange, fungible property, the absolutist conception, the hard core of the traditional notion of property—whatever one chooses to call it—exhibits the tensions within it that are often thought to constitute external limits on traditional property rights. Second, rather than focusing on different types of property (personal versus fungible), limiting the realm of commodification, or accepting a role for property in establishing the just social order, I have focused on the quality, character, and diversity of social relations. This approach relativizes both property and the relation between the public and private spheres and situates them within a context of multiple, contested, overlapping human relations.

By posing a conflict between a commodity conception of property and a noncommodified or proprietarian conception of property, critical models may suggest an internal coherence to the commodity image that does not exist and which they do not claim to find. My aim in this book has been to emphasize that there are tensions within the commodity or ownership model itself. Rather than understanding property as a conflict between commodified and noncommodified property or between a commodity conception and a proprietarian conception, I have sought to demonstrate that the commodity conception itself contains internal tensions. Those tensions partly involve conflicts among core property rights, such as free use versus security, rights of access versus rights to exclude, powers to transfer disaggregated rights versus rights to own consolidated, alienable estates, title versus possession. But those tensions also involve conflicts between self-interest and obligation, formal and informal sources of expectation, satisfaction of preferences and shaping of social relationships. Even when we are talking about commodities—the core image of fungible property within the realm of impersonal market exchange—we find not only ownership but also obligation. In other words, the conflicts that might be viewed as limits to traditional property actually exist at the heart of the ownership model.

Ownership does not and cannot mean absolute power within a rigid boundary. This conception of property is an inaccurate and distorted picture of the ownership rights that are at the core of a market system. It does not exist, because absolute property rights do not exist in a society that values individuals; property rights, like all legal rights, must be limited when they impinge on legitimate, legally protected interests of others. Because of the built-in tensions in the property concept, and between personal rights and property rights, there is no built-in structure to the market form of property. All property rights exhibit internal conflicts. For this reason, property is best understood as comprising limited and conflicting entitlements rather than absolute powers in title holders. Ownership is a concept we must reconceive. Because ownership rights are always limited, we should either think about multiple bundles of entitlements or conceptualize ownership as control of more limited estates. And if ownership comprises something less than absolute control of property, the problem of defining property rights becomes as central, and as difficult, as the problem of determining how to protect them.

Because property exhibits internal tensions, and because property rights are not the only entitlements in the world, the problem of defining entitlements cannot be separated from that of defining obligations. We cannot define obligations without having some sense of what people owe each other, and we cannot think sensibly about what people owe each other without understanding their relationships with one another. The obligations among family members are different from those among neighbors. Members of a political community owe obligations to each other that differ substantially from the obligations owed by landlords to tenants or by employers to employees. Owners have entitlements, but they also have inherent obligations to other owners, to nonowners, and to the community. Entitlements empower their owner by placing obligations or vulnerabilities on nonowners. Because of this power that owners have over nonowners, owners cannot exercise their entitlements without limit. Because each individual is of infinite worth and deserving of respect and common decency, entitlements can only be justified to the extent they are compatible with the legitimate interests of others. And because entitlements are various and often conflict with one another, we cannot escape from making difficult judgments.

JUSTIFIED EXPECTATIONS AND FAIR OBLIGATIONS

Ownership without obligation is a form of dictatorship. It is a claim to rule without regard for the needs or interests of others. Sometimes this claim is justified; often it is essential to personal autonomy and dignity. Ownership is a claim to entitlement, and entitlement represents claims that others should defer to the one who is entitled. But, as we have seen, entitlements place vulnerabilities on others. Claims of entitlement therefore represent claims that others should bear those vulnerabilities, that the obligations which are the correlative of entitlement are fair.

As John Rawls argues, we cannot reasonably expect individuals to honor the claims of others unless they are claims to which all could or should assent. One way to address this question is to consider whether one could accept the vulnerability associated with the entitlement if one did not know beforehand whether one was going to be entitled or rendered vulnerable. I have argued for an alternative approach. I have suggested we focus our attention on choosing property institutions and rules that shape the contours of social relations in a manner that accords with our considered judgments about the appropriate and defensible forms of social life.

Property confers power over others, but also obligation toward them. The two go hand in hand. Obligation limits power by directing it toward the fulfillment of others' needs; without obligation, power would indeed corrupt those who wield it. Power in turn limits obligation; one obligation we have is to defer, in appropriate cases, to the power of others. For property to be justified, it must be limited. Entitlements, including property rights, go both ways; they entitle and they obligate. You cannot have one without the other. To learn what entitlements we should have, we must ask what obligations we owe each other. This is the paradox of property.

I have criticized the ownership model of property, but not because it is without merit. The notion of ownership conveys a sense of entitlement, of legitimate power, of a place in the world and food on the table. It suggests a right (a strong moral claim) to have legal rights. But ownership cannot mean what it is often thought to mean: that one has a right to act without regard for others' interests, needs, and expectations. Ownership may be tempting, but obligation, as Christine Korsgaard reminds us, "is what makes us human."[34]

How should we understand the many tensions within property? Tension results when principles we accept seem to pull us in opposite directions. Property involves a tension between claims of liberty (free use of one's property) and security (protection against harm to one's property). We become aware of such tensions when we examine conflicts over property rights. When this happens, we feel pressure to reexamine the conflicting principles to see if they can be reconciled by an overarching principle. If we can construct one, it may resolve the tension by showing how the seemingly conflicting principles are actually consistent with one another. Each principle is put in its proper place and given its proper force.

I have suggested that the focus of property law should be on the justified expectations of the parties affected by the issue.[35] But this principle, as we have seen, does not really resolve the tension; on the contrary, it connotes a new set of tensions. Are expectations based on formal title or informal arrangements? If they are based on title, how do we interpret ambiguous contractual arrangements that may or may not transfer some or all of the rights associated with title? If they are based on informal arrangements, what do we do when the parties have different expectations of their relationship? And even if we can answer these questions about the actual expectations of the parties, we must ask whether the expectations are justified. To determine the answer, we must remember that expectations are not only claims of entitlements to control resources; rather, they are claims that others should be obligated to respect those claims. In other words, property claims are not only claims of entitlement but claims that it is fair to impose obligations on others to respect those entitlements. The importance of an entitlement to the claimant is never enough to justify it. Because entitlements represent legal relations among persons, they can only be understood and justified by reference to the fairness of imposing vulnerabilities or duties on those affected by the assignment of entitlements to other people.

This suggests that we understand property claims in their social context. Not all uses of property or assertions of exclusive rights have the same moral character. Context matters because the assertion and exercise of legal rights over property is almost never a fully self-regarding act. Because legal rights represent relations among persons, it is imperative that we understand the effects that alternative rules have on human relations. In turn, our considered judgments about the kinds of relations we want to encourage and discourage should be crucial to determining what rules the legal system should adopt. Relations are at stake not only at the local level. Rule choices do not only affect the parties to the dispute or similarly situated parties; rather, they often have a great impact on the shape of social life experienced by everyone in the community. Rule choices often involve choices about the kind of society we want to create. The systemic effects of alternative rules on a variety of norms, including justice and welfare, should be a central determinant of what the law should be.[36]

How then do we choose among possible property regimes? And how do we justify those choices? In my view, the central normative goal of property law is to protect justified expectations. Contrary to the tenets of the absolutist approach, protection of justified expectations does not mean that once someone is designated an owner, she is entitled to act in her own interest alone, without regard for the ways in which her uses of property affect others. Indeed, the very legitimacy of granting a person control over scarce resources depends on whether others have alternative means of meeting the needs that those resources could have met. An expectation cannot be justified, no matter how strong it is, if protecting it would leave others unduly vulnerable. One expectation we are entitled to have is that we may obtain the means necessary for a dignified human life.

Legitimate expectations sometimes place obligations on other individuals to meet them; in other cases the obligations rightly belong on the community as a whole. Since property rights constitute legal relations among persons, determining what expectations are justified translates into the related question of what obligations are fair to place on individuals to act in ways that will protect justified expectations.

Taking the protection of justified expectations as the central norm of property law leaves room for judgment in resolving conflicts among property claims. Protecting justified expectations is deliberately a more value-laden concept than the idea of maximizing satisfaction of human preferences. This norm invites critical inquiry into when expectations are justified, both from the standpoint of justice and from that of utility. It invites conversation about the circumstances under which it is fair to impose obligations on individuals to respect the interests and property rights of others.

Thus, when we reach the question of justification, we find new tensions. Sometimes we focus on satisfying whatever preferences an individual may have; when we do so, we promote interests in autonomy. But sometimes we judge those preferences to be immoral or unethical and refuse to satisfy them, as when we refuse to count interests in engaging in racial discrimination or in child abuse; in so doing, we protect the autonomy of those who would be the victims of the wrongful conduct. Sometimes we focus on individual interests or claims, and sometimes we focus on society as a whole. Sometimes we face conflicts between claims of individuals to protection of their interests and claims that such interests, if aggressively asserted, undermine the social conditions under which individuals can flourish. Sometimes we face conflicts between justifications that are based on fairness or justice and those that are based on promoting welfare.

The ubiquity of tension and contradiction among competing principles and among competing normative approaches may rise to the level of paradox. Tension becomes contradiction when two principles not only push us in opposite directions but counsel us to do opposite things. A paradox is a contradiction of a special kind—one that appears to be unsolvable because we cannot reconcile the contradictory principles, and yet we cannot abandon either one of them.

Two contrasting attitudes exist in the academy toward such paradoxes. The simplifiers seek a theory, value, formula, decision making procedure, or a normative framework that will resolve the paradox, either in general or in the context of particular problems. The complexifiers seek to acknowledge and express the contradiction and to articulate reasons for resolving it one way or the other without reference to a single overarching theory or formula. Some complexifiers take a pluralistic approach, suggesting that we have multiple values, or multiple ways of valuing, which must be considered in adjudicating any problem.[37] Others take a tragic approach, suggesting that we recognize a deep conflict between real values that we can neither discard nor reconcile.

The simplifiers argue that the tragic or pluralist perspective leaves judges without guidance and gives them too much discretion. The complexifiers counter that their approach constrains judges far better than the simplifiers' approach does; for it forces judges to consider multiple perspectives rather than appealing to a single, simplistic value, such as social welfare, and a single interpretation of that value, such as deferring to individual preferences without judging them. It also constrains judges by making them justify their decision and reveal their reasoning to the losing party. This duty is likely to constrain judges better than a theory that suppresses the truth of conflict and which protects judges from having to make the hard choices implicated in hard cases.

THE FIRST PROMPTINGS OF HUMANITY

It has been said that you are not your brother's keeper but your brother's brother. It is not the job of the law to force people to do everything they should do. It is the job of the law to define entitlements in a manner that is sensitive to the fact that individuals live in a world with other people. Ownership is partly about self-interest, but it is also about obligation. Owners have obligations—to other owners, to the community, and to nonowners. This observation should be both obvious and commonplace, but in today's political climate it is neither. Indeed, to talk about placing obligations on owners, as a necessary part of what ownership means, appears radical.

In his *Discourse on the Origin of Inequality,* Rousseau criticized Hobbes for thinking that human beings were ruthlessly egotistical. One of the principles that he identified as having escaped Hobbes's attention is "an innate repugnance at seeing a fellow-creature suffer."[38] This principle, which Rousseau called compassion, restrains people from acting out of pure self-interest. It is a part of human nature, but it is also fragile and can be suppressed. The most powerful tool to lock it away, Rousseau recognized, is reason:

> It is reason which . . . divides [man] from everything that could disturb or afflict him, and bids him say, at sight of the misfortunes of others: "Perish if you will, I am secure." Nothing but such general evils as threaten the whole community can disturb the tranquil sleep of the philosopher, or tear him from his bed. A murder may with impunity be committed under his window; he has only to put his hands to his ears and argue a little with himself, to prevent nature, which is shocked within him, from identifying itself with the unfortunate sufferer. Uncivilized man has not this admirable talent; and for want of reason and wisdom, is always foolishly ready to obey the first promptings of humanity.[39]

Rousseau's conclusion that humanity would be better off without reason is ironic, given his own attempt to reason his way to understanding the just basis of political power. What is not ironic is his suggestion that philosophers sometimes reason their way to counterintuitive conclusions, not because they are paradoxically true, but because they have unjustifiably excluded from consideration human impulses that have their own independent value.

We hear from academic lawyers that rules intended to help people in times of need are counterproductive. This is sometimes true, but often it is not. For example, when property rights conflict, it makes no sense to claim that regulation is counterproductive. When we must choose between competing property rights, the question is not whether to regulate but how to regulate.

Reason and experience may tell us that some of our preconceptions about how the world works are mistaken. Laws intended to help the poor may in fact wind up hurting them if we do not think through carefully how people will respond to those laws. But this does not mean that we are wrong to have those initial moral impulses. When regulation is counterproductive, in the sense that it produces negative as well as positive consequences, sometimes the right response is to go ahead anyway. The positive effects may outweigh the negative effects, or we may be able to deal with the negative effects in some other way than by rejecting the regulation entirely and insisting that we must live with whatever difficulty caused us to consider regulating in the first place.

I do not question the need to fashion programs that work, or to produce wealth, or to ensure that regulatory rules do not backfire and make the problem they were intended to solve even worse. But I do question the idea that it is a mark of immaturity to worry about the distributive effects of property law and the character of social life as it is shaped by legal rules that define the outer boundaries of allowable conduct. A good society that cares about justice and common decency must impose norms of conduct that ensure that no one is left out. Requiring owners to look out for the interests of others does not mean that those others have no personal responsibility. Personal responsibility and obligation are not opposites; we do not have to choose one or the other. We are responsible for ourselves, but it is also true that one personal responsibility we have is to respond to the needs of others, as well as to our own needs. We owe it to ourselves not to become the kind of people who are indifferent to the suffering of others. And we owe it to others to establish property institutions that work; good intentions do not ensure that public policies will be successful. This is part of what it means to treat people with common decency.

In defining the property rights that remain after one deregulates, one faces tensions within the property system itself that preclude one's finding a clear core of enforcible property rights that can be mechanically enforced without regard to judgments of a highly controversial nature. Judges cannot therefore defer to the legislature to make controversial distributive judgments while adopting a neutral baseline for judgments founded in technical criteria such as efficiency. There is no baseline free from judgment about the fair minimum standards for human relations.

Where does this leave us? It leaves us in the land of judgment.[40] Property is not just something we protect or invade, recognize or reject; it is something we collectively construct. We must give it its meaning, both social and legal. No definition of property, no conception or theory or formula, can contain it. Certainly it cannot be encompassed by a simplistic injunction to grant entitlements to those who would be willing and able to pay for them if we had a giant auction. Given the current unequal distribution of wealth, and its derivation from our unfortunate history of conquest, racial oppression, and gender inequality, such a distribution of rights would not have even a semblance of justice or justification.

I have not attempted to define a decision procedure for adjudicating the tensions I have identified. But I have said a great deal about how to ask the right questions about property, how to act in the face of these tensions. and how to choose among conflicting, overlapping, incommensurable goods. I have argued against one way of resolving these conflicts—the way of simplicity. Property is not equivalent to ownership, and it cannot be defined by reference to a unitary determinate theory, such as efficiency or the categorical imperative of formulating rules as maxims that could be made universal or which treat individuals with equal concern and respect. These unitary theories are distorting or tautological. The moral impulses behind them are real; they often suggest useful normative questions and paths of investigation, from approaches based on economics and utilitarianism to those based on justice and dignity and on postmodern descriptions of shattered wholes and inescapable contradictions. No single approach will be determinative; no formula can be decisive—if we act responsibly. No approach can relieve us of the burden of judgment, of further deliberation, conversation, or negotiation.

We should accept the responsibility of judgment, and we should understand our entitlements as obligations we owe others with whom we are in relationship. Those obligations determine the limits of what we can claim as our entitlements. The shape and character we want those relationships to have, as they exist over time, will determine the legitimacy of any property regime. The funny thing about obligations in relationships is that you cannot recite what they are by giving a list—even a long list. Relationships take place in time, and not all at once; what we owe others, and what we can legitimately claim for ourselves, depends on contingent and changing judgments about what we shall be to each other, what support we should give and what support we should withhold. The scope of the power we give owners gets its legitimacy from the relationships it enables and the forms of social life it creates. It gets its limits the same way. Owners have entitlements, but they also have obligations. The mix of entitlements and obligations we can legitimately claim depends on the kinds of human relationships we can defend, nothing more and nothing less.

Notes

PREFACE

Epigraph: Johan W. G. van der Walt, *The Twilight of Legal Subjectivity: Towards a Deconstructive Republican Theory of Law* 431 (Doctor of Laws Thesis, Rand Afrikaans University, 1995), on file at Langdell Library, Harvard Law School.

1. Robert Cover, *Narrative, Violence, and the Law: The Essays of Robert Cover* 239–48 (Martha Minow, Michael Ryan, and Austin Sarat, eds., Ann Arbor: University of Michigan Press, 1992).
2. Avivah Gottlieb Zornberg, *Genesis: The Beginning of Desire* 53 (Philadelphia: Jewish Publication Society, 1995/5755), quoting Richard Rorty, *Contingency, Irony, and Solidarity* 165 (Cambridge University Press, 1989).
3. Ibid. at 53.
4. Ibid. at 60–61.
5. Ibid. at 61.
6. Ibid. at 33.
7. Ibid.
8. Ibid. at 278.
9. Ibid.

INTRODUCTION

Epigraphs: Jonathan Larson, *You'll See,* from *Rent* (1996); Laura S. Underkuffler-Freund, *Property: A Special Right,* 71 Notre Dame L. Rev. 1033, 1046 (1996).

1. Paul D. Carrington, *The New Social Darwinism,* 1 Green Bag 2d 235 (1998).
2. Carol M. Rose, *A Dozen Propositions on Private Property, Public Rights, and the New Takings Legislation,* 53 Wash. & Lee L. Rev. 265 (1996).
3. The Private Property Rights Protections and Compensation Act, if passed, would have granted any private property owner the entitlement to compensation for "any . . . limitation or condition" imposed by a federal agency "on a use of property that would be lawful but for the agency action" and is "not negligible," defined as "any reduction in the value of the property equal to ten percent or more." H.R. 9, 104th Cong., 1st Sess. § 9002(a) (Jan. 8, 1995). H.R. 925, 104th Cong., 1st Sess. § 9002(a) (Jan. 8, 1995). This language is from the first version of the bill. *See* Joseph I. Sax, *Takings Legislation: Where It Stands and What is Next,* 23 Ecology L. Q. 509, 510 nn. 8–9 (1996); Joseph I. Sax, *Using Property Rights to Attack Environmental Protection,* 14 Pace Envt'l L. Rev. 1 (1996).
4. Sax, *Takings Legislation,* at 511.
5. S.R. 605, 104th Cong., 1st Sess. (1995). The Senate bill adopts a 33 percent figure rather than the 10 percent figure in the Contract with America.
6. H.R. 925, 104th Cong., 1st Sess. (1995). This bill applies only to devaluations of property caused by agency interpretation and enforcement of certain specific federal statutes, including the Clean Water Act, 33 U.S.C. § 1344 (Federal Water Pollution Control Act), and the Endangered Species Act, 16 U.S.C. §§ 1531–1544. As written, it would be deny a right to compensation if the prohibited land use were already illegal under local zoning law or unlawful under common law property norms (the law of nuisance). It also would have denied compensation for restrictions on property use when the primary purpose of the regulation was to prevent an "identifiable hazard to public health or safety or damage" to other specific property. H.R. 925, 104th Cong., 1st Sess. §§4 & 5(a).
7. Texas, for example, has passed the Private Real Property Rights Preservation Act, which grants owners the right to enjoin certain land use regulations that reduce the owner's market value by 25 percent or more. Tex. Gov't Code §§ 2007.001 to 2007.045. North Dakota has a similar statute that also grants owners rights to monetary compensation, as well as injunctive relief, if a land use regulation causes a 50 percent reduction in the market value of their property. N.D. Cent. Code § 28–32002.5. See Frank I. Michelman, *A Skeptical View of "Property Rights" Legislation,* 6 Fordham Envtl. L.J. 409 (1995); Rose, *Dozen Propositions* 265, 265*n1* (1996); Carol M. Rose, *Takings, Federalism, Norms,* 105 Yale L.J. 1121, 1121–22*n4* (1996). In 1988 President Reagan issued an Executive Order, kept in effect by President Clinton, that requires all federal agencies to conduct a "takings impact analysis" of all regulations that may affect the use of private property to avoid government actions that might result in an unconstitutional taking of property. Exec. Order No. 12,630, 3 C.F.R. § 554 (1988), reprinted in 5 U.S.C. § 601 (1994).
8. See, e.g., *Phillips v. Washington Legal Foundation,*—U.S. —, 118 S.Ct. 1925 (1998); *Babbitt v. Youpee,* 519 U.S. 234 (1997); *Dolan v. City of Tigard* 512 U.S. 374 (1994); *Lucas v. South Carolina Coastal Comm'n,* 505 U.S. 1003 (1992); *Hodel v. Irving,* 481 U.S. 704 (1987); *Loretto v. Teleprompter Manhattan CATV Corp.,* 458 U.S. 419 (1982); *Kaiser Aetna v. United States,* 444 U.S. 164 (1979).
9. Margaret Jane Radin, *Reinterpreting Property* 100 (Chicago: University of Chicago Press, 1993).

10. "In questions of ethics and public policy as in questions of law, it is always important—and surprisingly often determinative—which way the presumption lies, who has the burden of proof." Thomas C. Grey, *Property and Need: The Welfare State and Theories of Distributive Justice,* 28 Stan. L. Rev. 87 (1976).
11. Sir William Blackstone, 2 *Commentaries on the Law of England* *2 (1766; facsimile reprint edition, University of Chicago Press, 1979).
12. Isaiah Berlin, *Two Concepts of Liberty,* in *Four Essays on Liberty* 118 (Oxford: Oxford University Press, 1969).
13. Lawrence C. Becker, *Property Rights: Philosophic Foundations* (Boston: Routledge & Kegan Paul, 1977); Andrew Reeve, *Property* (London: Macmillan Education, 1986); Alan Ryan, *Property* (Milton Keynes, Eng.: Open University Press, 1987); Alan Ryan, *Property and Political Theory* (Oxford: Basil Blackwell, 1984); Jeremy S. Waldron, *The Right to Private Property* 3 (Oxford: Clarendon Press, 1988).
14. Waldron, *Right to Private Property* at 60.
15. Ibid.
16. Harold Demsetz, *Professor Michelman's Unnecessary and Futile Search for the Philosopher's Touchstone,* in *Nomos* XXII: *Ethics, Economics, and the Law,* 41, 43 (J. Roland Pennock and John W. Chapman, eds.; New York: New York University Press, 1982).
17. Ibid. at 44.
18. Ibid. at 44–45.
19. Ibid. at 46.
20. Ibid. at 46.
21. *See, e.g.,* Richard A. Posner, *Economic Analysis of Law* 30–33 (Boston: Little, Brown, 3rd ed. 1986). For a contrary view, see Duncan Kennedy and Frank Michelman, *Are Property and Contract Efficient?* 9 Hofstra L. Rev. 711 (1980).
22. Posner, *Economic Analysis of Law* at 32.
23. Robert C. Ellickson, *Alternatives to Zoning: Covenants, Nuisance Rules, and Fines as Land Use Controls,* 40 U. Chi. L. Rev. 681 (1973).
24. Louis Kaplow and Steven Shavell, *Why the Legal System Is Less Efficient Than the Income Tax in Redistributing Income,* 23 J. Legal Stud. 667 (1994).
25. Alice H. Amsden, Jacek Kochanowicz, and Lance Taylor, *The Market Meets Its Match: Restructuring the Economies of Eastern Europe* (Cambridge, Mass.: Harvard University Press, 1994).
26. Joseph L. Sax, *Takings, Property and Public Rights,* 81 Yale L. J. 149, 152 (1971).
27. Wesley Newcomb Hohfeld, *Some Fundamental Legal Conceptions as Applied in Judicial Reasoning,* 23 Yale L.J. 16 (1913), 26 Yale L.J. 710 (1917); Joseph William Singer, *The Legal Rights Debate in Analytical Jurisprudence from Bentham to Hohfeld,* 1982 Wis. L. Rev. 975.
28. Hohfeld, *Fundamental Legal Conceptions;* Arthur Corbin, *Offer, Acceptance, and Some of the Resulting Legal Relations,* 26 Yale L.J. 169 (1917); *Restatement of Property,* introductory note (Philadelphia: American Law Institute, 1936 Main Volume; the word *property* is used in this restatement to denote legal relations between persons with respect to a thing"); Thomas Grey, *The Disintegration of Property,* in *Nomos* XXII *Property* 69 (1980).
29. Roberto Mangabeira Unger, *What Should Legal Analysis Become?* 24–25 (New York: Verso, 1996).

30. See also Laura S. Underkuffler, *On Property: An Essay,* 100 Yale L.J. 127 (1990).
31. Underkuffler-Freund, *Property: A Special Right,* at 1033, 1034. See also Robert W. Gordon, *Paradoxical Property,* in *Early Modern Conceptions of Property* 95, 95 (John Brewer and Susan Staves, eds.; New York: Routledge, 1995; "What strikes the backward-looking observer as curious is simply this: that in the midst of such a lush flowering of absolute dominion talk in theoretical and political discourse, English legal doctrines should contain so very few plausible instances of absolute dominion rights").
32. Hannah Arendt, *The Human Condition* 7 (Chicago: University of Chicago Press, 1958).
33. Ibid.
34. Hohfeld, *Fundamental Legal Conceptions.*
35. Will Englund, *Russia's Oligarchy Tumbles Downward; Nation's Tycoons Lose Their Power in Wake of Ruble's Decline,* Baltimore Sun, Oct. 5, 1998, at 1A, 1998 WL 4987237; David Filipov, *Russians Protest Unpaid Fruits of Their Labor,* Boston Globe, Mar. 28, 1997 at A2, 1997 WL 6247352; Timothy L. O'Brien, *Voskresensk Journal; Russia's Factories, Prey of Bankers, Rust Away,* N.Y. Times, Oct. 16, 1998, at A4; Leigh Ann Roman, *High cost to reforms,* Memphis Business J., Oct. 2, 1998, at 3, 1998 WL 9783829.
36. Sharon LaFraniere, *Capitalist Reality Comes Home to Roost in Russia,* Wash. Post, Oct. 26, 1998, at A01, 1998 WL 16564652.
37. Carol M. Rose, *Trust in the Mirror of Betrayal,* 75 B.U. L. Rev. 531 (1995).
38. Carol M. Rose, *Property as the Keystone Right?* 71 Notre Dame L. Rev. 363 (1996).
39. Frank I. Michelman, *Ethics, Economics, and the Law of Property,* 24 Nomos: Ethics, Economics, and the Law 3, 31 (1982).

CHAPTER 1: PARADOXES OF PROPERTY

Epigraphs: Jiri Dienstbier, foreign minister of Czechoslovakia, quoted in William Echikson, *Euphoria Dies Down in Czechoslovakia,* Wall St. J. (Sept. 18, 1990), at A26, 1990 WL-WSJ 561114; Morris Cohen, *Property and Sovereignty,* 13 Cornell L.Q. 8, 16 (1927).

1. *Friendswood Development Co. v. Smith-Southwest Industries, Inc.,* 576 S.W.2d 21, 22 (Tex. 1978).
2. Ibid.
3. Richard A. Epstein, *Takings: Private Property and the Power of Eminent Domain* 60 (Cambridge, Mass.: Harvard University Press, 1985).
4. John Stuart Mill, *On Liberty* 69 (1859; Harmondsworth, Eng.: Penguin Books, 1974).
5. Tex Gov't Code §§ 2007.001 to 2007.045. Acts 1995, 74th Leg., ch. 517, 1, eff. Sept. 1, 1995.
6. See Louise A. Halper, *Why the Nuisance Knot Can't Undo the Takings Muddle,* 28 Ind. L. Rev. 329 (1995).
7. Paradoxically, by limiting the legislative power to protect property rights to traditional nuisance law, the Texas Real Property Rights Preservation Act may itself have taken property rights recognized under the prior common law of Texas.
8. *Restatement of the Law: Property (Servitudes)* (Philadelphia: American Law Institute, Tentative Draft No. 1, April 5, 1989; Tentative Draft No. 2, April 5, 1991; Tentative Draft

No. 3, April 5, 1993; Tentative Draft No. 4, April 5, 1994; Tentative Draft No. 5, April 5, 1995).

9. Robert W. Gordon, *Paradoxical Property,* in *Early Modern Conceptions of Property* 95, 107 (ed. John Brewer and Susan Staves; New York: Routledge, 1995). Gordon argues that the "power of the absolute dominion trope in political discourse, in fact, put tremendous pressure on the legal system to identify a single 'owner' of every species of property, and then to transfer to that owner as many sticks of the bundle of rights as possible."

10. Laura S. Underkuffler-Freund, *Property: A Special Right,* 71 Notre Dame L. Rev. 1033, 1046 (1996).

11. C. Edwin Baker, *Property and Its Relation to Constitutionally Protected Liberty,* 134 U. Pa. L. Rev. 741 (1986).

12. *Page County Appliance Center, Inc. v. Honeywell, Inc.,* 347 N.W.2d 171 (Iowa 1984).

13. *Second Restatement of Torts* §§827–828; W. Page Keeton, Dan B. Dobbs, Robert E. Keeton, and David G. Owen, *Prosser and Keeton on the Law of Torts* §§87–88 at 619–630 (St. Paul: West Publishing, 5th ed. 1984).

14. Roger A. Cunningham, William B. Stoebuck, and Dale A. Whitman, *The Law of Property* §7.2, at 418 (St. Paul: West Publishing Co., 2d ed. 1993).

15. *State v. Shack,* 277 A.2d 369 (N.J. 1971).

16. Laura S. Underkuffler, *On Property: An Essay,* 100 Yale L. J. 127, 128 (1990).

17. Ibid. at 129.

18. *Loretto v. Teleprompter Manhattan CATV Corp.,* 458 U.S. 419, 435 (1982). See also *Kaiser Aetna v. United States,* 444 U.S. 164, 179–180 (1979).

19. 483 U.S. 825 (1987).

20. 42 U.S.C. §§ 1981–1982.

21. 392 U.S. 409 (1968).

22. *Tioga Coal Co. v. Supermarkets General Corp.,* 546 A.2d 1, 5 (Pa. 1988), quoting Holmes.

23. For an analogous argument, see Carol M. Rose, *Crystals and Mud in Property Law,* 40 Stan. L. Rev. 577 (1988).

24. See Eyal Zamir, *The Inverted Hierarchy of Contract Interpretation and Supplementation,* 97 Colum. L. Rev. 1710 (1997).

25. *Mahoney v. Mahoney,* 453 A.2d 527 (N.J. 1982).

26. See Gregory S. Alexander, *The Transformation of Trusts as a Legal Category, 1800–1914,* 5 Law and Hist. Rev. 303 (1987).

27. Richard A. Epstein, *Notice and Freedom of Contract in the Law of Servitudes,* 55 S. Cal. L. Rev. 1353 (1982). See also Richard A. Epstein, *Covenants and Constitutions,* 73 Cornell L. Rev. 906 (1988), where he recognizes the holdout problem that might allow a recalcitrant owner to prevent change in a covenant unreasonably and suggests that it is usually solved by developers by granting home owners associations the power to alter covenants with majority or supermajority vote.

28. Frank I. Michelman, *Ethics, Economics, and the Law of Property,* 24 Nomos: Ethics, Economics, and the Law 3 (1982).

29. *See Northwest Real Estate Co. v. Serio.* 144 A. 245 (Md. 1929).

CHAPTER 2: FROM TITLE TO ENTITLEMENT

Epigraphs: Jennifer Nedelsky, *Reconceiving Rights as Relationship,* 1 Rev. Const. Studies/Revue d'études constitutionelles 1, 4 (1993); Gregory S. Alexander, *Commodity and Propriety; Competing Visions of Property in American Legal Thought, 1776–1970* at 1–2 (Chicago: University of Chicago Press, 1997).

1. *Breene v. Plaza Towers Association,* 310 N.W.2d 730 (N.D. 1981).
2. Morton J. Horwitz, *The Transformation of American Law 1780–1860* at 31–63 (Cambridge, Mass.: Harvard University Press, 1977).
3. Mill, *On Liberty* 70.
4. Ian Ayres, *Preliminary Thoughts on Optimal Tailoring of Contractual Rules,* 3 S. Cal. Interdisciplinary L.J. 1 (1993); Ian Ayres and Robert Gertner, *Filling Gaps in Incomplete Contracts: An Economic Theory of Default Rules,* 99 Yale L.J. 87, 94, 101–4 (1986).
5. The landlord may not be allowed to evict a tenant for nonpayment of rent if the tenant refuses to pay because the landlord has neglected her own legal obligations by failing to remedy a problem that stands in violation of the housing code.
6. *See* Eyal Zamir, *The Inverted Hierarchy of Contract Interpretation and Supplementation,* 97 Colum. L. Rev. 1710 (1997).
7. *Hill v. Fontaine Condominium Association, Inc.,* 334 S.E.2d 690 (Ga. 1985); *McElveen-Hunter v. Fountain Manor Association, Inc.,* 386 S.E.2d 435 (N.C. Ct. App. 1989).
8. Jeremy Paul, *The Hidden Structure of Takings Law,* 64 S. Cal. L. Rev. 1393 (1991).
9. Jeremy Waldron, *The Right to Private Property* 292 (Oxford: Clarendon Press, 1988). Waldron's emphasis.
10. Jacqueline P. Hand, *Right-to-Farm Laws: Breaking New Ground in the Preservation of Farmland,* 45 U. Pitt. L. Rev. 289 (1984).
11. 276 U.S. 272 (1928).
12. Ibid. at 279.
13. Underkuffler-Freund, *Property: A Special Right.*
14. *Southern Burlington County, NAACP v. Township of Mount Laurel,* 336 A.2d 713 (N.J. 1975).
15. In some cases a city or town might be obligated to induce developers to construct low-income housing by conditioning building permits on the developer's agreement to offer a certain number of units for low-income occupants. The municipality might relax other restrictions in exchange; it might, for example, allow the developer to add an extra story on the building in exchange for reserving some units for low-income families. The rule could still be understood as deregulatory since the town is lifting a restriction on development in exchange for the provision of affordable units.
16. Many of these statutes, however, were interpreted to allow racial segregation in seating or service. See Joseph William Singer, *No Right to Exclude: Public Accommodations and Private Property,* 89 Nw. U. L. Rev. 1283 (1996).
17. Charles T. McCormick, *The Rights of the Landlord upon Abandonment of the Premises by the Tenant,* 23 Mich. L. Rev. 211, 221–222 (1925), quoted in *Sommer v. Kridel,* 378 A.2d 767, 772 (N.J. 1977).

18. Echikson, *Euphoria Dies Down in Czechoslovakia.*
19. D.C. Code §§45-1631 to -1642; N.J. Stat. Ann. §§2A:18-61.22 to .39 (applicable to senior citizens and tenants with disabilities).
20. On the distinction between personal and fungible interests in property, see Margaret Jane Radin, *Reinterpreting Property* (Chicago: University of Chicago Press, 1993).
21. Wesley Newcomb Hohfeld, *Some Fundamental Legal Conceptions as Applied in Judicial Reasoning,* 23 Yale L.J. 16 (1913), 26 Yale L.J. 710 (1917); Arthur Corbin, *Offer, Acceptance, and Some of the Resulting Legal Relations,* 26 Yale L.J. 169 (1917); *Restatement of Property,* introductory note (Philadelphia: American Law Institute, 1936, Main Volume; the word *property* is used in *Restatement* to denote legal relations between persons with respect to a thing); Thomas Grey, *The Disintegration of Property, in Nomos* XXII: *Property* 69 (1980).
22. Jeanne L. Schroeder, *Chix Nix Bundle-O-Stix: A Feminist Critique of the Disaggregation of Property,* 93 Mich. L. Rev. 239 (1994). Schroeder argues that the legal-realist image of disaggregated property failed to deprive the concept of property of operative significance.
23. See Jennifer Nedelsky, *Private Property and Limits of American Constitutionalism: The Madisonian Framework and Its Legacy* (Chicago: University of Chicago Press, 1990). Nedelsky suggests that it will not be easy to reform the property concept.
24. See john a. powell, *New Property Disaggregated: A Model to Address Employment Discrimination,* 24 U.S.F. L. Rev. 363 (1990); Laura S. Underkuffler-Freund, *Takings and the Nature of Property,* 9 Can. J. L. and Juris. 161 (1996).
25. *Rodrigue v. Copeland,* 475 So.2d 1071 (La. 1985).
26. See john a. powell, *New Property Disaggregated: A Model to Address Employment Discrimination,* 24 U.S.F. L. Rev. 363 (1990).
27. Joseph William Singer, *Jobs and Justice: Rethinking the Stakeholder Debate,* 43 U. Toronto L.J. 475 (1993).
28. Joseph William Singer, *Property Law: Rules, Policies, and Practices* 323 (New York: Aspen Law and Business, 2d ed. 1997).
29. *Friendswood Development Co. v. Smith-Southwest Industries, Inc.,* 576 S.W.2d 21, 33 (Tex. 1981) (Jack Pope, J., dissenting).
30. 239 U.S. 394 (1915).
31. 239 U.S. at 410.
32. Robert Nozick, *Anarchy, State, and Utopia* 150–52 (New York: Basic Books, 1974).

CHAPTER 3: PROPERTY AND SOCIAL RELATIONS

Epigraphs: Jennifer Nedelsky, *Reconceiving Rights as Relationship,* 1 Rev. Const. Studies/Revue d'études constitutionelles 1, 16 (1993); Martha Minow, *Making All the Difference: Inclusion, Exclusion and American Law* 10 (Ithaca, N.Y.: Cornell University Press, 1990).

1. *Rase v. Castle Mountain Ranch, Inc.,* 631 P. 2d 680, 682 (Mont. 1981).
2. Ibid.
3. Ibid. at 683.
4. Ibid.

5. *See* Grant S. Nelson and Dale A. Whitman, *Real Estate Finance Law* §1.3 at 7–9 (St. Paul, Minn.: West Publishing, 2d ed. 1985); A. W. B. Simpson, *A History of the Land Law* 141–143, 242–247 (Oxford: Clarendon Press, 2d ed. 1986).
6. Simpson, *History of the Land Law* 243.
7. Ibid. at 246.
8. 83 P. 808 (Cal. 1908).
9. Ibid.
10. Ibid.
11. Ibid.
12. *Black's Law Dictionary* 551 (St. Paul, Minn.: West, 6th ed., 1990).
13. Ibid.
14. Steven H. Gifis, *Law Dictionary* 213 (Woodbury, N.Y.: Barron's Educational Series, 1975).
15. The easement may be limited to a specific time period. Such easements are permanent only in the sense that they are not revocable at will.
16. These approaches have been supplemented in recent years by approaches based on pragmatism or communitarianism.
17. Jeremy Waldron, *The Right to Private Property* 3 (Oxford: Clarendon Press, 1988).
18. Roberto Mangabeira Unger, 1 *Politics, A Work in Constructive Social Theory: False Necessity: Anti-Necessitarian Social Theory in the Service of Radical Democracy* 34 (Cambridge: Cambridge University Press, 1987). "A framework of social life becomes stable only when it is reimagined as an intelligible and defensible scheme of human association."
19. Waldron, *Right to Private Property.*
20. *Black's Law Dictionary* 1485 (St. Paul, Minn.: West Publishing, 6th ed. 1990).
21. Mark Kelman, *Consumption Theory, Production Theory, and Ideology in the Coase Theorem,* 52 S. Cal. L. Rev. 669, 678–679, 681–82 (1979). Emphasis in original.
22. Elizabeth Anderson, *Value in Ethics and Economics* (Cambridge, Mass.: Harvard University Press, 1993).
23. Nedelsky, *Reconceiving Rights as Relationship* 1, 7–8.
24. Duncan Kennedy, *Toward an Historical Understanding of Legal Consciousness: The Case of Classical Legal Thought in America, 1850–1940,* 3 Research in Law *and* Sociology 3 (1980).
25. Nedelsky, *Reconceiving Rights as Relationship* 1, 7–8.
26. Ibid. at 8.
27. Jennifer Nedelsky, *Reconceiving Autonomy: Sources, Thoughts and Possibilities,* 1 Yale J. L. and Feminism 7 (1989).
28. Nedelsky, *Reconceiving Rights as Relationship* 1, 8.
29. Ibid.
30. Wesley Newcomb Hohfeld, *Some Fundamental Legal Conceptions as Applied in Judicial Reasoning,* 23 Yale L.J. 16 (1913), 26 Yale 710 (1917)
31. Ibid. at 32.
32. Ibid.
33. Nedelsky, *Reconceiving Rights as Relationship* 1, 13.
34. Robert C. Ellickson, *Order Without Law: How Neighbors Settle Disputes* (Cambridge: Mass.: Harvard University Press, 1991).

CHAPTER 4: SYSTEMIC AND DISTRIBUTIVE NORMS

Epigraphs: Frank Michelman, *Liberties, Fair Values, and Constitutional Method,* 59 U. Chi. L. Rev. 91, 99 (1992); Johan W. G. van der Walt, *The Twilight of Legal Subjectivity: Towards a Deconstructive Republican Theory of Law* 166–67 (Doctor of Laws Thesis, Rand Afrikaans University, 1995; on file at Langdell Library, Harvard Law School).

1. The power exercised by those ten families would be enormous. Even in the United States we see the role that money plays in politics, allowing wealthy candidates to compete more effectively for public office than candidates of modest means.
2. Alex Poinsett, *Economic Apartheid Haunts South Africa,* Chicago Tribune (May 18, 1998), at 15, 1998 WL 2857246.
3. Van der Walt, *Twilight of Legal Subjectivity* at 166–167.
4. Frank I. Michelman, *Anti-Negativity as Form,* 21 Law and Soc. Inquiry 83, 84 (1996).
5. Ibid. at 84–85.
6. *Oxford American Dictionary* 696 (1980).
7. *See* Cornelius J. Moynihan, *Introduction to the Law of Real Property* (St. Paul, Minn.: West Publishing, 2d ed. 1988); Joseph William Singer, *Property Law: Rules, Policies, and Practices* 523–49 (New York: Aspen Law and Business 2d ed. 1997).
8. I do not mean to argue that the system always functions this way in practice. Until recently, land ownership in Hawaii was extremely concentrated, with fewer than one hundred owners claiming much of the land in the state. See *Hawaii Housing Authority v. Midkiff,* 467 U.S. 229 (1984). This concentration of ownership persisted until the state passed a land reform act forcibly redistributing property from landlords to tenants. I mean to argue that the policy behind the estates system rules is to combat the kinds of social hierarchy and centralized power over land associated with feudalism.
9. Moynihan, *Law of Real Property* at 34–39.
10. They are not infinite if one can get the law changed to allow the current owner of a fee tail to convert it to a fee simple. This is exactly what happened in England.
11. 245 U.S. 60 (1917).
12. 334 U.S. 1 (1948).
13. It is often claimed that Apple got its ideas from other companies, such as Xerox. See *Apple Computer, Inc. v. Microsoft Corp.,* 799 F.Supp. 1006, 1032–34 (N.D. Cal. 1992).
14. James Boyle, *Shamans, Software, and Spleens: Law and the Construction of the Information Society* (Cambridge, Mass.: Harvard University Press 1996).
15. Of course, there are disputes about both these claims.
16. *See e.g., Dunafon v. McDonald's Corp.,* 691 F.Supp. 1232 (W.D. Mo. 1988).
17. 682 N.E.2d 1357 (Mass. 1997).
18. 682 N.E.2d at 1358.
19. 682 N.E.2d at 1359.
20. 682 N.E.2d at 1360.
21. See Richard A. Posner, *The Economics of Justice* 66 (Cambridge, Mass.: Harvard University Press, 1983), explaining the moral difference between purchase and theft of a necklace by arguing that a buyer's monetary offer "was in all likelihood accumulated through productive activity—that is, activity beneficial to other people besides himself," while the

thief "provides no benefit to the owner of the necklace or to anyone else"; *International News Service v. Associated Press,* 248 U.S. 215 (1918), recognizing a property right in news partly because "the acquisition and transmission of news require elaborate organization and a large expenditure of money, skill, and effort"; see also Carol M. Rose, *Possession as the Origin of Property,* 52 U. Chi. L. Rev. 73, 73–74, 80 (1985), explaining the labor theory of the origin of property rights and arguing that "the common law of first possession, in rewarding the one who communicates a claim does reward useful labor; the useful labor is the very act of speaking clearly and distinctly about one's claims to property."

22. Cf. Posner, *Economics of Justice* 66 and John Locke, *The Second Treatise of Government* 18–30 (Oscar Piest ed., Indianapolis: Bobbs-Merrill, 1952).
23. Richard Epstein, *No New Property,* 56 Brook. L. Rev. 747, 749–50 (1990). "As inheritors of the Lockean tradition, the basic theory [in the United States] was that property rights emerged from first possession, from first occupation, from homesteading, and not from state grant."
24. Victor R. Fuchs, *Women's Quest For Economic Equality* 84–89 (Cambridge, Mass.: Harvard University Press, 1988.
25. Ibid. at 4, "women's weaker economic position results primarily from conflicts between career and family, conflicts that are stronger for women than for men." See also Paul Weiler, *The Wages of Sex: The Uses and Limits of Comparable Worth,* 99 Harv. L. Rev. 1728, 1779–88 (1986), arguing that a significant portion of the difference between the overall wages of women and men can be attributed to the fact that many women work part-time or interrupt their work careers to care for children.
26. There is still a lot of old-fashioned sex discrimination going on as well.
27. Fuchs, *Women's Quest* 86.
28. Ibid. at 94, 107.
29. Cheryl Russell and Margaret Ambry, *The Official Guide to American Incomes* 278 (1993).
30. Fuchs, *Women's Quest* 107.
31. Ibid. at 107–8.
32. Russell and Ambry, *American Incomes* 280–81.
33. Ibid. at 58–64. I get this phrase from Marlene Booth.
34. Mary Joe Frug, *Securing Job Equality for Women: Labor Market Hostility to Working Mothers,* 59 B.U. L. Rev. 55 (1979).
35. See Kathryn Abrams, *Gender Discrimination and the Transformation of Workplace Norms,* 42 Vand. L. Rev. 1183 (1989); Mary Becker, *Barriers Facing Women in the Wage-Labor Market and the Need for Additional Remedies. A Reply to Fischel and Lazear,* 53 U. Chi. L. Rev. 934 (1986); Nancy E. Dowd, *Work and Family: The Gender Paradox and the Limitations of Discrimination Analysis in Restructuring the Workplace,* 24 Harv. C.R.-C.L. L. Rev. 78 (1989); Lucinda M. Finley, *Transcending Equality Theory: A Way Out of the Maternity and Workplace Debate,* 86 Colum. L. Rev. 1118 (1986); Sylvia A. Law, *Women, Work, Welfare, and Preservation of Patriarchy,* 131 U. Pa. L. Rev. 1249 (1983); Martha Minow, *Justice Engendered,* 101 Harv. L. Rev. 10 (1987), Joan Chalmers Williams, *Sameness Feminism and the Work/Family Conflict,* 35 N.Y.L. Sch. L. Rev. 347 (1990).
36. See Alice Kessler-Harris, *A Woman's Wage: Historical Meanings and Social Consequences* 117 (Lexington: University Press of Kentucky, 1990).

37. Fuchs, *Women's Quest* 137. "Women 'childcare workers' earn only about two-thirds as much per hour as other women at comparable levels of education."
38. Elizabeth V. Spelman, *Inessential Woman: Problems of Exclusion in Feminist Thought* (Boston: Beacon Press, 1988).
39. *Coppage v. Kansas,* 236 U.S. 1 (1915).
40. 236 U.S. at 17.
41. *Armstrong v. United States,* 364 U.S. 40, 49 (1960).
42. Louis Kaplow and Steven Shavell, *Why the Legal System Is Less Efficient Than the Income Tax in Redistributing Income,* 23 J. Legal Stud. 667 (1994).
43. There may, of course, be efficiency reasons to prefer a damages remedy to an injunctive remedy.
44. Lani Guinier, *The Tyranny of the Majority* (New York: Free Press, 1994).
45. James K. Galbraith, *Created Unequal: The Crisis in American Pay* 263–70 (New York: Free Press, 1998).
46. Roberto Unger has made this argument. See Roberto Mangabeira Unger, *Democracy Realized* 140 (New York: Verso, 1998).
47. *The Little, Brown Book of Anecdotes* 395 (Clifton Fadiman, ed., Boston: Little, Brown, 1985).
48. Jeremy Waldron, *The Right to Private Property* 329 (Oxford: Clarendon Press, 1988).
49. Ibid.
50. Robert Nozick, *Anarchy, State, and Utopia* (Englewood Cliffs, N.J.: Basic Books, 1974).
51. It has been far less successful as an accurate description of legal and social practice.
52. Locke, *Second Treatise of Government* 18–30. A second significant proviso was that the use of money allowed and enabled a market system to operate in which individuals could legitimately acquire more resources than were necessary to satisfy their immediate wants. Exchange of resources meant that the property would not be wasted. For my purposes, this argument is peripheral to the underlying moral basis for initial acquisition, which itself is qualified by the proviso that individual property rights are only justified if the system is administered so as not to exclude any individual from the opportunity to acquire property in the first place.
53. Waldron, *Right to Private Property* 127. See also ibid. at 176, "Locke has to explain 'how a bare corporal Act' such as labouring on an object 'should be able to prejudice the right and power of others' without their consent." Waldron argues that granting property rights can impose "onerous obligations" on nonowners because they can be excluded from scarce resources that may be urgently needed—indeed, "the use of material resources is a matter of life and death." Ibid. at 267. It is hard to see how an individual act of appropriation can legitimately place a duty on others if it deprives them of equal opportunities to acquire property or, worse still, places them in a position of peril. For a sympathetic critique of Waldron's theory, see Jeremy Paul, *Can Rights Move Left?* 88 Mich. L. Rev. 1622 (1990; review of Waldron, *Right to Private Property*).
54. Alan Brudner, *The Unity of the Common Law; Studies in Hegelian Jurisprudence* 74 (Berkeley: University of California Press, 1995). "Specifically, an owner's right against takings of property is now inwardly limited by the equal right of all persons to the material prerequisites of self-determined action."

55. Frank Michelman, *Liberties, Fair Values, and Constitutional Method,* 59 U. Chi. L. Rev. 91, 99 (1992).
56. Ibid.
57. Ibid.
58. Jeremy Waldron, *Homelessness and the Issue of Freedom,* 39 UCLA L. Rev. 295, 296 (1991).
59. Richard Middleton, *Colonial America: A History, 1607–1760,* at 131–32 (Oxford: Basil Blackwell, 1992). Other proprietary colonies included North Carolina and South Carolina. Ibid. at 172.
60. Lawrence Friedman, *A History of American Law* 230–34, 414–19 (New York: Simon and Schuster, Touchstone Book, 2d ed. 1985).
61. Robert A. Williams, Jr., *The American Indian in Western Legal Thought: The Discourses of Conquest* (New York: Oxford University Press, 1990). See also Robert A. Williams, Jr., *Documents of Barbarism: The Contemporary Legacy of European Racism and Colonialism in the Narrative Traditions of Federal Indian Law,* 31 Ariz. L. Rev. 237 (1989), quoting Locke's argument that in America "there are still *great tracts of ground* to be found, which (the inhabitants thereof not having joined with the rest of mankind, in the consent of the use of their common money), lie waste, and are more than the people, who dwell on it, do, or can make use of, and so still be in common."
62. Richard Epstein, *Simple Rules for a Complex World* (Cambridge, Mass.: Harvard University Press, 1995); Nozick, *Anarchy, State, and Utopia.*
63. Nozik, *Anarchy, State, and Utopia* 151. His third principle of rectification only comes into play if the principle of fair initial acquisition is violated.
64. Epstein, *Simple Rules* 53–70.
65. Nozick, *Anarchy, State, and Utopia* 153–60.
66. For a similar argument, see van der Walt, *Twilight of Legal Subjectivity* 431.
67. Nozick, *Anarchy, State, and Utopia* 160–64.
68. Jonathan Macey, *Externalities, Firm-Specific Capital Investments, and the Legal Treatment of Fundamental Corporate Changes,* 1989 Duke L. J. 173.
69. Gerald E. Frug, *City Services,* 73 NYU L. Rev. 23, 30–35 (1998); Cass Sunstein, *After the Rights Revolution: Reconceiving the Regulatory State* 47–73 (1990); William H. Simon, *Contract versus Politics in Corporation Doctrine,* in *The Politics of Law: A Progressive Critique* 387 (David Kairys, ed., New York: Pantheon Books, 3d ed. 1998); James Boyd White, *How Should We Talk about Corporations: The Languages of Economics and of Citizenship,* 94 Yale L. J. 1416 (1985).
70. I get this hypothetical from one like it by Randall Bartlett. On the relation between ideology, social structure, and economic and political power, see Randall Bartlett, *Economic Foundations of Political Power* (New York: Free Press, 1973).

CHAPTER 5: REPARATION

Epigraph: Elie Wiesel, quoted in Lance Morrow, *The Justice of the Calculator: A Symmetrical Deal: Let the Swiss Remember, So the World May Begin Forgetting,* Time (Feb. 24, 1997) at 45.

1. Gary Moore, *Wiped Off the Map,* Miami Herald (Mar. 7, 1993), at 15. See also William Booth, *70 Years Ago, a Town Disappeared in a Blaze Fueled by Racial Hatred. Not Everyone Has Forgotten,* Wash. Post (May 30, 1993), at F1.
2. Fla. Laws 1994, ch. 94–359 (preamble). See Fla. Stat. Ann. §240.4126.
3. Act of 1946, ch. 949, 60 Stat. 1049 [formerly codified at 25 U.S.C. §§70–70v-3]. See Robert N. Clinton, Nell Jessup Newton, and Monroe E. Price, *American Indian Law* 721–24 (Charlottesville, Va.: Michie, 3d ed. 1991).
4. See, e.g., Robert Hochstein, *Jewish Property Restitution in the Czech Republic,* 19 B.C. Int'l & Comp. L. Rev. 423 (1996).
5. Civil Liberties Act of 1988, Pub. L. No. 100–383, 102 Stat. 903.
6. See Martha Minow, *Between Vengeance and Forgiveness: Facing History after Genocide and Mass Violence* (Boston: Beacon Press, 1998); Eric Yamamoto, *Friend or Foe or Something Else: Social Meanings of Redress and Reparations,* 20 Denv. J. Int'l L. & Pol'y 223 (1992).
7. *State v. St. Francis,* No. 1170–10–86Fcr, slip op. at 1 (Vt. Dist. Ct. Aug. 11, 1989), *rev'd,* State v. Elliott, 616 A.2d 210 (Vt. 1992), *cert. denied,* 113 S. Ct. 1258 (1993).
8. Ibid. at 91–92. Whether recognition of original Indian title would give the Abenaki Nation the right to evict non-Indian residents from Abenaki land or to collect rent from them is a separate question not addressed by the court.
9. Ibid. at 96.
10. 616 A.2d 210 (Vt. 1992), *cert. denied,* 113 S. Ct. 1258 (1993).
11. Ibid. at 218; see also ibid. at 213–18, describing the way in which Indian title was extinguished by historical events.
12. 25 U.S.C. § 194.
13. *County of Oneida v. Oneida Indian Nation,* 470 U.S. 226, 247 (1985) [hereinafter *Oneida II*].
14. *United States ex rel Hualpai (Walapai) Indians v. Santa Fe Pacific Railroad,* 314 U.S. 339, 354 (1941) *(Walapai Tribe).*
15. *Oneida II,* 470 U.S. at 247–48.
16. Ibid. at 248.
17. 616 A.2d at 213.
18. Ibid.
19. Ibid. at 215–17, 220.
20. Ibid. at 217, 220–21.
21. Ibid. at 218.
22. *Trade and Intercourse Act of 1790,* ch. 33, 1 Stat. 137 (expired 1793; codified as amended at 25 U.S.C. § 177).
23. See 616 A.2d at 214–21, arguing that "cumulative effects leading to statehood" extinguished Abenaki title.
24. Ibid. at 218.
25. Ibid. at 220.
26. Ibid. at 218–19.
27. For an explanation of the importance of the Proclamation of 1763, see Robert N. Clinton, *The Proclamation of 1763: Colonial Prelude to Two Centuries of Federal-State Conflict over the Management of Indian Affairs,* 69 B.U. L. Rev. 329 (1989).

28. 21 U.S. (8 Wheat.) 543 (1828).

29. See 616 A.2d. at 220, concluding that "Vermont's admission to the Union . . . eliminat[ed] any remaining ambiguity about who had dominion over lands once controlled by the Abenakis."

30. Ibid. at 218.

31. "Once a determination has been made that a particular statute affects Indian tribes or individuals, courts have invoked canons of construction favoring creation and preservation of tribal rights." Robert N. Clinton, Nell Jessup Newton, and Monroe E. Price, *American Indian Law* 230 (Charlottesville, Va.: Michie, 3d ed., 1991).

32. Lawrence Friedman, *A History of American Law* 230–34, 414–16 (New York: Simon and Schuster, Touchstone Book, 2d ed. 1985), discussing the Homestead Act of 1862.

33. Brian Dippie, *The Vanishing American: White Attitudes and U.S. Indian Policy* 48–60 (Middletown, Conn.: Wesleyan University Press, 1962); Reginald Horsman, *Expansion and American Indian Policy 1783–1812* at 62 (1967; Norman: University of Oklahoma Press, 1992).

34. Horsman, *Expansion and American Indian Policy* 53–65.

35. William A. Haviland and Marjory W. Power, *The Original Vermonters: Native Inhabitants, Past and Present* 225–39 (Hanover, N.H.: University Press of New England, 1981).

36. See *County of Oneida v. Oneida Indian Nation,* 470 U.S. 226, 24748 (1985), requiring congressional intent to be "plain and unambiguous."

37. Ibid.

38. See *Elliott,* 616 A.2d at 220.

39. Ibid.

40. Lori S. Robinson, *The Price of Justice: Blacks Seek Compensation for Past Wrongs,* News and Observor (Feb. 23, 1997) at A19, 1997 WL 7823980; Irma Jacqueline Ozer, *Reparations for African Americans,* 41 How. L. J. 479 (1998).

CHAPTER 6: EXPECTATIONS AND OBLIGATIONS

Epigraphs: Avivah Gottlieb Zornberg, *Genesis: The Beginning of Desire* xviii (Philadelphia: Jewish Publication Society, 1995/5755); Jennifer S. Nedelsky, *Law, Boundaries, and the Bounded Self,* 30 Representations 162 (1990).

1. Josh Simon, *Heroes of the Moment: The Mensch of Malden Mills; When Fire Destroyed a Mill and Threatened the Jobs of His Workers, Aaron Feuerstein Heeded an Ancient Rabbinic Teaching: "Where There Is No Man, Be a Man,"* Life (May 5, 1997), at 4a, 1997 WL 8498482.

2. Ibid.

3. Bruce Butterfield, *Mill Owner Feuerstein Vows to Pay Idled Workers for Another Day,* Boston Globe (Feb. 10, 1996), at 58, 1996 WL 6849522.

4. *Owner of Burned Mill Promises to Continue Paying His Workers,* Providence Journal-Bulletin (Dec. 15, 1995) at A13, 1995 WL 13244698.

5. Ann Scales, *Malden Mills Owner Gets Seat of Honor,* Boston Globe (Jan. 24, 1996), at 6, 1996 WL 6847438.

6. For a trenchant critique of this image of the shareholder, see Daniel J. H. Greenwood, *Fictional Shareholders: For Whom Are Corporate Managers Trustees, Revisited,* 69 S. Cal. L. Rev. 1021 (1996).

7. Interview with Aaron Feuerstein, March 5, 1999.
8. Richard Jerome and Stephen Sawicki, *Holding the Line: After Fire Wrecked His Mill, Aaron Feuerstein Didn't Let His Workers Down,* Time (Feb. 5, 1996) at 122.
9. Bruce Butterfield, *Lawrence Will Mark Malden Mills Rebirth: Complex Destroyed in December 1995 Fire,* Boston Globe (Sept. 13, 1997), at F2, 1997 WL 6269327; *Malden Mills Rebuilt in Inner City,* Dallas Morning News (Sept. 13, 1997), at 11f, 1997 WL 11520076.
10. *Factory Owner Invited to State of Union Event,* All Things Considered, National Public Radio (Jan. 23, 1996), 1996 WL 4369720.
11. Patricia McLaughlin, *After a Fashion: Fabric Firm Finds Loyalty Wears Well All Around,* Harrisburg Patriot (Dec. 10, 1996), at D1, 1996 WL 5713000.
12. Samuel Heilman, *Looking In: A Shining Example of Orthodoxy; Selfless New England Mill Owner Helps Atone for Transgressions by His Coreligionists,* Jewish Week (Feb. 2, 1996), at 24, 1996 WL 15747037.
13. Simon, *Heroes of the Moment.*
14. Ibid.
15. Laura Meade Kirk, *Museum Offers Lesson in Value of Work: Aaron Feuerstein, Who Kept His Employees on the Payroll When His Malden Mills Plant Burned Down, Tells Hundreds at a New Woonsocket Museum That Urban Employment Is Essential for the Financial Health of the Nation,* Providence J.-Bulletin (Oct. 13, 1997), at B01, 1997 WL 13863537.
16. Bruce Butterfield, *Malden Mills to Cut 300 Jobs in Velvet Unit: Vows To Rehire Workers Within 2 Years,* Boston Globe (Feb. 26, 1998) at D1.
17. Ibid.
18. Ibid.
19. Edward D. Murphy, *Honored Businessman Decries Values of Today's Corporate World: Mill Owner Aaron Feuerstein Tells an Audience in Portland That Loyalty Pays Off Over the Long Term,* Portland Press Herald (Dec. 4, 1997), at 1A, 1997 WL 12537662.
20. Robert Charles Clark, *Corporate Law* §3.1.2, at 96 (Boston: Little, Brown, 1986) (shareholders have the power to sue managers for breach of their duty of loyalty to shareholders; Robert A. G. Monks and Nell Minow, *Corporate Governance* 182 (Cambridge, Mass.: Basil Blackwell, 1995) (corporate directors owe shareholder-owners legally enforceable duties of loyalty and care).
21. Feuerstein explained: "I own my company, but it's unfortunate that CEOs, who are maybe professionally far better than me, are being forced today, because of [the] power in the hands of these Wall Street funds, they're being forced today to make short-term decisions to improve the bottom line. As a result of it, they are cutting and killing the very labor that this country needs for its future." *Profile: No Longer Needed: Aaron Feuerstein, Corporate America's Layoff Policies and How They Affect the United States,* Sunday Morning (Jan. 14, 1996), CBS transcript, 1996 WL 8065770.
22. Joseph William Singer, *Jobs and Justice: Rethinking the Stakeholder Debate,* 43 U. Toronto L.J. 475 (1993).
23. In recent years some exceptions to the employment-at-will doctrine have gained currency, such as the public policy doctrine and the implied duty of good faith and fair dealing. These exceptions are very narrowly construed, however, and do little to limit managerial discretion. Of course, employers cannot fire employees for racially discriminatory

reasons, but this limit on the right to fire is in a class by itself. Jack Beermann and Joseph William Singer, *Baseline Questions in Legal Reasoning: The Example of Property in Jobs,* 23 Ga. L. Rev. 911 (1989).

24. The sole exception is Connecticut. Conn. Stat. Ann. §33–756 provides that "a director of a corporation . . . shall consider, in determining what he reasonably believes to be in the best interests of the corporation, (1) the long-term as well as the short-term interests of the corporation, (2) the interests of the shareholders, long-term as well as short-term, including the possibility that those interests may be best served by the continued independence of the corporation, (3) the interests of the corporation's employees, customers, creditors and suppliers, and (4) community and societal considerations including those of any community in which any office or other facility of the corporation is located. A director may also in his discretion consider any other factors he reasonably considers appropriate in determining what he reasonably believes to be in the best interests of the corporation."
25. *Friendswood Development Co. v. Smith-Southwest Industries, Inc.,* 576 S.W. 2d 21, 33 (Tex. 1981) (Jack Pope, J., dissenting).
26. Robert W. Gordon, *Paradoxical Property,* in *Early Modern Conceptions of Property* 95 (John Brewer and Susan Staves, eds., New York: Routledge, 1995).
27. *The American College Dictionary* 878 (C. L. Barnhart ed., New York: Random House, 1966).
28. Martha Nussbaum, *The Fragility of Goodness* 49–50 (1986). See also Duncan Kennedy, *A Critique of Adjudication (Fin de Siecle)* (Cambridge, Mass.: Harvard University Press, 1997).
29. *Aristotle's Ethics* 5 (John Warrington ed., New York: Everyman's Library, 1963).
30. Nussbaum, *Fragility of Goodness* 242.
31. *Aristotle's Ethics* 5.
32. Margaret Jane Radin, *Contested Commodities: The Trouble with Trade in Sex, Children, Body Parts, and Other Things* (Cambridge, Mass.: Harvard University Press, 1996); Margaret Jane Radin, *Reinterpreting Property* (Chicago: University of Chicago Press, 1993).
33. Gregory S. Alexander, *Commodity and Propriety; Competing Visions of Property in American Legal Thought, 1776–1970* (Chicago; University of Chicago Press, 1997).
34. Christine Korsgaard, *The Sources of Normativity* 5 (Cambridge: Cambridge University Press, 1996).
35. Joseph L. Sax, *Liberating the Public Trust Doctrine from Its Historical Shackles,* 14 U.C. Davis L. Rev. 185, 186 (1980). "The essence of property law is respect for reasonable expectations."
36. Ibid. at 187. "The root values that inhere in the maintenance of an established community have much in common with the established expectations that underlie the recognition of private property rights."
37. Stephen R. Munzer, *A Theory of Property* (Cambridge: Cambridge University Press, 1990).
38. Jean Jacques Rousseau, *A Discourse on the Origin of Inequality,* in *The Social Contract and Discourses* 175, 223 (G. D. H. Cole, trans., 1950; New York: Dutton, 1950).
39. Ibid. at 226.

40. On the meaning of judgment, see Martha Minow and Elizabeth V. Spelman, *Passion for Justice,* 10 Cardozo L. Rev. 37 (1988); Martha Minow and Elizabeth V. Spelman, *In Context* (with Elizabeth V. Spelman) 63 S. Cal. L. Rev. 1597 (1990); Todd D. Rakoff, *The Implied Terms of Contracts: Of "Default Rules" and "Situation-Sense,"* in *Good Faith and Fault in Contract Law* (Jack Beatson and Daniel Friedmann, eds., Oxford: Clarendon Press, 1995).

Index